T0086039

CLOVEN COUNTRY

CLOVEN COUNTRY

the Devil and the English Landscape

Jeremy Harte

REAKTION BOOKS

For Sophia, a devilish good companion

Published by Reaktion Books Ltd
Unit 32, Waterside
44–48 Wharf Road
London N1 7UX, UK
www.reaktionbooks.co.uk

First published 2022
First published in paperback 2023
Copyright © Jeremy Harte 2022

All rights reserved

No part of this publication may be reproduced, stored in a retrieval system,
or transmitted, in any form or by any means, electronic, mechanical,
photocopying, recording or otherwise, without the prior permission
of the publishers

Printed and bound in Great Britain
by TJ Books Ltd, Padstow, Cornwall

A catalogue record for this book is available from the British Library

ISBN 978 1 78914 833 6

CONTENTS

INTRODUCTION

I gazed down the chasm, its rocky walls receding below me as if the cleft would continue forever to the lowest smoking pit. This was the Devil's Chimney, they said. Whoever named it, named it well. What ancient pagan rites, what passionate missionary sermons, what stubborn Puritan struggle against the allure of the dark had gone into the making of that place-name?

Once I was home, I checked through all the historic maps of Ventnor that I could find. The Devil's Chimney first appeared in 1978. Before then it had just been a crack in the ground.

From that moment I began to look at the Devil in a new light. It wasn't just place-names: wherever I turned – to legends, ballads, superstitions, the lore of uncanny places – he always turned out to have been a late arrival at the board of folklore. Yes, there was a vivid canon of Devil stories, but some of them had first been told about giants, and others were stolen from the fairies. Perhaps that explained the cheerful turn of the lore, in which the Devil seemed more buffoon than fiend: bumbling, easily fooled. Even in the more sinister tales it was easy to see how the one Devil of modern narrative had taken over plot lines originally sketched out for the innumerable devils, demons or uncanny spirits of medieval tradition.

This was a surprising development in the history of folklore, but it is there for anyone to see once you appreciate that folklore actually has a history. Within the last generation we have turned away from talking about legend and tradition as if they came from the immemorial past, and realized instead that oral narrative develops and changes just like written literature. Because it is the spoken word, it can live and fade away untraced – no doubt many flourishing cycles of storytelling are now lost beyond recall – but there have always been a few curious literate people who wrote down what they heard. The records of past folklore are a fragment, but they are a representative fragment.

England never saw the systematic collecting of local lore that was carried out in other countries. Instead, in a typically English way, our stories have come down to us in a muddle of guidebooks, scribbles in the corners of maps, amateur poetry and notes for antiquarians. These sources speak in many voices, but mostly middle-class ones, because it was gentleman amateurs who recorded and retold the stories. Comic verse by country vicars may not be to everybody's taste, but that is what survives from the eighteenth and nineteenth centuries; for authentic transcripts of what people really said, we must turn to the more modern collections of Scotland and Ireland.

In any case, authenticity is something of a will-o'-the-wisp when we are tracking these traditions, because they have passed through written channels as often as oral ones. Much of our Devil lore derives from memories of the Grand Tour, copy-writing for visitor hot-spots and half-remembered German ballads. With this in mind, I have not scrupled to retell the stories myself, one more link in the long chain of oral and written technique. I hope that I have done them justice by giving a feeling of what the stories themselves are really like, without the period dress of yesterday's prose style.

For stories exist independently of the words in which they were told, or the occasions on which they were performed. Given the bare bones of who and where and when, a skilful performer can tweak the narrative a little to change the atmosphere or the sympathies of the audience, but each story has a grain of its own which determines what is possible in performance. Even the laboured efforts of the Victorian moralist cannot disguise an underlying flippancy in much of our Devil lore. The masks of comedy and tragedy are not interchangeable.

This story-Devil is the demotic brother of the sermon-Devil, both of them children of popular Christianity, but quite different in their character and the company they keep. Occasionally, it is true, a flash of hellfire reminds us that the popular Devil has something in common with his theological twin. Not wanting to disappoint the cultists of folk horror, I have marshalled my Devils on a darkening spectrum from cheerful to dreadful. The grimmest stories are the rarest, and lie under suspicion of being worked up for the literary market. What looks like blood on Satan's claw usually turns out to be blackberry juice, and most of the time he is just kidding: a trickster whose wiles are easily out-witted by the little man. This is not a book for the Christmas stocking of the Satanist, and it may disappoint religious people for whom the Devil is a real and terrible presence, but for anyone who likes good-humoured drama and (mostly) happy endings against the backdrop of the English countryside, I hope it will be a damned good read.

The Devil's Dyke, Brighton.

HIS WORK UNDONE:
THE DEVIL'S AMBITIOUS
PROJECTS FAIL

Mighty works have been attributed to the Devil – great rifts in the landscape and wonderful feats of road-building – but his industry always ends in failure. Outwitted by clever mortals, he leaves a half-finished monument. Sometimes his plans are purely destructive and he sets out to drop a small hill on a town, but then he will be talked out of it by a clever cobbler. If he builds a bridge, the work will be finished on time but he never gains the soul he hoped to win this way. These stories spread around the country wherever local features were renamed as diabolical landmarks.

The Devil's Mighty Works

Leave Brighton's urban growth behind, cross the A27 on the outskirts of town, and suddenly you are on unbroken downland. Away to the south, the long sea sprawls; always the same view, grey-blue down there and green up here, the grand simplicity of chalk, until you come to the golf course, which some imaginative club secretary has marked out with little red Devil flags. Go across a field, past hedges drooping under the weight of old man's beard, until suddenly the world drops from your feet and stretching away before you is the vast panorama of the Weald. Cloud-like against the northern sky rise the ridges of the further side, Leith Hill and Box Hill and the Hurtwood. Fields and woods and farms, churches, pubs and pastures cluster at your feet, 'the most extensive and beautiful prospects', as John Cary the atlas-maker put it in 1787.[1]

The Devil likes a good view; he once took his business rival to a high place just to point out details of the vista. Now the National Trust helps out with two concrete blocks framing panoramas, so that we can make out the names of villages in the vale all by ourselves: Fulking, Edburton, Bramber, Steyning. The view is what draws everyone to the Devil's Dyke, and it rather upstages the Dyke itself, tucked behind the ridge and easily passed without noticing as you head to the viewpoint. It is what the geologists call a re-entrant valley, in plan like a backwards quiver of a pencil tracing the line of the South Downs. Long, straight and incredibly steep-sided, this is a remarkable valley but not unique – simply a larger version of the other combes cutting into the fretted escarpment.

There's another wider break in the scarp line a little to the east at Poynings, where the road from London comes through, and traditions of the Devil's Dyke may owe something to that road. John Cary, he of the *New and Correct English Atlas*, is the first to mention the name; since you can't see the view from the valley, he may be thinking instead of the earthworks on the spur of the hill, just east of the Devil's Dyke pub. Banks and ditches are still conspicuous there. Everywhere else along the south coast – at Aldworth, Moulsford, Boxgrove and St Mary Bourne – Ditch or Dyke is a name for earthworks attributed to the Devil, not for valleys, and that may have been the original intention here. In 1778 the hill fort was known as Poor Man's Walls, but that is a very local kind of name, the sort that would need to be explained to visitors who weren't aware that 'the Poor Man' is Sussex dialect for the Devil.[2] And visitors were plentiful enough. From the 1770s onwards an ever-increasing throng took the turnpike road to Brighton, hungry for sea air and scenery. They loved a quaint local tradition and were probably generous in their tips when they heard one. Legends flourish in an environment like this.

By 1810 it must have been decided that the Dyke was definitely the long cleft valley, not the hillfort, because in that year a visitor from Birmingham, William Hamper, heard a story about how it had come to be. He was so charmed that he put the tale into verse. In those days, gentlemen liked to versify the legends they were told about local landmarks; it let them tell the story once again in a lively imaginative way, while making it subtly obvious how much cleverer they were than the unlettered people who had given it to them in the first place.

Still, Hamper's poem is short, effective and not too cluttered by literary ambitions.[3] In days of yore, he says, Old Nick looked out over the Weald and saw with dismay that it had been studded with new churches. Bells rang, people gathered outside the doors, every Sunday saw another service. The Devil looked grimly on these holy places, built to cheat him out of his revenue of souls:

> He mutter'd twenty things beside;
> And swore, that night the foaming tide,
> Led through a vast and wondrous trench,
> Should give these pious souls a drench!

So, waiting till the sun had sunk in the west, confident in his monstrous strength and armed with an equally monstrous shovel,

> Old Nick began, with much ado,
> To cut the lofty Downs in two.

Hurling a thousand wagonloads to right and left with each pitch of the spade, the Devil begins to carve a trench that will let in the sea to drown the Weald. But just as he is getting somewhere, in the very middle of the night, an old woman happens to get up in her little cottage, which lies at the foot of the escarpment. Though it is dark, she can hear that something is going on. She looks up and sees a black outline against the stars, dim and shadowed against the line of hills, but unmistakeable in his horns, his burning eyes. And she realizes that something must be done.

> Swift 'cross her mind a thought there flew,
> That she by stratagem might do
> A deed which luckily should save
> Her country from a watery grave.

Lighting a candle, she picks up her hair sieve from the kitchen, boldly flings open the window and holds the sieve out with the candle behind it. The flame shines through the mesh, looking like a faint bright orb. If it isn't dawn, it's something very like it, and the Devil is not taking any chances;

> Behold – he fled – his work undone –
> Scar'd at the sight of a new Sun;
> And muttering curses, that the Day
> Should drive him from his work away!

A happy ending to a vivid story, and who would complain? Certainly not the smiling locals or the appreciative tourist. Though a child might ask, in the penetrating way of young children – yes, but why didn't the Devil come back the next night? That superficially silly question hands us a thread which, if we follow it all the way, will unravel many of the mysteries of the Devil's Dyke, and ultimately of the Devil himself.

On the face of it, our awkward child has misunderstood the way that narrative works. Within the story-world, Devil and danger belong to the night, sun and safety to the day. Bridge that distinction with an artificial sun, courtesy of the old lady and her candle, and the contest is won: there can be no second match. But however satisfactory from a structural point of view, this answer begs another question: why is the Devil lined up in this way with night? What is there to stop him being diabolical in the daytime?

Biologically, we are creatures of the day, and although we may try to think of supernatural beings in the abstract, to embody them in any detail we must fall back on the prompts provided by our own nature. So there are ancient reasons to imagine creatures who could only do harm in the night hours, and who were nullified as soon as day arrived. There is a hint of this in a tradition heard by John Aubrey, the pioneer of English archaeology and folklore, when he was picking up local lore in the 1680s. He was told it at Ockley, which makes sense when you remember that Ockley stands at the Surrey end of a very long, very straight stretch of road, 'by some called the Devill's Causeway'. Even today this road, the A29, stands out as something artificial in a winding landscape, and it would have been much more obvious in the seventeenth century, when it was the only raised ground in an area subject to winter floods.

> The Common people do say it was made by the Devil. Scilicet [that is to say], that the Devil made one of the Causeways for a faire Lady, a great man's daughter, whom he should have, if he could make it before Sun riseing: and then they made a great fire to make the Devil believe the Sun was up: and the Devil then let fall a lap-full of Stones, which made a Hill at one of the causeways.[4]

This is both like and unlike the Devil's Dyke story. Yes, we have a work that must be undertaken in one night, an artificial sun, a Devil baulked of his wicked design, but this time he is building, not destroying, and the story is set in motion not by his malice but by a prior agreement. This Devil, one suspects, had come courting, and was fobbed off with a promise that he could marry the great man's daughter if he accomplished the impossible, building a road in one night, which he was in a fair way to achieve until he was tricked into thinking he'd lost. The trick seems to have been the work of the common people, 'they', and not the 'great man'. Further than this we cannot go, because after Aubrey's time the story seems to have been forgotten completely.

But it was not an isolated tradition, for another story with a very similar plot line had been told many centuries earlier in a different country, by people who had never even heard of the Devil. This is the story of the construction of Asgard in Norse mythology, which tells how a giant bargained to build the stronghold, to be paid with the sun and moon and Freyja the goddess if he completed in time, and how he was defeated by the cunning of Loki.[5] Very similar tales survive to this day in Scandinavia, associated not with the mythical Asgard but with real-life magnificent buildings. These are usually churches that are to be built by a troll in one night (not in winter, as in the Edda, but winter is simply the night of the year), and the work is to be done in return for the same reward, the sun and moon, together with the life of the protagonist. The hero escapes through good luck and trickery, and the troll architect hurls himself from the spire of the almost-completed building.[6]

Sometimes a stone is shown as proof of the truth of the story, and this matches up with another of the legends that survived in the pagan literature of the North. Thor is matched against the dwarf Alvis, who has been promised an unwilling bride from Asgard, and the god tricks his opponent into a contest of wits that lasts all night and lingers past sunrise, when at once the dwarf stiffens into stone.[7] Like the story of the giant builder, this tale has survived in less lofty local traditions: Norway and Sweden are full of boulders that were once trolls, who were caught in the rays of the sun and turned to stone. Some elements of this old myth – the stolen bride, the deception of a supernatural enemy – are still present in the story from Ockley. And both the Devil's Causeway and the Devil's Dyke have preserved in their legends the overriding importance of night and day. The reason why the Devil must finish his work by sunrise lies not within the plot of the story, but in its history. Once, he was not the Devil of Christianity at all, but a troll; he had to flee the sunrise, or he would perish.

So in one sense the story told to Aubrey in the 1680s was very ancient, going back to the pagan past of Northern Europe. But in another sense it was not ancient at all, because traditions are continually in flux. They are like the Irishman's old hammer, which had been in the family for generations but with three new heads fitted to it and five different handles. Because they are being continually renewed by storytellers, it is impossible to say at what point in its combinations and recombinations a tradition stops being one story and becomes another. The legend of the Devil's Dyke looks very much as if it was worked out under the influence of the Ockley story, which was told only a few miles away, and on a road that took travellers down to the Sussex coast. Folk tales in which the Devil's work is cut short by an artificial sun are not common – there is only one other example in England, at Buckland Abbey in Devon – and the repetition of this motif in nearby places is probably not accidental. But even if the Ockley legend is the original of the Sussex one, it is unlikely to have been told for many years as that particular story, at that particular place. We know this from one minor detail: the naming of the road as the Devil's Causeway.

Names like this are prompt-lines for stories. They are the rough surface on which a stranger's attention is snagged; Aubrey asks what the long raised road is called, locals tell him, he naturally wonders why it should have such an odd name, and out comes the story. Names give a heavy hint that stories once existed, even in the centuries before anyone was writing them down, while the absence of names can be taken as negative evidence.

It turns out that Devil's Causeway is not a name found in any early records. Ockley is the earliest of a group that associates Roman roads with the Devil, and there are four others – the Devil's Causeway in Northumberland (1717), the Devil's Highway in Berkshire and Hampshire (1761), the Devil's Pavement at Soyland in the West Riding of Yorkshire (1775) and the Devil's Causeway at Ruckley in Shropshire (1841).[8] It is not as if these names could have somehow escaped notice until the seventeenth or eighteenth century. Roman roads are not easily overlooked, and they appear in documents going back to the Anglo-Saxon period, often with their own distinctive names; but these names have nothing to do with the Devil. Only in recent times did people learn to associate him with ancient monuments, and when they did so, they were grafting his personality onto tale-types that had previously figured a giant or troll as the enemy of man.

This is why the earliest versions of stories have come down to us in slightly incoherent form, as if the tradition were still pulling itself together. Consider what seems to be the first reported legend about the Devil in the English landscape, a story told about three – originally four – massive upright standing stones at Boroughbridge near Ripon. They stand on the outskirts of the village, in some old hayfields by the River Ure. At 18 feet high, these monoliths are a local wonder and have been pointed out to visitors for centuries, first as the Devil's Bolts and then as the Devil's Arrows, which are much the same thing, a bolt being the thick, stocky arrow that you fire from a crossbow. A Yorkshire gentleman, Richard Shanne, mentions the story in his common-place book. 'My owne selfe have hard this taile verie often tould,' he says, which would push the date back to the late sixteenth century.

A spirit was sekinge an auncient citie harde by called Aldburrowe, who metinge with some by the way did aske howe farre it was to such a citie, and they tould him they knewe it not. And the spirit said, 'I have beene sekinge of the same so manie years and yet could never fynd it', and in a rage shott those boults away and so fled and was never hard of anie more.[9]

Not the Devil, you notice, but 'a spirit', though this was the kind of spirit who totes large rocks around, evidently with no good intent. We can deduce as much from a comment by William

The Devil's Arrows, Boroughbridge.

Camden, the founder of British landscape studies. He wrote in 1590, about the same time as Shanne, but instead of jotting down a private note, Camden addressed his fellow scholars in Latin, the international language. He had evidently heard the stones called 'Devils Bolts', but he wrote, in translation, 'frankly I am leaving out the local story, which calls these the arrows of evil spirits, with which they bombarded the cities of old.'[10] Though the story is still vague – not the Devil, but devils – it is clear that here, as at the Dyke in Sussex, the aim was to destroy homes and lives. And here, too, the demons or spirits have been deflected by trickery, for when the locals said that 'they knewe not' Aldborough, they can't have been straight-faced: the little town is only a mile down the road.

Was this an old story? It is curious that John Leland, Camden's predecessor as a field antiquary, visited Boroughbridge earlier, in about 1540, and took careful notes on the standing stones; he describes them not as the Devil's (or devils') Bolts, but just as '4 great maine stones'. Of course he was recording monuments, not folklore, but this would have been made easier by using their distinctive name, if that had existed then. Perhaps the name came into use after his visit and the legend followed.[11]

A Crafty Cobbler

Two hundred years go by and then we hear once more about a destructive Devil, a deceitful wayfarer and an enduring monument. This time we are on the outskirts of Wyre Forest, west of Kidderminster, and the landmark is the Devil's Spittleful. It is a sandstone hillock, a great knob of red rock that looks quite out of place on the farmland a mile outside Bewdley, and the story tells us why.

Spittleful is Worcestershire dialect for 'spadeful', and this hill was indeed being carried by the Devil on his spade. He was making his way with great purposeful strides from the western regions when he saw someone coming the other way. The traveller was a poor man, tramping the countryside with a sack on his back; but the Devil is no respecter of persons, and besides, it would be nice to take a break from carrying that enormous spade-ful. So he shifted the weight to his other hand and stopped for a chat. The Devil is a proud spirit, so his conversation was rather one-sided: he told the stranger everything about his plans and ambitions, while the poor man never got to say much in reply about his own line of business. There was, said the Devil, a certain godly town in the heart of England that had resisted all his rec-ommendations to vice. Its folk were incorrigible; they were beyond hope of damnation; there was nothing to be done but to drop this hill in the River Severn and let its floodwaters totally sub-merge the people of Bewdley. Bewdley! said the poor man, so shocked that even the Devil stopped in mid-monologue. You'll never make it to Bewdley – why that's where I came from, when I first set out – and look, I've worn out this pair of shoes since I started (he pulled a pair out of the sack) and this one as well, and this pair, these, these too . . . The Devil watched while the split and broken shoes tumbled out of the sack, and his spadeful seemed heavier and heavier as he thought of the road ahead. Finally he could take no more and, tipping his massive burden out by the roadside, he slung the great spade over his shoulder and returned to his native place. The poor man watched that mighty form retreat into the distance, then picked up the shoes carefully, two by two. He was a travelling cobbler, and had been taking his customers' orders home to repair when he met the unexpected stranger.

Such is the story, as it was told independently by two local antiquaries in the 1850s, but it was older than that.[12] When George Griffith wrote one of those versified adaptations that were popular in the nineteenth century, he explained that he had heard the story from a third source, his wife; she had been told it by her parents, who first heard it when they ran a pub at Bewdley that was a stopping-off point for the boatmen who carried goods up and down the Severn.[13] That takes us back to the late eighteenth century, a date which is confirmed by the appearance of the name 'Devil's Spittleful' on Isaac Taylor's 1772 map of Worcestershire, so that the story must already have been familiar then.

But not far away was another hill and another story – or, if you like, the same one. The hill is the Wrekin, that unmistakeable conical mount which dominates the landscape of Shropshire, and the story proceeds on exactly the same lines: a huge spadeful of earth, plans to dam the Severn (except now it is Shrewsbury which is to be annihilated), a meeting with a cobbler, the worn boots shaken out of the sack, a retreat in confusion and the town saved. Only this time the great antagonist of the story is not the Devil but a giant. First published in 1860, this continued to be told as the tale of how a giant was fooled until the 1880s, when versions with a spade-bearing Devil began to creep in. Hiram Howell, in his versified *Wrekin Legend*, preferred the Devil, but an old woman interviewed by the great folklorist Charlotte Burne said, with the air of one who has long since ceased to be surprised at the waywardness of youth, 'They generally call it the devil nowadays, but the older people say it was a giant.'[14] And since Burne preferred the version with the giant in her *Shropshire Folk-Lore*, it has become canonical and nobody tells one featuring the Devil any more. It is likely that the story at Bewdley had also developed, at an earlier date, from an original in which it was a giant who dropped the spittleful. After all, the plot depends on the adversary being huge – so huge that he can casually carry a whole hill's-worth of earth on his shovel: and great size is something that you associate more naturally with giants than devils. The older form of the story survives in northwest Wales, where it involves a giant couple planning to bridge the Menai Strait. When deceived by the cobbler, Mr Giant discards two huge stones and Mrs Giant drops the mound of earth she is carrying in her apron, so their encounter is marked by a mound called Barclodiad y Gawres, 'the apronful of the giantess'. If the place-name is an old one, then giants had always been the protagonists.[15]

But it was the Devil who caught the popular imagination, and his version of the story began to spawn imitations. Why some legends should be told invariably of only one spot while others get repeated at place after place is a mystery of the narrative mind; several different factors must come into play before a story gets legs. At the basic level, the tale has to fit some common cultural template, if not of how things could possibly be (like ghosts), then at least of how they could be imagined (like dragons). The legend of the giant/Devil and the cobbler classifies as a folk tale, but it was not confined to the folk, if by that is meant predomin-antly rural workers. 'It is a story current among all classes,' observed Charlotte Burne. 'You all know the story of the Spadeful,' said Benjamin Gibbons to the worthies of Bewdley.

Legends belong to everybody, not just to rustics with prodi-gious but illiterate memories or to a few trained storytellers; that is why they are always at risk of breaking down. You have to remember the plot, and even one as simple as the Wrekin story could be distorted by people who only recollected in a confused way that it was somehow about shoes. Sometimes the cobbler is omitted, and the people of Shrewsbury set out themselves with bags of worn-out footwear to convince the giant he is a long way from his destination. Sometimes the trick is left out, and the hill is supposed to consist, in hugely magnified form, of shoes dropped by the frightened cobbler.[16] Most people need a lot of reinforce-ment before they can repeat a story pat, with all its incidents. That is why, even in a country with communications as good as nineteenth-century England, local legends seldom spread further than walking distance. You needed to hear the original version more than once, in the ordinary round of work and leisure, before its imitation could be successfully grafted onto a new site.

Most of all, the story needed prompts from the landscape itself. For this tale to really work, you need a hill that looks as if it might, in some fantastic alternative reality, have dribbled off a huge spade. You need a town with a famous river that might be blocked by the spadeful: some versions skip this and rewrite the plot so that the Devil/giant is going to obliterate a town directly by dropping the earth onto it, but even fantasy needs consistency, and a hill is obviously too small to cover a town. And there needs to be a road, running hard by the hill itself, on which the two protagonists can meet.

Pyon Hill in Herefordshire meets all these requirements: in fact it looks like a miniature Wrekin, about 30 miles away from the original. Hereford was the city targeted for destruction because of its virtue – although a malicious variant says that the Devil was talked out of his purpose, not by a cobbler's ruse, but when he discovered that the people of the city were in a fair way towards Hell already. Another sharp-edged version is told at nearby Shobdon, where the Devil's wrath was aroused by the beauty of the parish church. He is foiled by the cobbler in the usual style but the villagers, suspecting that they may not get away so easily the next time, pull down the offensive church and studiously avoid anything that might give the place a reputation for piety. Shobdon is an unexpected site for this legend: it is not a city, it doesn't have a river and there isn't even a suitable hill, although a small mound behind the village war memorial was pressed into service as the Devil's Shovelful. But it did have a dynasty of cobblers, living opposite this mound on the outskirts of the village, who may have introduced the legend.[17] Cobblers are not noted, as a trade, for their heroism but they were professional itinerants, prepared to tell a story wherever they stopped to pick up shoes, so they would have cherished a tale that put their profession in a good light.

If the legend was indeed leapfrogging from one conical hill to another, then its next stop was Cam Peak, overlooking the Vale of Berkeley on the east side of the Severn. This is a dramatic outlier of the Cotswold escarpment, just the sort of hill to attract a legend, but the story had only been imperfectly adopted by 1904, when a scholar writes of 'how the Devil, on his way to dam the Severn, found the distance trying, and, tipping up his load in a fit of disgust, formed the hill': no cobbler, no trick. Later in the twentieth century, the full version would be told here, as elsewhere.[18]

A wheelbarrow would make sense (if an immaterial spirit trundling a barrow some 800 yards long over an Area of Outstanding Natural Beauty can ever be described as sensible) but it is a novelty in the story. Maybe it was just the invention of a practically minded storyteller, but if you go over to the other side of the Cotswolds, to Fairford church with its magnificent fifteenth-century windows, you will see a blue devil pushing a wheelbarrow of sinners headed, literally, to Hell in a handcart. Though this was a common motif in medieval paintings of the Day of Judgement, Fairford is one of the few places where it is still visible; perhaps this window provided some curious traveller with the necessary detail.

At Cley Hill, on the Somerset side of Wiltshire, the storyteller dispensed with both spade and wheelbarrow; here the Devil just staggers along with the weight of the hill on his back. Other details from this version, recorded in 1893, suggest an imperfect imitation; the Devil is on his way to destroy Devizes, and stops to ask for instructions from a traveller (so far, so expected), but 'the man replied, "That's just what I want to know myself. I started for Devizes when my beard was black, and now it's grey, and I haven't got there yet"' – which doesn't, logically, prove anything about how far off the town is: he should have said 'started from Devizes'.[19] In any case, the obvious focus for destruction would be Warminster, which is only 2 miles away, so the teller seems to have got his hill muddled up with another landmark further to the northeast.

Here the story comes in two flavours depending on whether you are from Marlborough or Devizes. The two market centres for the Wiltshire Downs have never seen eye to eye, so it is not surprising that Devizes folk talk about the time that the Devil was enlisted by the Marlborough people to drop a load of earth on their community, while at the other town (keeping a discreet silence over who motivated him) they dwell on his zeal for destroying Marlborough. First, the Devizes version: the Devil heads westwards along the A4, the townspeople panic, St John (patron of their church) steps forward to give good advice, a man with a sack of shoes sets out and meets the fiend about halfway along the road, near Avebury. The usual dialogue ensues, the Devil drops his burden, and there it is, Silbury Hill.[20]

Or, if you want to hear it as told in Marlborough (and in the richness of Wiltshire dialect), then begin with the Devil heading eastwards – unburdened, this time – along the A361, where about halfway along he meets a shepherd:

> Zo Maister Nick comes to'n an' zays 'Howdydo?'
> Shepherd says 'Tarblish! I hope you be, too;
> An' wher' be 'ee boun' vor at this time o' day?'
> 'To Marlboro', says Nick, 'but I caint vind my way!'

The shepherd panics and runs to Marlborough, the townspeople are in consternation; a wise man steps forward and tells them all to give him their old shoes, and off he goes. He meets the Devil, who is still asking the way, and

The wise man did zay – vlingin' down his girt pack –
'I caint zay how vur 'tis, but miles an' miles back!
When I come vrom Marlboro theäm shoes were al' new,
An' I wore 'em all out travellin' this vur, snaw you!'

Despairing of ever reaching Marlborough, the Devil departs to his own place, while the wise man chuckles to himself and sets off home, ignoring the bag of shoes, which he has dropped in the road. This, like any pile of rubbish, gradually accumulates until in time it becomes Silbury Hill.[21]

The Devizes version is roughly contemporary with the versified accounts from Bewdley and the Wrekin, while its Marlborough counterpart is later, but both are manifestly imperfect – one has forgotten the cobbler and the other is missing even the pile of earth, which is a pity since Silbury, unlike all the other hills which we have visited so far, really is earth piled up, a man-made construction; it also lies just where it ought to according to the story, slap in the middle of the highway, because the old Roman road is aligned on it. There is another version in which the Devil sets off to smother Avebury in earth until he is forced to drop his spadeful by the charms and incantations of priests at the old temple – but this, despite all its intimations of an older paganism, is a twentieth-century elaboration.[22]

It is not easy to prove a negative in folklore but Silbury Hill offers a rare chance. One of the major prehistoric monuments of England, it has attracted archaeologists since the seventeenth century, many of whom were inquisitive for legends and traditions. John Aubrey was here in 1670, when he was told that the mound was the burial place of King Sil. According to later elaborations, the king was interred on horseback in golden armour or in a golden coffin.[23] These traditions have a romantic ring to them, but we are still in the world of historical speculation, accepting the mound as an ancient earthwork rather than bringing in the

Silbury Hill.

fantastic. If they had been told stories about the Devil, Aubrey and his antiquarian successor William Stukeley would have written them down, for they were trying every possible key to open the mystery of the pre-Roman world, and did not scruple to use folk traditions. But they heard nothing about the Devil. He arrived after their time, probably in the 1860s.

We mistake the age of legends when we pay too much attention to their landscapes. Because a story is told about a prehistoric mound, we think of it as being very old, quite possibly prehistoric. Now, it is true that motifs, the raw material of stories, have been knocking around the world for countless ages, and stones, for instance, must have featured as petrified people ever since there were human beings with imaginations and words for 'people' and 'stone'. But actual stories, the narratives with incidents and a plot, often turn out to have spread in quite recent times. The Devil and cobbler tale-type has every appearance of having migrated through a limited area of southern England between the mid-eighteenth century and the closing years of Queen Victoria's reign.

The Price of a Bridge

A legend does not need natural or prehistoric monuments for its focus: it can as easily fasten onto works of the Middle Ages. The River Lune descends from the Lake District to Lancashire, and, where it begins to run through the green lands below the fells, it is crossed by an elegant fifteenth-century bridge with three rising spans. This replaced earlier masonry of the thirteenth and fourteenth centuries, and the river crossing is evidently the nucleus around which the village of Kirkby Lonsdale has grown.

But in the story, it is the other way round: imagine a village of Kirkby but no bridge. There is good grazing on the eastern side of the river, and every morning the villagers drive their cattle through the rough waters of the Lune and leave them in the meadows until nightfall, when they are rounded up and swum home again. Until one night a cow gets left behind – the only cow of a poor old widow woman. The waters are in spate, so she has no chance of getting over for many days, and who knows what will have happened by then.

Looking across the river in the evening murk, she can see a strange figure on the far side, darkly outlined against the darkening night. Desperate for anyone's assistance, she calls to him – can he help? – and the stranger shouts back – yes, he will be delighted to help her, and might a bridge across the river be the thing she needs? Then she can walk her cow over every morning and walk it back again in the evening, no problem. He is sure that he can fix something like that for her. This very night, as it happens.

The old woman, who like many old women was not born yesterday, fixes a steely gaze on the black shape over at the further bank and asks if there's a catch. Dear me, no, says the shadow, nothing but a small consideration: in the morning, when the bridge is built, the first to cross it will be mine. That's all, and just think of the convenience. The old lady does indeed think for a bit, and then she shouts a loud Yes! – and the Devil sets to work.

Say what you like about him, he builds to a very high standard and doesn't waste time on the job. By first light the bridge is complete, with its three graceful arches spanning the wild waters, and as the old lady walks down to the edge, she can see the black architect on the far side, bowing to her and beckoning. Out of her pocket she pulls a savoury bun, and after waving it quickly in front of the half-starved dog by her side, she bowls it across the bridge. The dog runs after, the Devil clutches at it, and finding that he has gained nothing but an underfed household pet for his pains, he vanishes in flames with a howl that wakes up half the village. They rush down to the river to see what can have happened, and there is their neighbour, complacently driving her cow back across the new bridge.

That's 'the legend which nearly all Kirkby people will tell you' in 1898, and which they continue to tell today.[24] Different renditions keep closely to the basic story-line, if you allow for some ambiguity at the last moment: for dog-lovers, the mutt was left behind as not worth the Devil's attention; others didn't mind him going up in flame, as long as no human beings were harmed in the making of the story. The first recorded version, printed in a local magazine for 1821, adds a pony to the cow, so that the Devil can say:

> 'To raise a bridge I will agree,
> That in the morning you shall see,
> But mine for aye the first must be
>   That passes over;
> So by these means you'll soon be able
> To bring the pony to his stable,
>   The cow her clover.'

This version was evidently written by a Lancastrian, who misses no chance to remind us that the woman was an incomer from Yorkshire, hence her preternatural sharpness at a bargain.[25] Like so many of the local legends that were versified around this time, its brisk rhythm and bouncing rhymes bring a smile to what is, after all, a rather sinister plot redeemed at the last minute by a happy ending.

There is something a little uncanny about a bridge. There were stories in which the stonework fell down, night after night, until human life had been built into the foundations. At some remote period, the story of the Devil's Bridge may have been fused from stories of the church-building troll who is tricked out of the life he demands as his fee, and the tragic legends in which a life must be paid before a bridge will stand firm. Perhaps the fusion happened in a region, such as Germany, where the Devil had already replaced the troll as antagonist, and afterwards spread to England.

If so, it had not reached the Lune by 1781, for that was the year that John Hutton set out on a tour of the Yorkshire Dales, and like many tourists (to use a newly coined word) he was curious about everything he saw. Since there were as yet no guidebooks to the Dales he relied on oral tradition, and when he asked about the bridge in Kirkby Lonsdale he was told 'that it was built by the devil one night in windy weather; he had but one apron full of stones for the purpose, and unfortunately his apron-string breaking as he flew with them over Casterton-fell, he lost many of them out, or the bridge would have been much higher'.[26] No old lady; no cow.

The story told to John Hutton was the same as that recounted of the Devil's Bridge over Hell Gill beck in Wensleydale: just as he was flying down from the mountainside with the necessary materials, the straps of the Devil's apron broke. Some of the stones tumbled in a heap near the bridge, and the rest crashed into the bed of the river, creating the hollow that locals call the Kail Pot, an unfathomable pit of seething waters.[27] There is a third Devil's Bridge in the Dales, at East Witton near Richmond, and this one already had its name in 1804, although it had previously been called Kilgram Bridge after a nearby hamlet.[28] It was built by the Devil all in one night, they said – tales like this often celebrate the instantaneous construction of landmarks, a storyteller's embodiment of the way things can appear all at once in the imagination. But the Devil was not quite as quick as had been thought, and at the end of the night one stone was still missing from the parapet. Since then the work has been left undone, with no human builder willing to enter into partnership with the black architect in case they found themselves spending more time with him later on. The tradition, already current in the 1850s, was never forgotten; when the bridge was repaired in 1997, the missing stone was carefully left that way.[29]

But by 1894 the reputation of the Kirkby Lonsdale bridge had spread, and it inspired people at East Witton to a more elaborate tradition. The bridge reverted to its original designation, now deformed to Kilgrim Bridge to support one of those heavy-handed puns which explain the names of places. The Devil offered, and the locals accepted, that this bridge should be built on con-dition that he take the first living creature to cross it. Once his work was done, the dalesfolk clustered at the near end, under-standably reluctant to put the matter to the test, until an old shepherd with more sense than the others swam across the stream, put his fingers in his mouth and whistled for his dog to follow. Over the bridge bounded the dog – Grim, he was called – to be instantly killed, hence the name.[30]

This is not altogether satisfactory as a transfer of the Kirkby story. The idea of someone swimming across the river and then standing on the other side, presumably behind the Devil's back, brushes aside the analogies that made the original tale so effective – the framing of its surface narrative upon a pattern of something deeper. Until the Devil is defeated, this side of the bridge should be as far from the other as life is from death. So in structural terms, the version with the old lady and her cow is the better one.

Nevertheless, Hutton's travel notes shows that this story did not arrive at the bridge over the Lune until sometime between 1781 and 1821. But then it did not need any polish from local talent; it arrived ready-made, copied and pasted from another Devil's Bridge, across the Mynach near Aberystwyth. At this beauty spot, visitors were being amused from the 1810s onwards with a legend in jingling rhymes that began:

Old Megan Llandunach,
Of Pont y Mynach,
    Had lost her only cow;
Across the ravine
The cow was seen,
    But to reach it she could not tell how.[31]

It is exactly the same story, in very much the same style, as the 1821 Kirkby poem – even down to some of the wording. But the Cardiganshire tradition is older, already being told to visitors in 1787, while the name Devil's Bridge is recorded from 1734.[32] It cannot be much older than that, for the language of the name betrays its eighteenth-century origins. We are in Welsh-speaking Wales, where an English place-name could only have been adopted to please visitors, and originally the crossing was simply Pontarfynach, 'bridge over the Mynach'.

What did the bridges at Pontarfynach and Kirkby have in common? One thing: tourists. The Welsh village lay on turnpike roads that brought the mountain landscape within easy reach of Shrewsbury and London; the Westmorland one was the gateway to the Lake District for travellers coming from Skipton on the Kendal road. But the scenery was certainly more dramatic at the

DEVIL'S BRIDGE 17750

The Devil's Bridge, Aberystwyth.

Welsh Devil's Bridge, at least before 1753, when the county magistrates prioritized safety over picturesqueness by giving the original bridge a second tier. A narrow gorge of sharp split rocks, a stream of raging mountain water breaking through the cleft, the thin single span of the bridge in grey outline above the flood: there was nothing to compare with it, unless you had crossed the Teufelsbrücke across the River Reuss. Which, of course, a lot of the tourists had done, since the Schöllenen Gorge was their route across the Alps and into the cultural splendours of Italy. They were not likely to forget this slender ancient bridge, almost the twin of the falls of the Mynach but in the dramatic and more dangerous passes of the Swiss Alps. 'The most hazardous part is the bridge on the Rus,' wrote Thomas Nugent in 1749, 'called the bridge of hell from the horrid noise the water makes as it tumbles from the rocks, and from the slipperiness of the bridge which renders it difficult even to foot passengers who are obliged to creep on all fours, lest the fury of the wind should drive them down to the rocks.'[33]

As we saw with Devil and cobbler stories, migratory legends usually make their way across the country a step at a time; that is why the Devil's Bridges of Kirkby, Hell Gill and East Witton are all found within a small area of Yorkshire and its borders. But this is not a consequence of geography, simply of human nature, and when people who are familiar with a story in one place find themselves reminded of it somewhere else, distance is no object. In this way the legend told to explain the Teufelsbrücke – old woman, cow and all – made the jump to rural Wales. Even at the time this did not go unnoticed. 'The Devil's Bridge, par excellence,' writes Askew Roberts in his *Gossiping Guide to Wales*, 'is the one on the St Gothard's pass on the (very) high road between Fluellen and Milan; and the tradition connected with it is so like that told of the Cardiganshire one, that Mr. Longfellow's version, in the Golden Legend, might serve for the two.'[34]

A Taste for Scenery

By the time Alpine tourists had recovered from their terror, listened attentively to the mountaineer's tale and perhaps tucked an engraving of the scene into their portfolios, they would have a clear image of what a Devil's Bridge should look like if they met one back at home. Supposing there was a medieval bridge nearby spanning a chasm, so much the better; if not, then one could be supplied. Scattered follies of this kind reflected the new taste for landscape gardening, at first confined to England, though the craze rapidly spread across Europe. A freshly weathered Devil's Bridge improved the *jardin anglais* laid out in the 1780s by the Comte d'Albion; having married the daughter of a financier, the *comte* could afford more improvements than most, and his château at Franconville also boasted a Temple of the Muses and two rustic huts, along with an obelisk, pyramid, hermitage and half-ruined grotto.[35]

A few years later, the French Revolution would brush aside these sham ruins to create new ones much more realistic in their execution. Meanwhile, on the conservative side of the Channel, estate gardeners continued to dot each vista with some picturesque or folkloric building. Not every park could boast a deep romantic chasm, but the name of the original bridge proved quite adaptable and was applied to all sorts of features: in the 1790s the owners of Steephill on the Isle of Wight placed a seat to command the magnificent sea view on their Devil's Bridge, which was simply a rock shelf jutting out from the cliff.[36] On the cliffs near Whitby, the 1st Earl of Mulgrave consulted Henry Repton on landscape design before marking the extremes of his property with a Wizard's Glen, Eagle's Nest and Devil's Bridge.[37] If you wandered along the burn at Castle Eden Dene just after the woodlands had been laid out in 1800, you would have passed the Devil's Bridge near Black Bull's Hole and then the Devil's Scar upstream from the Seven Chambers and Dungeon Bridge before finally coming to the Devil's Lapstone – that is, a stone from his lapful; as at Kirkby and Hell Gill, he was flying with the burden in his apron when the strings broke and precipitated it by the waterside.[38] Perhaps the legend existed before the landscaping; perhaps it was simply encouraged to grow in these wild surroundings, like moss on a garden seat.

With the rise of a more natural style of gardening in the nineteenth century, it was no longer necessary to build these devilish features. Instead, the romantically minded landowner relied on names alone when he wanted to induce an appropriate shiver at some gloomy corner. Devil's Grove was a division of Chicksands Wood in the grounds of Haynes Grange, marked out in 1835 with rides and an obelisk. You could pause here or continue to Long Grove, Temple Grove or Druid's Grove, whichever best suited your programme of meditations for that day's ride.[39]

Devil's Den was a wood in the grounds of Prestwood Park in Kingswinford.[40] There is another Devil's Den on the island of Brownsea in Poole Harbour. Since Brownsea had no permanent inhabitants – it was the private domain of George Cavendish-Bentinck, who improved the grounds between 1873 and 1891 – the Den is likely to reflect his personal taste in landmarks, along with St Michael's Mount, Harlequin and Pantaloon Hills, and Piper's Folly.[41] It's true that William Benson of Brownsea might have left a whiff of the diabolical behind him: after working on the gardens at Stourhead, he moved to the island and developed it as a private estate before losing his mind in 1741, when he took to black magic and sacrificed a servant girl in the nearest thing he could find to a grove. Or so they said on the waterside at Poole, but then Poole merchants were never very well affected to the gentry anyway.[42]

Are rumours like this real folklore? Does a gentleman's choice of a name for his rustic bridge count? Or the decision by that gentleman's valet, retired at last, to open a tea-shop by the local beauty-spot and sell little handbills with a copied legend? If we are searching for the authentic, unmediated voice of the folk, we will probably brush all these aside as illegitimate, but it is our search that is at fault and not the facts. Traditions of the Devil do not rise from the national subconscious; they are oral literature, drawn from sources here and there like any other literature, and just as capable in the end of moving our emotions.

2

DOWN TUMBLED THE STONES: LANDSCAPES SHAPED BY THE DEVIL'S HAND

The Devil watches over treasure hidden at ancient landmarks. The landscape itself is said to have been carved into mounds and embankments by his efforts, and otherwise inexplicable piles of stone turn out to have been accidentally dropped by him. Where the historical record is detailed enough, we can see these stories developing in modern times, and replacing the quite different lore of the Middle Ages. Storytellers worked up narratives from local peculiarities: any isolated boulder had been thrown by the Devil, and his prodigious leaps left an imprint on hard stone.

Treasure and Its Guardians

The Ashmolean Museum is full of light. It floods the atrium, spills downs the stairwells and shines off the marble and glass; this museum was prized in its earliest days for classical antiquities, and something of that serene order survives in the Grecian facade and the high ceilings of the statue hall. Nowadays children run along with their colouring sheets where once the periwigged virtuosi of Oxford swapped tags from Virgil, but it is all illumination of a sort. This is not what we have come for, however; an unkempt line of scholars, like the Hogwarts faculty in mufti, we push on through the bright galleries until we come to a black wall, which looks much more promising, because it carries the word SPELLBOUND in yard-high gold letters, and in the dimmed galleries behind is the Ashmolean's exhibition of magic and witchcraft.[1]

Two hundred objects have been gathered to illustrate this theme. Some have been beautifully crafted in silver, ivory and gold; others are squalid little horrors. Yet they are all charms and countercharms. Once they compelled love, secured children, promised fame, inflicted witchcraft or repelled it; all were wicked powerful things in their day, now pinned and labelled behind glass, as danger-free as the tigers at the zoo. But magic is one of those themes, like sex and war, that can never feel really dead and dispassionate, not even in a museum case. We may peer at a row of talismans, squint closely at their sigils, make out the crabbed Gothic lettering – this is a private view, and we are a tremendously learned lot. Still, even at the heart of museum enterprise and in a selected band of historians of magic, nobody actually reads out the demon names. That would be a little too close to ritual, and while not expecting it to work we still feel a shiver of unease about bringing back to life the words that held such power for our historical shadows, the magicians themselves.

Here, for instance, is a copy of the Sworn Book of Honorius next to a brass medal with the Sigillum Dei. Honorius, or someone pretending to be him, has left very clear instructions for the Sigillum: you are to draw a circle, and inside that a heptagon, and inside that a heptagram, and inside that another heptagon, and inside that a pentagram, and inside that a cross. Then you fill in the spaces with names – the ineffable name of God, the unutterable names of the planetary intelligences – until every gap is filled, after which you will have a talisman that will force spirits of every kind to appear in an attractive and docile form and to grant your every request. Unless you copied a letter wrong, in which case you have only a short time left to regret ever getting into magic at all.

That is probably why, facing the brass medal, we can see a metal matrix for casting copies of the Sigillum. Armed with a

The Devil's Ditch, Newmarket.

red wax version, perfect in every detail, operants could open their ritual without fear. The matrix, made in the sixteenth century, has survived in the collections of the Museum of the History of Science down the road because it was found buried in the Devil's Dyke. This is not the Sussex valley, but an embankment which runs for 7 miles in a straight line west of Newmarket. Its height to the top of the bank is a good 30 feet, making it the largest of the dykes that defended East Anglia from Mercia in Anglo-Saxon times.

Why should a mould for making magical talismans get lost in the Cambridgeshire countryside? It's not the sort of thing that would drop out of a pocket. It must have been buried, probably for safety, and not just for the safety of the object either, because anyone found with materials for performing the rites of the Sworn Book would be liable for discipline and penance before the ecclesiastical courts, perhaps worse. The magical paraphernalia had to be hidden until the hue and cry had died down, and where better to bury it than in the Devil's Dyke, where the Devil could look after it?

Or if not *the* Devil, then at least *a* devil, because it was common knowledge in the sixteenth century that buried treasures were guarded by demons. These might be one of the spirits called keepers, who were tethered to the spot like a kind of psychic guard-dog, bound by a magician's art and fated to remain there until some greater magician overpowered them. Or they might be independent spirits whose subtle senses, far more acute than those of mortal men, could detect the metal that was buried underground. Treasure-hunters often wavered between these two interpretations, a tribute to the relative unimportance of the surface narratives; what really mattered was the subliminal link between gold and the demonic. Though the Sworn Book and other occult works had promised that contact with the forbidden would reveal the secrets of the spiritual world, what the magicians really wanted was cash.

George Dowsing, a schoolmaster of Norwich who was 'seen in astronymye', was enlisted by a treasure-hunting consortium in 1521 because he could raise up 'in a glasse a little thing of the length of an ynche or ther about'. In 1539 William Wycherley joined with four Sussex companions to call up the spirit Baro in search of treasure. Though they used the Circle of Solomon, a consecrated sword and holy water, Baro stayed away.[2] Perhaps it was the high failure rate, or some other change in the spirit of the times, but as the years pass these stories of devil-guarded treasure lose what little realism they ever had and grow fantastical. At Skenfrith Castle near Monmouth 'the voice of the country goeth there is a dyvill and his dame, one sets upon a hogshead of gold, the other on a hogshead of silver,' according to an opportunistic Welshman in 1589. Though currently lodged in the Tower of London, as soon as he was set free he would serve notice on Mr and Mrs Devil and make over the money to Elizabeth I; some of it, anyway.[3]

At Glastonbury, that tireless tourist Celia Fiennes was shown what we now know as the vault of St Joseph's Chapel, presented

St Joseph's Chapel, Glastonbury.

to her as 'the cellar or vault which if they cast a stone into the place it gives a great echo, and the country people sayes its the Devil set there on a tun of money, which makes that noise least they should take it away from him'.[4] By Aubrey's time the traditions had developed that catch, popular in folk tales, of the self-confessed impossibility: on St Anne's Hill in Chertsey 'lies a huge Stone ... which they call the Devil's Stone, and believe it cannot be moved, and that Treasure is hid underneath'. Not much use to know, if it can't be lifted. Only one speculator is said to have delved round this immoveable stone in search of its treasure, and the longer he dug the less it yielded, which is hardly surprising as it is an outcrop of the natural rock: he was trying to dig up the hill on which he stood.[5]

In their nineteenth-century versions, stories about hidden treasure had lost any clear connection with the demonic. Nothing was left but a sense that some ill-defined 'they' did not want you to get at the hidden wealth, that attempts with pick and shovel would be brought to an end by strange appearances and unseasonable weather, and that even if by some lucky chance you did get a glimpse of the gold, then uttering a holy word, just swearing in amazement, would cause it to dive out of reach forever. If it were not for the earlier historical records, we would think it very far-fetched to imagine that such scattered traditions, all told very much in the spirit of fancy, derived from actual practice.

In the same way, the patron of the Devil's Dyke rapidly evolved from whatever elemental horror was supposed to be guarding the buried Sigillum into a much more mythical figure. The earliest mention of the name – in fact, the earliest record of any landmark being named after the Devil – comes from 1574, when a local historian says (in Latin, of course; he was a Cambridge man) that it is so called 'because the common people think it made by devilish art, not by human labour'.[6] William Camden was uncertain, as he had been at Boroughbridge, whether there was one Devil or many; 'they foolishly call it Diuelsdyke, as it were the work of devils and not of men.'[7] The name carries overtones of horror and wonder, although as time passes the horror fades out and the Devil begins to seem a quite jovial character.

Remaking the Landscape

Perhaps this was caused by familiarity, for East Anglia has a lot of Devil's Dykes – or Ditches (there is no real difference, it just depends on how faithfully map-makers took down the local pronunciation). They are all bank-and-ditch earthworks dating from the Iron Age to the early medieval period. One runs along the boundary of Garboldisham, another along that of Beeston; another ends at Wayford Bridge in Stalham.[8] After digging the ditch in Narborough the Devil finished off his job, like a tidy workman, by cleaning his spade. A large lump of earth fell off, which formed the barrow of Hangour Hill.[9] At the Devil's Ditch in Weeting he scraped the mud off his boots, and that was the origin of Thetford Castle Hill.[10]

'Tis frequent with us to give the Honour of such great Trenches, which they think was never worth the while for Men to dig, to the Devil, as if he had more leisure, or that it was less trouble to him than to a whole Army of Men,' wrote Daniel Defoe in the 1720s.[11] It was the casualness of these works, the idea of vast strength idly employed, which appealed to storytellers. 'One day the Devil, having nothing to do,/ Built a great hedge from Lerryn to Looe,' say the Cornish.[12] No longer the adversary of the human race, this Devil is simply a scaled-up everyman; whatever most needs doing in any particular region, he does it, and on a gigantic scale. On the Norfolk clay he digs drainage ditches, in the West Country he clears stones for a Cornish hedge and on the Berkshire Downs, where there are neither stones nor clay, he turns ploughman. The Devil's Ditch along the northern edge of the downs, from Lowbury Hill to Cuckhamsley, was ploughed in one night, a single furrow. By the time the Devil had got in sight of Wantage, the ploughshare was clogged, and he bent over to scrape off the dirt, throwing it across the Ridgeway, where it landed as what is now the barrow of Scutchamer Knob. Others have pointed to a pair of barrows as the plough-scrapings, while a third one is the clod of earth which the Devil threw at his imp for leading the team crooked.[13]

It's not what you'd call a story; you have to be there, as they say, to appreciate a tradition like this. But when you stand on the Ridgeway, with the long swell of the hills under an arch of sky, it all falls into place and you can almost see a wave of grass being turned up as the plough cuts through with tireless superhuman strength behind it. Stories like this are set in a world where reality and imagination still overlap, where sheer demonic will can impose new forms on hill and rock and hollows.

Every country has stories of how supernatural beings created mountains and valleys in the first days of the world, what the Australian Aborigines call the Dreamtime. So the traditions from

Moulsford and Weeting and Narborough fit a very ancient template, and so do the more elaborate legends from Brighton and Bewdley: all of these explain strange features of the landscape as the Devil's work. But even though they have this archaic character, the stories as told can't be all that ancient. None of the Devil's Dykes is recorded before the nineteenth century apart from the Newmarket one, and even that was known for most of the Middle Ages as the ditch of St Edmund, because it formed a property boundary for the abbey at Bury St Edmunds. The Devil's Dykes at Narborough and Beeston had quite different names in the eleventh century – Bichamdic and Lawendic. Two of the Devil's Ditches, at St Mary Bourne in Hampshire and Wheathampstead in Hertfordshire, appear in Anglo-Saxon charter boundaries with merely mundane names, 'the great ditch' and 'the high ditch'.

Devil traditions continued to grow in modern times at sites like the massive earthwork running across St Briavels Common in Gloucestershire, locally known in the 1890s as the Devil's Ridge or Devil's Dyke, but now identified as the southern stretch of Offa's Dyke. Having lost all memory of who Offa was, the villagers simply replaced him by another remote figure famous for his ditch-digging. First came the name and then the tales; whereas a visitor in 1902 reported that 'the people have no stories about it,' by 1994 it was confidently claimed that it was 'cut in a single night with a plough drawn by a fox and goose'.[14] This story came from further north, in Shropshire, where it was said earlier that the Dyke was turned up by the Devil in a single night with a plough drawn by a gander and a turkey.[15] Any pair of animals would do, as long as they were ill-matched enough for their partnership to seem wonderful. At Wansdyke in Wiltshire the tradition, noted again by our friend William Camden, was that 'it was dug by the Devil on a Wednesday': here the similarity of words has led people to assign the built-in-a-night tradition to a specific day of the week.

Before Camden's time, however, great embankments were associated not with the Devil but with someone called Grim. Who he was nobody knows, especially now that his diabolical rival has usurped so many of the earthworks assigned to him. At Aldworth in Berkshire, Crowmarsh and Spelsbury in Oxfordshire and Berkhamsted in Hertfordshire the names Devil's Ditch and Grim's Ditch compete to label the same earthwork, some of the adjoining villages preferring one and some the other. At the boundary earthwork that divides Dorset from Wiltshire, the name Grim's Ditch disappeared completely from memory. When in 1872 Charles Warne asked after it, the locals were baffled. 'No one had ever heard of such a work; we were well nigh in despair, when meeting one of the magnates of the village ... at last he said "Do you mean the Devil's Ditch?" – we assented, and were at once put on its track.'[16]

A writer in that unimaginative publication *Philosophical Transactions* sneered in 1694 at the natives who told him about supernatural origins for natural features: 'as for such, that will ascribe it to Giants, or Daemons, I think do not deserve any Answer.'[17] Whenever we follow these stories further back in time, we find less of the demon and more of the giant. We can do this through the evidence of place-names, but narrative details themselves will also give a clue.

We have already seen how some of the Devil's Bridges – the one across the River Lune, and the less elaborate crossings of the Hell Gill beck and the Castle Eden burn – stood near piles of rock that had been accidentally dropped in the Devil's construction projects. He was bringing a great pile of stones in his apron, the apron-string broke, out they all tumbled and the Devil, who is easily discouraged, went away and left them; the heap stands there to this day, to be pointed out indignantly if anyone claims these old stories are not true.

Occasionally the legend gives us a little more detail. Between Bacup and Rawtenstall the River Irwell breaks through a narrow passage in the rocks. This deep gorge is known as Hell Gill, and the valley upstream as the Devil's Bathtub, for the rocky passage is said to have formerly been a solid block, forming a retaining wall for a huge basin or lake. One night of storm and thunder, the Devil had just made himself comfortable in the bath, soaping down his shaggy back while lightning flickered on the scrubbing-brush, when he noticed that the wind was beginning to whistle a bit around his thighs. The rock plug had fallen out of the gill and all the water was rushing downstream. Getting out of the rapidly emptying bath, the Devil put on his apron and filled it with gravel and small stones with which he could mend the hole, But just as he got to the gorge, the apron-strings broke, and out fell all the rubbish, making a little hill that can still be seen by the curious visitor.[18]

Aprons and Accidents

The ways of Hell are hard to fathom, but it is fair to say that most of us, getting out of the bath in a hurry, would not reach for an apron as the first thing to wear. Evidently the motif is exercising a mysterious pull that brings it into a tale even when it does not make narrative sense. This may reflect a pre-existing place-name which must be honoured in the telling of the story. A cairn at Barden, south of Richmond, was the Devil's Apronful, and so was another near Clitheroe.[19] Near Wellington in Somerset another mound of stones was the Devil's Lapful. 'The country people inform me with great gravity that, "the Devil brought them there in one night in his leathern apron,"' wrote a traveller in 1792, while the five smaller earthen barrows which stood nearby had been shaken out of his glove.[20] On the edge of the cliff at the Lizard there is a heap of stones known as the Devil's Apron-Strings (a part standing in for the whole) and attributed to his generous desire to make life easier for Cornish smugglers: 'they wor broft here by the devil in his apurn, to build a bridge across to France, so they do say, and the apurn string broke, and down tumbled the stones, and there they are.'[21]

The Devil is not a farrier or a Freemason – well, not a farrier, anyway – so why is he wearing an apron? A clue to this otherwise incidental detail of costume can be found in other traditions that have exactly the same storyline: stones are gathered for some purpose, carried in an apron, tumble out when the string breaks and shown today as proof of the tale. The only difference is that the protagonist is not the Devil but a giantess. On Ilkley Moor the wife of the giant Rombald, after a little (but gigantic) tiff with her husband, went out and filled her apron with stones so that she could hurl them at him, but he was saved by the broken apron-string, and the rocks remain on the moor in two piles, the Skirtful of Stones and the Little Skirtful.[22] In Wales, where we have found the traditions to be generally older than in England, there is one mention in Flintshire of a Ffedog y Diawl, Devil's Apron, but this was more generally known as Arffedogaid y Wrach after a mythical witch. There were two other cairns with the same name, meaning Witch's Apron, and an Arffedogaid y Gawres. We have already met with a Barclodiad y Gawres at Conwy, Apronful of the Giantess, and there is another mound with the same name on Anglesey.[23] In Ireland these stories are always told of the witch-giantess called the Cailleach, and never of the Devil.[24] It seems that, as at the Grim's Ditches, the Devil has stepped into the shoes of another character, and into her apron as well. The stories carry on being told in the old style, but with a new character and a breezy disregard for the illogical join in the narrative.

Gradually a pattern is beginning to emerge from all these migrations of tale-types and sequences of place-names: at some point between the sixteenth and eighteenth centuries, the Devil – or at all events the Devil-in-the-landscape, the one who is busy with spade and wheelbarrow – took over as the lead character for stories that had previously featured heroes or witches or giants. But this argument is based very much on hints and inferences, and it would be stronger if we had clear evidence of succession at a single site associated with the Devil. There is indeed an ancient monument with an unbroken succession of tale-telling from the high Middle Ages to the present day: it is Stonehenge, and it bears out the sequence perfectly.

Already when we hear of Stonehenge in the 1130s, it has two names: one meaning 'the stone gallows' (which has survived) and another 'the giants' ring' (which has not). Shortly afterwards, that agreeable romancer Geoffrey of Monmouth worked up a story about the site, probably drawing on local lore. Aurelius Ambrosius, king of the Britons, wants to raise a memorial for his followers who have been treacherously slain. He asks Merlin for advice, and the magician says that only one monument would be worthy, and that is the Giants' Ring in Ireland. Having subdued the Irish, Aurelius is at a loss how to get the stones back to Wiltshire, but Merlin smiles and employs his art to transport them home at once. (Here, as often in medieval romance, magic and technology lie on a spectrum, and it's not clear if Merlin just clicks his fingers or brings up pulleys and sheerlegs.) Once they have been set in place, Merlin explains why only these stones would do: there is a healing power in the water that gathers in their hollows. Geoffrey's story caught the popular imagination, though in some retellings the giants, Irishmen and Merlin all fused with each other: a fourteenth-century manuscript shows Merlin as a giant himself, easing a lintel into position as easily as if he were stacking up haybales.

In Leland's time this was still the accepted story, and it was not until the 1670s, when Aubrey was out talking to the shepherds of Salisbury Plain, that they told a variation on it: 'when Merlin conveyed these Stones from Ireland by Art Magick, the Devill

hitt him in the heele with that stone, and so left the print there.'[25]
The story must have been much the same in 1724, when William
Stukeley jotted down: 'they say the devil threw it at the builders.
They don't say the devil built this place as commonly of stupen-
dous ... stones,' so that Stukeley, grasping at straws in his attempt
to make some sense of the great monument, thought the absence
of any traditions about the Devil as builder should be taken as 'a
sign 'tis a temple'.[26]

This demonstrates how dangerous it is to base your archaeology on supposedly timeless traditions, because even as Stukeley
was writing the locals had begun to claim just that. Twenty years
later, Gaffer Hunt, the garrulous self-appointed guardian of the
stones, was telling a version that had lost Merlin altogether. The
stones came from Ireland – he carried that much over from medieval tradition – but as the gaffer told it, they were the property
not of warlike kings but of an old woman who was not at all keen
to part with them. Temptingly, the Devil came to her with a large
bag of money, and offered to pay her as much of it as she could
count while he was removing them. She took him up on his offer,
which if you think about the size of Stonehenge must have
seemed like easy money; then she shook the bag and was sorely
puzzled, what with the 13*d.* shillings and the 4½*d.* groats that
came tumbling out. But before she could add the first two coins
together, pfft!, instantaneously the Devil transported his whole
burden eastwards and she got nothing for her pains. He hurtled
the stones through the air to Wiltshire, losing a couple along the
way (which is what comes of being hasty), before sitting down
with the jumble of sarsens and bluestones and starting to slot
them into position. Feeling a bit cocky, he boasted that nobody
who saw the completed monument would ever be able to imagine
how such immense rocks ever came to stand on the lonely plain.
Up jumped a friar, who had been lying hidden in a hollow all the
while, sneering at the Devil and announcing (he was a Wiltshire

friar) 'That's more than thee canst tell!' Furious, the Devil tossed a vast stone at the man, but this was in the days of old, when friars were made of tough stuff, and it just bounced off his heel. You can still see the imprint. And then the Devil, having more or less finished the job that he came for, spread his wings and flew off to do devilish stuff somewhere else.[27]

Here are fragments of stories that we already know, but muddled up like events in a dream. There is an old woman who strikes a bargain with the Devil, but this time she gets the worst of it; there is the instantaneous making of some great structure; there is an interruption of the Devil at his work, which causes him to leave in a fury. But as in so many dreams, none of it makes sense. Why has the Devil decided that he urgently needs to transport some stones from Ireland to rural Wiltshire? What is a friar doing concealed in the middle of Salisbury Plain – not the best of landscapes to hide in? These inconsistencies are there because the story has been reworked from two quite different origins: the history of Geoffrey of Monmouth, and a stone pointed out to tourists because it showed a heel mark. This wasn't the present Heel Stone but another block entirely, probably the archaeologists' Stone 14.

The changes show how, in the years around 1700, landscape legends were being reworked to replace their older heroes by the Devil. But why? Perhaps that's more than we can tell, but there are some clues in the way in which the narrative revisions spread. It seems to have been the largest monuments that were renamed first: the Newmarket Devil's Dyke in 1574, the Boroughbridge Devil's Arrows and the Wansdyke in 1586 and in 1595 the Stiperstones, a great stone ridge on the west borders of Shropshire that was briefly known as the Devil's Bridge (evidently in the older sense of 'causeway', as the rocks don't bridge anything).[28] Similar connections at Stonehenge and Avebury followed in the seventeenth century until by 1724 Stukeley was treating stories like this as 'common'. There seems to be a feedback loop between Devil traditions and the emerging tourist industry. A comedy of 1662 mocks a typically solemn German traveller who has taken everything told to him at Stonehenge and elsewhere as gospel truth: 'There are many other sights in England: the rocks which the Devil has assembled right in the country; the ditches, also made by the Devil, at New-Market.'[29]

This pre-eminence of the Devil was very much an English, or rather an Anglo-Scots, tradition. Right up to the edge of the language barrier, the Devil or Deil is responsible for hills, ditches and anomalous stones, but when you cross over into the Welsh- and Gaelic-speaking regions, the traditions and place-names change, and instead it is heroes from the native tradition who toss great boulders across the country as if they were so many pebbles. Arthur and Fionn mac Cumhaill take the parts which in older English stories had been played by Grim and other giant figures. Just as the leading figures from Welsh and Irish epics were responsible for shaping the landscapes of Celtic Britain, so characters from Germanic legend must have featured in the local traditions of medieval England. We know this because a handful of them continued to be celebrated until the eighteenth century, such as Wada of Wade's Causeway in Yorkshire and Weland of Wayland's Smithy in Oxfordshire, the last survivors of the old lore. But their other companions have all been erased from popular memory. Bringing in the Devil as a protagonist who hurled stones and heaped hills was not just an innovation: it was also a structured forgetting.[30]

The Riddle of the Rocks

Still, this Devil was more than a cipher: theologians and the folk could agree about his mysterious power, if nothing else. In the Wergin Meadow north of Hereford stands the Devil's Stone.

Here for once we can be confident that its name has not replaced some older mythological reference, for there was nothing remarkable about this stone until the night of 17 February 1642, when it picked itself up, seemingly without human intervention, and moved to the far end of the meadow. As the stone was a boundary marker, they had to haul it back again, which took the best part of a day and a yoke of twelve oxen. After that, it was known as the Devil's Stone, for who else could have interfered so capriciously with the landscape?[31]

The movement of the Wergin stone really was a mystery, but when genuine anomalies were lacking, the storytellers knew how to fabricate them. The Devil's Thumb on the edge of Delamere Forest in Cheshire was a huge boulder that was eventually shifted for land clearance. This took a work gang of dozens, but it had been no problem for the Devil to toss it into position, and the marks of his claws could still be seen: or, if you were less romantically inclined, it was a glacial erratic with traces of ice scratchings on the surface.[32] In the same way, geologists pointed to a rent in the slate cliffs at Polperro as a good example of a fault, but locals knew it was the Devil's Doorway: 'As he arose from below in his fiery car, drawn by a gigantic jet black steed, the rocks gave way before him,' until 'his horse, delighted with the airs of this upper world, reared in wild triumph, and, planting again his hoof upon the ground ... left the deep impression of his burning foot behind,' creating a hoof-shaped pool that was shown to curious strangers.[33]

Further west along the same coast, the rocks at Tolcarne above the church of Newlyn are known as the Devil's Leap. There are different stories to explain why, but the most detailed version starts when the Devil took it into his mind to go fishing. This was not a field in which he had much experience – there was fishing for men, of course, but that was very much in the hands of the rival organization. Still, how difficult could it be? All you needed was a net, and there were lots of them soaking in tan-water at the barking-house down by the harbour. So he raided the building, piled all the nets on his head in one great bundle and set off with hasty strides in the direction of Penzance.

But the Devil had not gone unobserved. In those days nearly all the men of Newlyn were fishers, and all the fishers were in the church choir. They were great strong outdoor types, and their voices could carry for miles. So they set off after the Devil, some chanting the Apostles' Creed, others the Lord's Prayer, while a few with good memories threw in the Responses and even a Collect or two. This made the Devil very uncomfortable, and in his hurry to get away he jumped straight across the valley behind Newlyn, landing on Tolcarne in a single stride. That was a bit of an effort, and his foot sank down into the granite slab; besides, he lost his balance, and the nets slapped down onto the outcrop, hitting it so hard that they too left a mesh-like imprint on the rock. On came the choir, roaring a medley of morning and evening prayer in voices that could be heard above an October gale. There was nowhere left to run, so the Devil turned at bay, raised

Newlyn Harbour.

himself to a terrifying height, flapped his wings in fury and took off, but not before hissing, in a voice mixed with flame, three words: 'Buckah! Buckah!! BUCKAH!!!' Which, interpreted, means: 'You are doomed to be destroyed by a foreign power.' And this came to pass in the summer of 1595, when two hundred men from the invading Spanish fleet burnt the churches of Paul and Mousehole and Newlyn.[34]

That is how the story was told by an old fisherman of Newlyn whose version reached print in 1879. His mysterious 'Buckah!' hints that here, as at so many sites, there was a pre-Devil version, for bucca has nothing to do with destruction or foreigners: it is the name given to a Cornish spirit, equivalent to the Middle English bugge or pouke. The old fellow must have been very well read for a fisherman if he remembered the year when the Spanish came – folk tales aren't usually so exact about dates – so perhaps there was some working-up from the original performance, but for all that it's an impressive piece of storytelling to build out of little more than a hollow and some reticulated marks on a granite slab.

It is not just the Devil who has left prints in solid stone, for the same motif appears in tales about otherworldly beings of many different kinds, the only common denominator being the narrator's desire to round off an improbable story with concrete proof that it must be true – look, you can see the mark to this day! But unlike saints, witches, fairies and giants, the Devil has the advantage of a mixed physique, sometimes human, sometimes animal, as the needs of the story require it. When the mark looks like a foot or hand, he can be credited with stamping or clutching the stone, but when it is round or scratched, then the storyteller can just as easily make it a trace of his hoof or claws.

Some of the marks, to be honest, look like nothing anatomical at all, but then the Devil may have been in a hurry, or perhaps he slipped during his exertions. At Huddersfield he hopped from West Nab to Broadstone on Honley Moor, then strode to Scar

Top at Netherton, and finally jumped to Castle Hill at Almond-bury before disappearing into the maze of subterranean passages well known to underlie the hill, in which he may or may not still be wandering (depending on whether you come from Almondbury).[35] As at Moulsford or Narborough, the story isn't much in its own right, but when you are there, looking across the valley of the Holme at the crags where the Devil leapt from hill to hill and tracing his scorched footprints at each point, it all falls into place.

Swift Leaps and Sudden Falls

In Dorset's Marshwood Vale, the Devil's Jumps record a less dignified episode. Back along, as they say in those parts, there was a great abbey on the edge of the Vale at Forde, staffed by good and pious monks. The Devil was sniffing round the cloisters to see if there were any chinks in their virtue when he was caught by the abbot, a muscular Christian who wasted no time on remonstrations but gave him a mighty kick just at the base of his tail. The Devil soared through the air to land uncomfortably on the ground, bounced, bounced once more, hit the ground one last time and shot off into the sea.[36] This is the part that everyone agrees on, but there is much uncertainty about the details. Some say that the three jumps are marked by three tree clumps on a hill near Birdsmoorgate. Others are certain that this hill was just the first bounce in a sequence that ended at Colmer's Hill just outside Bridport, or that he hit the ground at Pilsdon Pen, Lewesdon Hill and Thorncombe; some have him landing on Langdon Hill, then Thorncombe Beacon, from which he would end at West Bay (depending on whether you come from West Bay). In short, everybody names hills that are seen on the horizon where they live, so that they can stitch the story into a familiar landscape.

Probably someone with a literary background brought in the abbot of Forde, since monks and monasteries don't usually have such good press in English folk memory. If so, the story has become indigenized, just like Geoffrey of Monmouth's romantic fabrication about Stonehenge, and it would be churlish to deny either of these the status of tradition. After all, an 'authentic' folk tale is simply one where we haven't found out who made it up in the first place. The Marshwood story is certainly true to the popular spirit in its undignified revelations about the Devil, a fallen angel in the most literal sense. The print of cloven feet marks the Devil's Rock between Birtley and Bellingham, where he braced himself to jump across the Tyne, failed and plunged into the Leap Crag Pool to drown.[37]

There is something very comforting about pointing out the spot where the Devil drowned; I suppose it gave the Northumbrians one less thing to worry about. This was not the only occasion on which the Devil died. He perished of the cold at Windwhistle in Somerset – or was it Northlew in Devon? – or 'Stow-on-the-Wold, where the Devil took cold'? Every county in the West of England seems to know of one place so cold that the Devil died there of sheer exposure and is buried somewhere about the village.[38] Of course this was a temporary arrangement, for like his old sparring partner Mr Punch, the Devil never stays dead for long. By the time he got to the North York Moors he had learnt from experience, and as the wind rose he took refuge in the old Saltersgate Inn on the Whitby road. He was not exactly welcome company for the drovers and carters who had gathered there to wait out the storm, and by one means or another their prayers and curses got the Devil out of the parlour into the kitchen. This put him in a high rage, and he vowed not to leave one stone of the building on another when he got free. Luckily the landlord was one of those men who knew a thing or two, and he bound the Devil into the kitchen fire so that for as long as a drift of smoke rose up from the fireplace, he should not be able to break out. From then on, through every summer and winter for a century or more, the peat fire was kept banked up. All was well until in our own days someone decided that the pub was no longer paying its way. The brewery redeployed the manager, workmen boarded up the windows and that was the last flicker of the peat fire. Now the Saltersgate Inn is a derelict shell by the A169 and the prophecy is in a fair way to be fulfilled, either from the simmering rage of the Devil or through the workings of an unfettered market economy, if there is a difference.[39]

It must be rather uncomfortable to be conjured into a wisp of smoke, just as it is miserable to freeze to death (even on a temporary basis), undignified to be kicked all over the landscape and embarrassing to collapse down a rock face scraping at the boulders. All these stories put the Devil in a contemptible, often comic light: they are pantomime, slapstick. They would not be told specifically about the Devil, the common enemy of man, unless there was something more to him than pantomime – but who is responsible for this mixed atmosphere? When it comes

The Devil's Elbow, Saltersgate.

to these older stories, with their strange havering between terror and laughter, it is a challenge to tell which parts of a narrative circulated locally and which were added for the press by gentlemen.

For instance, what are we to make of the Devil's Humps on Bow Hill above Chichester? They are four prominent barrows, the sort you would expect to have a local folk story about them, but none is told, and they were not even called the Devil's Humps until 1934.[40] It is easy to see where the name came from, though, because 5 miles north on the Downs are the Devil's Jumps. Very well, what are we to make of the Devil's Jumps at Treyford? Here legend is not lacking. In days of old, the god Thor used to sit here and watch the web of fate weave itself in the world of men. It's pretty tiring being a god, and on summer afternoons, when the air was still, he would put his arms behind his head, lean back on the end barrow and have a nap. Along came the Devil, and of course, compared to the ancient pagan gods, the Devil is a bit of a youngster, with lots of surplus energy. He couldn't keep still and started playing a private game up and down the barrows, a hop and a jump here, a jump and a hop there. Thor woke and grumbled, but the Devil took no notice, skipping to the barrow at the further end and thumbing his nose at the god. 'Look at you, you old snooze! Don't you wish you were young like me and full of go?' Well, old he may have been, but Thor was still mighty as ever, and hot-tempered with it. In a rage he seized the nearest convenient boulder and hurled it at the Devil, who doubled up in mid-jump. And he never came back there again, which is useful to know if you live in the neighbourhood of Treyford.[41]

Told as it is now, this story is pretty light-hearted, but could there be more to it than that? After all, one of the two characters is Thor, and while he is slumming it a bit by appearing in a folk tale rather than myth, Thor is still a god with twelve centuries of history behind him, back to the days when Viking sails spread terror on the Sussex coast. Alas, scholarly daydreams about echoes of an older paganism are dashed when we find that exactly the same story was being told about the Devil's Jumps in Surrey. This must be the original version, because unlike Treyford, the Surrey Jumps have an actual Thor's Stone on the heath nearby. Furthermore, the nearest village is Thursley, which looks as if it might have originally been Thor's Lea.

So, let us begin again. What are we to make of the Devil's Jumps at Thursley? The name is certainly older here than it is in Sussex: it is first recorded on a map of 1765, along with the nearby Devil's Punchbowl, a dramatic hollow on the road through Hindhead. On the other hand, you can't compare a valley to a punchbowl until punchbowls exist for it to resemble, which means that the second of these two names, at least, is no older than the eighteenth century. There is a hint that the Devil is an interloper at his Jumps, as he is at so many other places, because a traveller recorded in 1799 that 'the country people (particularly the aged) relate many tales of these eminences, and hold them in a kind of awful reverence (the revels of the Fairies yet linger in the tales of the aged rustic).'[42] That sounds as if they were originally fairy hills. As for Thor, it is suspicious, to say the least, that as late as 1895 an antiquarian writer was combing the neighbourhood for evidence that the village name Thursley contained that of the god. If the story of Thor's contest with the Devil had been known then, he would have made much of it, and the fact that he didn't suggests that the tradition was rooted in his speculations and not the other way round.[43]

Once again, our attempts to get at an authentic original folk tale peter out in a tangle of influence and transference. There is no core stratum untouched by literary speculation: from their first rise to popularity around 1700, these legends of the Devil are told in a medley of different styles, sometimes tricked out with learning from the scholar's study, sometimes dressed up for the lady's parlour, sometimes spun plain enough to suit the servants' hall. Luckily there are travellers' notebooks that have preserved the vernacular for us, voices like that of the old Shropshire countrywoman who explained the Devil's Causeway at Ruckley in 1899: 'It was the Devil as builded un up in one night, and when cock-crow come er dropped they stwuns down in a hurry out of's apern, and flew away to his own place.'[44] But this understated foolery of the Devil who breaks his apron-strings is no more or less true to the tradition than the fun and games that Richard Harris Barham had, fifty years earlier, with the dazzling metrics and anachronisms of his 'Brothers of Birchington':

> Hanging his ears, Yet dissembling his fears.
> Ledger in hand, straight 'Auld Hornie' appears,
> With that sort of half-sneaking, half-impudent look,
> Bankrupts sport when cross-question'd by Cresswell
>   or Cooke . . .[45]

Barham was playing the fool with a purpose, to send up the pretensions of contemporary nostalgia for the Middle Ages, but he was a churchman himself. His Devil is still, after all, the Devil, and Hell, to which the elder brother is sent by that mistaken ledger entry, really is Hell, which is why after resuscitation he

> Could never thenceforth bear the sight of a fire
> Nor ever was heard to express a desire
> In cold weather to see the thermometer higher.

The comic verses turn on something dark, as comedy always does – death, judgement, Heaven and Hell, the four last things.[46] If Christianity weren't serious, there would be no point in fooling about with it. Barham's playfulness went beyond verbal pyrotechnics, however, for he is under grave suspicion of planting this folk tale himself at the two towers of Reculver; nevertheless, his tale of two identical brothers, one of whom gets snatched away to the afterlife by mistake for the other, is a real migratory legend, with a pedigree extending as far back as Late Antique Rome.[47] Adoption, not parentage, is the real test of folklore – a test which this story has passed ever since it was taken up as a tradition in the Birchington neighbourhood.

At the end of it all the Devil is worsted by St Thomas Becket, but this plot development pushes at the boundaries of the acceptable in English folk tale. It is rare for saints to appear as the protagonists of popular stories. St George has his place, of course, and St David for the Welsh; saints Crispin and Clement appear in origin legends for shoemakers and blacksmiths; St Peter has his seat beside the Pearly Gates. But in England (though not in Wales or Cornwall), the Reformation wiped out living traditions of saints in story. It is usually a mark of learned interference when they appear as dramatis personae in traditions about the Devil.

Most of the people who retold these legends were town and village historians. They knew all about the saints who featured locally in monastic chronicles and miracle lists, and they thought it a pity that their stories should die out completely, even if nobody in the neighbourhood had ever heard of them. So we find Harrison Ainsworth pulling St Cuthman out of the limbo of Sussex hagiography and giving him a star part in the legend of the Devil's Dyke, to replace the humble old lady with her sieve and candle. The story needed female interest as well, so Ainsworth invented a pious anchoress called Ursula de Braose.[48] This is not how folk tale works. Apart from a few lead characters like Robin Hood and Dick Turpin, the protagonists in folk stories are mostly anonymous: an old woman, an honest farmer, a soldier returned from the wars. If they need a name to tell them apart from the next character, 'Jack' or 'Mary' will do, names that might belong to anybody, for these stories are set in a kind of idealized everyday and have none of the period trappings that appeal to the historical novelist. An anonymous abbot of Forde is close enough to the popular style in storytelling for people to repeat the version of the Devil's Jumps story in which he features, and even in England the mighty Thor is instantly recognizable as an antagonist. But when a legend of the Devil and his deeds has characters invented solely for the sake of the story, with fustian medieval names – when it has a Sir Guy de Gravade, Brother John of Hulton Vale, wicked Rainaldus, Hugh of Bury the sacristan, young Edgar Astley or Lady Sybil of Eagles Crag – then their presence betrays the tale as a fabrication.[49] Not that this would matter, if a story had caught the popular taste, for then it would soon have been worn down to the plot line and passed on from mouth to mouth, but these Gothic romances never achieve that kind of anonymous immortality. Nobody remembers them, and nobody passes them on.

3

HAVE AT THEE! CHURCHES SHIFTED, TARGETED AND RAIDED BY THE DEVIL

The Devil is interested in churches, naturally enough, though not for good reasons; he likes to move a new build from its original, accessible site to a hilltop or other difficult location – though sometimes, with the typical confusion of tradition, these are said to have been carried the other way. Sometimes the church is already built, and the Devil throws great stones at it, but fails to hit the target; sometimes he makes off with the bells, and though he is forced to drop them, fate takes a hand and they can never be restored to the steeple from which they came.

A Place for the Church

People who say that the traditional English village is dead have never visited the Isle of Wight. Wheelchair-friendly and trim, Godshill Model Village provokes gasps of amazement as families recognize the buildings that they have just walked past in the real village, itself an attraction that can be seen pretty thoroughly in under an hour. Under the dwarf conifers and bonsai maples, the people of a smaller Godshill go about their business at a scale of 1:10. Miniature thatch protects little roofs and the Griffin Arms has fretwork bargeboards and smokeless knobbly chimneys. They are playing cricket outside the manor house and the local football team has just scored on the edge of town, beside the Gypsy field with its scaled-down cobs and pygmy wagons.

Less vigorous citizens sit or snooze as the brass band plays, while little people tower over the model village of the model village, where their smaller counterparts are also admiring the shop windows, laughing at the dog on the bandstand and pointing out *their* model village in an infinite regress where it is always summer and forever 1939.

Just like the real thing, the gift shop has two signs at each side of the bay windows, one saying 'To the Church via the Hill', the other 'To the Church via the Steps'. Either route looks pretty steep, even in miniature, but this is because of the Devil. He is missing from the Model Village, an Eden purged at last of its serpent, but without him none of this would make sense, at least not the social geography of the real Godshill. Outside the porch of the model church, you have only to take a step backwards – cautiously – and look up, and you will see the real church matching it just above, picked out against the skyline where it was built in spite of the Devil.

Once you have left the garden and toiled up the steps, the actual church reveals itself as a fourteenth-century building probably replacing an earlier structure of the late eleventh century. At this point history gives out, and legend picks up the thread.

Once there was no church in the village at all, and it was a long time before the villagers could be persuaded to build one. At once they began quarrelling violently (which was probably why they needed a church in the first place), mostly over the question of where to build it. The row was at its height when an outsider joined the meeting; nobody knew him but he seemed to know everyone, and he spoke like a gentleman with many years of experience. Surely there was no point in an ostentatious building, that would just be virtue-signalling . . . Better to have something practical and modest on low ground, just below the road. That would save on haulage costs, had they thought of that?

They all claimed they had, and the thing was as good as done. After the first cartload of stone had been delivered, two masons got to work on the level, by the square, with a great air of mystery. All day they paced to and fro, supervising the laying-out of the church, and at night they returned to the inn, tired but proud. Next morning they woke and washed and strode down to the field, ready to marshal their workforce where – there was nothing. Nothing but unbroken grass and, on the skyline of a neighbouring hill, the broad outline and raised voice of a peasant proprietor wanting to know what all these stones were doing on his land.

So the villagers had to drag the masonry back down on skids and sleds, until by sunset everything was where it had been before. On the dawn of the next day they found it had happened all over again. This time they ended the day's work by putting men on guard, but at first light on the third morning, the watchmen stumbled in with a wild story. They had seen the stones go bouncing and jumping upwards, the little blocks helping the slabs up over the ruts, the marker pegs marching along to chivvy the slackers and the levelling cords snaking up behind. They had crept after this strange procession and seen every stone fall obediently into its place on the hilltop site, with a last tap from a flying mallet to square up the corners.

The masons were more shocked than surprised, miracles being commoner in those days than they are now. It was the will of God, and there was nothing to do but fall in line: so they called the new site Godshill and doubled quantities on the stone contract. Course after course they built, parapet, gable and wall, until the flashing cross on the summit could be seen eastwards to Shanklin and southwards to Ventnor, and the wicked plan of the old gentleman was altogether defeated.

> The church there today on the top of the mound
> Lifts its pinnacled tower to sky,

While a mile to the south 'Devil's Acre' is found –
Which maids in the dark are afraid to pass round –
Two proofs to you legends don't lie.[1]

A fine moral story, and it makes a change from all those roads and bridges and ditches whose construction had kept the Devil hard at work for no apparent purpose at all. By contrast, it makes sense for him to be interested in religious buildings, if not for pious motives. Of course, the Devil is a wily old serpent and you cannot expect him to play the same trick twice, or not exactly. At Churchdown in Gloucestershire, another village whose name is taken from its hilltop church, the sequence of events is the same – work starts on building the church at the bottom of the hill, stones appear mysteriously at the top every night, and eventually the villagers accept the inevitable – only here it is the uphill site that is favoured by the Devil, and he continues to carry the stones uphill until he gets his way.[2]

At Brentor, at the western edge of Dartmoor, you can have it both ways. In one version, the villagers decide to build their church at the foot of the tor, but after the Devil has moved all the materials upwards, they give in and finish the work on the craggy summit – in a bit of a hurry, it seems, as the building is one of the smallest churches in England, less than 40 feet long. Still, they are determined to finish the job properly and get the Bishop of Exeter to do the honours at the church's consecration, which sets the Devil off into a fury again. Hardly has he appeared to rage at the congregation than the skies part and down on a shaft of light comes their patron St Michael. Still smarting from his defeat before the beginning of time, the Devil is ready for a return match with the archangel, but it ends just as before, with Michael tossing his old adversary down over the cliff edge, then hurling a stone after him for good measure, like a heavenly Thor.

Others, however, say that a wealthy merchant was caught at sea in a mighty storm, the Devil's work. As the ship drifted closer and closer to the fatal rocks, the merchant kept his gaze steadfast on the highest landmark that he could see and vowed that if his life was spared, and the crew alongside him, he would make its summit unmistakeable with a tall church tower. All at once came St Michael to calm the raving winds, so that the ship came safe into harbour, where the honest merchant spent all he had in fulfilling his vow. (Yes, I know that Brentor is 18 miles inland from Plymouth Sound, and that any merchant who tried to use it as a seamark would almost deserve to go to wreck – but hush! This

Brentor.

vow-of-the-merchant story is a migratory legend about coastal chapels that has been grafted onto the other version: that's how legends work.) So the merchant called workmen from all over and paid them enough for a dozen churches, which was just as well, because every time they built on that rocky hill, the Devil knocked the walls back down again. At his wits' end, the wealthy man prayed to St Michael, who had not forgotten him, and appeared on a shaft of light as before. This is why the church is so small: the money had run out.[3]

These stories do not have to be about hills. As long as the final site is out of the way somehow, it can be explained as the work of the Devil, who wanted to make things as inconvenient as possible for the parishioners. At Hollington, inland from Hastings, he chose a location so deserted that it became known as the Church in the Wood. With no parish other than a few farmhouses, and those a quarter of a mile away, the little church lies alone among the trees with only birds for a congregation. If the Devil wanted to discourage regular churchgoing, he could hardly have chosen a better spot.[4]

And yet there are other places where this obvious explanation is lacking. At Duffield, between Derby and Belper, the church lies just beside the village, in a field overlooking the Derwent. Here it is the first-proposed site that occupies a hill, opposite the old castle of the Ferrars, earls of Derby. Night after night the Devil removed the building to its present situation, until the masons gave in and finished it on the less awkward spot.[5] At Checkendon in the Chilterns the church is in the heart of the village, while the proposed site lies in a wood at the edge of the parish, an ancient enclosure sheltered by a ring of dark yews and still known as the Devil's Churchyard.[6]

So many variations, but you get the general story – it is like one of those Picasso drawings where there are three eyes and two mouths but all recognizably come from the same face. There must be a first proposed location, and a final one where the church is built; there should be repeated attempts at building before the final reconciliation; one of the sites should stand out geographically (it is uphill, or in a wood, or just a long way out of the village) while the other should be marked by something special that the storyteller can point to, an old ruin perhaps, or earthworks, or maybe just a curious name, like Devil's Acre or Devil's Churchyard.

The Haunter of the Dark

There is another Devil's Churchyard at Minchinhampton, a few miles outside Stroud, and here again building work was pulled down each night until at last the church was built in the village. The place never lost its bad reputation.

> You are supposed to see men without heads there (so one of my jobbing gardeners confessed), and dogs, and unknown horrors. A man who works on the roads tells me that once he and a friend were poaching round there after midnight, and were terribly scared by 'a noise like bagpipes'.[7]

The reasons for its name are not hard to find. This was a field cluttered with large flat blocks of oolitic limestone, which lay around like so many toppled tombstones and got in the way of agriculture. In about 1870 they were cleared, with the largest stones taken to the rectory and stacked up round the stable yard, later to be identified by more than one antiquary as a misplaced stone circle.[8] With the most obvious reason for its name removed, the Devil's Churchyard was then supposed to be so called because of fiendish things that happened there.

The Devil is a spirit of negation; he features in place-names whenever somewhere is not really what it claims to be. The Devil's

Churchyard was not a churchyard, just as the Devil's Armchair is not furniture and the Devil's Frying Pan is useless for culinary purposes: they're a large rock on the beach at Paignton and a collapsed cave near the Lizard. But the two 'churchyards' offer the additional irony of endowing the Devil with land which, of all kinds of property, must be the least use to him. There is a rectangular earthwork on the Sussex Downs, east of Brighton, which from its appearance might easily be called a book, or perhaps the book of the Devil; but it was much more piquant to call it the Devil's Bible.[9] To most people this must have seemed merely ridiculous, because what would he be doing with a Bible? But those with an ear for the sinister would remember spellbooks and grimoires; they were called Devil's Bibles, and so were the proselytizing texts (mostly imaginary) of libertine atheists.

In the same way, Devil's Pulpit might be just a quirky name for a square upright rock. But in the fading light, when shapes are uncertain, it would be easy to imagine a gaunt occupant taking possession, to deliver such a sermon as we are told was given in 1591 by the lord of the witches at St Andrew's Auld Kirk, east of Edinburgh, who,

> Clad in a blak gown, with a blak hat upon his head, preachit unto a great number of them out of the pulpit, having like light candelis round about him. The effect of his language was till knaw, what skaith they had done, how many they had won to their opinion sen their last meeting.[10]

There were two Devil's Pulpits in Lincolnshire: one at Hemswell, where it was the children's game to stick it with pins to make it speak, and another at Tealby, which lumbered down to drink at the stream when the Devil heard the clock strike. But when was that? 'No one knows – so no one knows just when he is to be expected. But I've known those that wouldn't venture in that part of the Park for anything, for fear he might be there.'[11] It is the old uneasy compound, sometimes laughter, sometimes terror. In the Forest of Dean, the scowles or old iron workings, long since deserted by the ancient miners, were shown off to visitors as the domestic quarters of the Devil. He had a kitchen and seven chambers as well as a pulpit, and a chapel to go with them.[12] It was all very light-hearted, and yet . . .

One day at dusk a man gathering firewood there heard rustling in a great oak tree above his head, and saw a figure

The Devil's Chapel,
Forest of Dean.

climbing down. Soon it leapt to earth, and there was just enough light for the man to make out horns and cloven hoofs. He did not stay to ask questions.[13]

Like most of the other place-names we have met so far, this was coined in the nineteenth century, but the idea of a Devil's chapel is much older. It already appears in the closing episode of the fourteenth-century poem *Sir Gawain and the Green Knight*. Gawain's quest for his unearthly antagonist is coming to an end, and he has set out from the castle, where he has been splendidly entertained, to their appointed rendezvous at the Green Chapel, but this place turns out to be not at all what he had expected. As he walks around a craggy old hill honeycombed with caves,

> 'We! Lorde', quoth the gentyle knight,
> 'Whether this be the grene chapelle?
> Here myght aboute mydnyght
> The Dele his matynnes telle!'[14]

Already an uncanny place, its atmosphere is soon roused to terror pitch by the sound of an axe being honed to a cutting edge – and then as suddenly dissipated, for Gawain's mysterious adversary turns out not to be the Devil after all, but his jovial host from the castle. Bercilak is delighted to see his guest, and it is only Gawain's bad conscience about three days of temptation with his host's wife that has made him so sensitive to ideas of evil. Bercilak, with his glamorous castle in the wilderness and his mysterious comings and goings, is more elfin than mortal, and his testing of Gawain has the arbitrary moral quality of Faërie.

Fairies, devils . . . we place them in opposite pigeonholes of the legendarium, but the further back you go, the less confident people seem to have been about this. We have already seen how the Devil stepped into the shoes of the fairy folk at Thursley, and this may have happened also at Godshill, for despite the splendid confidence of the story with which we began, the earliest version, going back to the 1770s or thereabouts, told how the church was moved by fairies.[15] At Winchester they said that the whole city, not just a church or two, had first been erected on Old Winchester Hill, but that all the buildings were carried down night after night into the valley of the Itchen; some said it was done by fairies, others blamed the Devil. At Hartland, the stones of the church were moved at night by the Devil, or by pixies (we are in pixy country here, on the north Devon coast), or possibly by angels. When St Clement's Church at Worcester was moved away from its parish across the Severn, it was definitely done by angels.[16] In short, these night-time shifts of a church from its first proposed location to the final one can be ascribed to any number of different supernatural agents. The obvious explanation, that the Devil is doing it because he wants to make the church hard for the villagers to get to, is simply a gloss added to provide some kind of plausibility to otherwise motiveless interference from the other world. Adding up all the local variants of this tale (and they are legion) shows that the Devil is only responsible in a third of them.

Significantly, he does not feature in any of the Welsh-language versions. Just as the Celtic regions retained giants in their stories of the dropped apronful of stones, and heroes in their traditions of footprints marked in bare rock, so they resisted the English trend of blaming the Devil for interference with churches. The Welsh stories, like the Irish, are much closer to the earliest versions found in the lives of medieval saints. Here we are told that the holy founder was looking for a place to establish his cell in the wilderness, and picked on one spot that seemed suitable, but was then warned off it by some marvellous token, such as the demolition by night of everything he had built by day. Humbly he waits for a sign from Heaven, and hears a voice telling him to go to another location, distinguished by a name, or a particular growth, or the presence of a white animal. Several of these motifs survive in the older storytelling traditions of the British Isles, but once the Reformation had removed the central figure of the saint, the logic of the older tales fell apart and their core elements were reconstituted around a new narrative theme: the Devil's hostility to places of worship.[17]

Hurling Great Stones

Sometimes the Devil is frustrated; sometimes he never even gets near the church. Beside the road that runs into Staple Fitzpaine, a few miles south of Taunton, there is a large boulder of hard sarsen. Because it was lying there with no obvious purpose or explanation, it became known as the Devil's Stone, and once it had that enticing name, a story had to follow. They say that when Staple folk first decided to build a church, rumour of their plans got around and eventually reached Hell. Naturally this news rocked the evil empire to its core (we're looking at things from a Staple Fitzpaine perspective here) so responsibility for tackling it went right to the top. Off sets the Devil, with a satchel of stones just the right size and shape to throw at the workmen; that should cure them of their godly ways, he thinks. Finally at day's end he arrives at the village. It's a long way from the bottomless pit to Taunton Deane, and the stones had been uncommonly heavy, so on arrival the Devil settled down to a long nap by the roadside, the better to summon up strength for the next day's exertions. But in the meantime the villagers had not been idle. When dawn came, the Devil blinked and looked down the street, and there he saw the church all perfect and complete, its fine tower shining in the first light of day. He was so surprised that he dropped his satchel, and as its strap broke the stones all tumbled away, which put him into such a huff that he flounced off and never came back again.

That is the story, or rather it's a version of the story, which no two people in the village seem to tell the same way. You will recognize fragments of other tales that we have met before – the dropped stones, the frustration of the Devil caught by the arrival of morning. Other accounts mention the holes left in the rock by the Devil's hands when he first gripped the rock. Maybe he was rolling it along, and that was what left him so tired. Or the stone was not dropped, but thrown at the church, only luckily it fell short. Perhaps he was standing on Castle Neroche, the nearest hill on the far side of the village, when he aimed his missile. There might be one stone, or there might be three, each one in a different spot on the outskirts of the village. Some call them the Devil's Stepping Stones, others the Devil's Three Jumps, because he jumped from one to another instead of throwing them.[18] There is no one story of the Devil's Stone (or Jump) that you can tell as the proper, authentic version; instead the imaginative details are left to each individual teller, a kind of jazz improvisation on the key diabolical theme.

The necessary conclusion – the keynote on which any improvisation must end – is that the village is saved and the Devil returns to his own place, never to trouble them more.[19] This is what remains when a tale has been otherwise completely remodelled. In the seventeenth century, the Devil's Arrows at Boroughbridge had featured in a version of the cobbler story, in which villagers fool the Devil into thinking he is so far from his destination that he throws away the great stones with which he was going to destroy it. But the Victorian version is quite different and draws on the same kind of setting that led the Somerset storytellers to imagine their Devil menacing them from Castle Neroche. In the Yorkshire tale, the Devil takes his stand on How Hill, about 8 miles away from the village, picks up the first gigantic arrow, and declares

Borobrigg, Borobrigg,
Keep out of the way,
For Auldboro' town
I'll ding down to-day.

Luckily the first arrow falls short, and so do the second and third.[20] As with so many of these Devil's Dykes and Doorways, the landscape itself is just as important as the story. You have to take your stand on How Hill, look over the valley and line up the three stones in order to appreciate that the Devil was a good shot, if not unerring. His skill in Yorkshire dialect poetry is less expected, but then it is a convention of all these folktales that the fiend or ghost or pixy or whatever should speak in rhyming couplets. Within the framework of the tale, verse is a sign that the super-natural is speaking to us; for the storyteller, it provides a kernel of remembered words that jog the memory for the rest of the story.

But why did Boroughbridge need to be told to keep out of the way? The Devil does not have a social conscience: he is not like a golfer shouting 'Fore!' in case anyone gets hurt. The whole point was to hurt people, in this case the inhabitants of Aldborough. But presumably he had a soft spot for the other village, or it was locally suspected that he might. Another great stone, on Gatherley Moor to the north of Richmond, was marked by the grip of the Devil's hand as he raised it to hurl at another obnoxious village, only once again it missed its target; here his words are remembered as:

Have at thee, black Hartforth,
But have a care o' bonny Gilling![21]

which sounds very much like a story told by Hartforth people at the expense of their neighbours in Gilling West, a village wicked enough to get preferential treatment from the Devil.

Because it was important in all these tales to show how near the Devil's miss actually came to landing, the storytellers would select a hill from which the stone lined up with its target. This sort of judgement would come naturally to people who were used to throwing the hammer or tossing quoits or playing at any of the other games that combine strength and aim. In fact, stones are routinely known as the Devil's Quoits – at East Harptree in the Mendips, where he threw them at the church from Widcombe Hill; at Stanton Harcourt in Oxfordshire, another trio of pre-historic standing stones; at Avebury; and at Tidenham by the Severn.[22] It tickled the fancy to imagine this everyday pastime being played on a colossal scale back in the childhood of the world, whoever was doing the throwing, and in fact a dolmen at St Columb Major in mid-Cornwall was indifferently known as the Devil's, the Giant's and Arthur's Quoit.[23] So it seems that when stories give the Devil a motive, and have him trying to annihilate the village church with a hurtling missile, this is simply part of the tidying-up process by which narrative motifs from different sources were brought into a more coherent tradition. Originally he was trying to win, not destroy.

This is hard to believe when you look at somewhere like Rudston in the Wolds of East Yorkshire. Here an immense mono-lith, the tallest standing stone in Britain, dominates the churchyard. Visitors look up in awe and ask how two such incompatible symbols, the brute dignity of paganism and the Gothic artifice of the church, could coexist in such a small space. Legend, always the tourists' friend, explains that when the church was newly built the Devil shot this great stone arrow to bring down the hated building but, as usual, missed.[24] This story has become part of the interpretation of the site, even for people who have never been near Rudston, since it can be read allegorically, pitting the oppos-ing forces of paganism and Christianity against one another in a single coherent vision. The arrow falls short, the Devil's power

Rudston Monolith.

fails, and in the place where the old religion once flourished, a new faith asserts its dominion.

It is a powerful myth (I mean the myth about the legend, not the legend itself) but it is not true. The native paganism of the British Isles died out a long time ago, and the kaleidoscope of story has been shaken too many times since then for any one narrative to have been attached unchanged to a particular place since those remote days. Before you can imagine the Devil as the 'old god' – the object of a pagan cult, the embodiment of awe at nature's powers, the master of old stones and ancient hills – a lot of historical water must pass under the bridge. First, of course, to even think of 'religions' as a plural you need to lose what was self-evident to medieval people, that Christianity was real and everything else just parody or perversion. Then this world-view must be turned completely inside out, so that paganism becomes the natural religion of the land and Christianity an artificial suppression of it: that was unthinkable before late Victorian times. Until the Romantic movement transformed the way we felt about 'nature', it would have been absurd to prefer it to 'artifice'. And to give the lead role in this recomposed paganism to the Devil, of all dark beings, implies a fondness for rebellion and subversion which best fits the twentieth century. Unsurprisingly, the Rudston story is not recorded until 1975.

For a wider understanding of folklore, we need to look at tale-types rather than particular instances, and we need the kind of historical depth vision which, instead of assuming that every story is as old as can be, looks instead for changes and shifting influences of the sort that we have seen in Devil lore over the past three or four centuries. Stories get other stories caught onto them, like tangles of goosegrass. When the people of Egloshayle, on the outskirts of Wadebridge, say that the Devil threw a stone at their church, this is something we have come to expect; but when we find he was throwing it at the church tower because he feared most of all that this would carry a peal of bells, it looks as if one tradition has got mixed up with another.[25]

The Church Bells Ring No More

There is something magic about bells. They are dead metal with a speaking voice, centuries old but still alive with music every Sunday, the only things in the holy church that are to be handled by laymen. The voice of bells is not noise but neither is it quite music: instead it is almost pure sound, a kind of auditory prayer. In the Middle Ages, bells were honorary people, baptized like children and under the protection of the saints whose names they bore. They provided safe passage for the dead, broke the power of lightning and thunder, and – most to our purpose – dispelled evil spirits. Down to the end of the nineteenth century we find people telling folk tales that hint at the old exorcizing powers, such as the story about a goblin family who have to move house because they cannot abide the sound of a newly installed peal of bells. It follows that the Devil, too, will be angry and afraid when he hears the bells ring.

In Cranborne Chase, on the northeastern borders of Dorset, there is a church without a village. It has no windows or roof either, just the bare shell of a building, and there are no parishioners but the dead, for Knowlton lies among the barrows of the bare downland; old as it is, the church is ringed by earthworks raised by the men of a far older age. However, it was not always like this, at least not according to the story. Imagine that ruin in its first splendid state, highest above a skyline of towers and spires. Imagine wide streets running between the seven churches of Knowlton, and each street lined with shops and houses, yards and inns. From dawn to dusk there rises up the noise of a great city, songs, curses and prayers, but above it all serenely floats the chime of the one great bell. This was the bell that sent the Devil into a frenzy, so that one autumn night he raised a great wind, the sort of wind that flattens trees and plucks the roofs off houses and turns a chimney-stack into brick artillery. People hid indoors, too scared even to open a window, and when day came and the wind dropped they found that a ragged hole had been torn out of their church tower and the great bell was gone. The Devil had carried it off over field and fence for 7 miles, but in the end the agony of touching holy things had been too much even for him, and he let it drop in the water meadows of the River Stour, where it rolled down and sank into the bed of the stream. On a clear day, flickers of sunlight still reflected off the grey metal, so near the surface that the men of Knowlton had great hopes for recovering it, with ropes and chains and a great team of heavy horses bracing their knees to take the strain; but the bell did not move an inch. In fact, the harder they pulled it the more it seemed to pull back, and they realized that there was more against them than brute strength could overcome. So they called on a wise man, listened carefully to everything he said and got rid of the horses. Then they scoured the country until they had built up a team of white oxen, each one pure and unblemished. The oxen were yoked in line, a rope was thrown round the bell, and with only a little goading and tugging it sucked free of the mud to slide up the riverbank. It was hovering on the very edge when the foreman shouted:

Now we've got out Knowlton bell
In spite of all the devils in Hell!

At once the ropes snapped and, with a dull clang, the bell rolled back into the water, over and over into the deepest and most inaccessible part of the stream. After that there was nothing more they could do. They went home to try and rebuild their lives, but their hearts were not in it. The damage was done, and people began to drift away from the shattered city. Walls and towers fell into decay, grass grew in the streets and today there is nothing left but the stub of its principal church, with a ragged hole still in the side of the tower.[26]

This strange story was believed, or half-believed, because it intersected at so many points with real, commonsense knowledge about the world. Those lost streets, for instance, are an imaginative extrapolation of the real earthworks around Knowlton; people who work in the fields from dawn to dusk become very sensitive to the low shadows that mark out archaeological features. As for the terrible possibility of the Devil ripping out your city bell, this is simply a heightened rendition of the loss felt by communities whose bells really were taken. Bells continued to be confiscated and melted down for armaments in time of war, to be looted as portable assets or sold to make good a deficit in parish finances – but this loss was always remembered bitterly, for the sound of your village bells was part of who you were.

Stories distort realities, although it doesn't necessarily follow that the legend told at a particular place derives from events that happened there; folklore doesn't work like that. At Halvergate on the Norfolk Broads, legend has it that the village church was ravaged by a fire which only the bells survived, hanging precariously from their charred headstocks. Should they be propped in a timber cradle while the tower was repaired around them, or could they be sold off to augment the building fund? The parson and churchwardens were arguing this point when the clouds grew dark around them, a bolt of thunder split the sky and the Devil himself seized the bells. The full ring, this time: which may have been a bit ambitious, for almost immediately he dropped them in a boggy field, from which they have never been recovered, and that is why this field has always been known as the Bell Hole.[27] So they say: but the story looks as if it derives, not from a real dispute among parishioners, but from a play of words on a local field-name. Holes are much more likely to get their name because they are bell-shaped than because they hold sunken bells, but that's not so tempting to the imagination. Rivers also contain deep hollows with a bell profile, places that are important to name so that swimmers can be warned away from them, and a name like this may provide the seed crystal around which a legend can grow. Significantly, the resting-place of Knowlton bell is a long way from the church – not even in the nearest river – and that may be because it was the closest example of the place-name.

Sometimes we can follow a legend as it grows. Outside the church at Newington, near Chatham, is a stone marked by a single shoeprint. Shoe, not hoof; but as it is known as the Devil's Stone, we can go along with the tradition that he has one human foot and one bestial. In Edwardian days the villagers of Newington liked to show this off to strangers and explain that the Devil once passed this way when they were building a church. He took a dim view of this, naturally, but as he had several other engagements going to and fro in the earth and walking up and down in it, by the time he returned to the village the work was complete and the church already standing. Nothing loath, the Devil braced his back against the tower, one foot against the stone, and pushed ... and pushed. It didn't budge; such is the strength in construction when faith is the mortar. Having achieved nothing but the raising of a shoe-shaped weal on the stone, the Devil went on his way and that was that.[28]

Except that, by the end of the twentieth century, this story had blossomed into a much more complicated version. Now the Devil was outraged not by the sight of the tower but by the sound of its bells, and, forgetting the use of his wings, he shinned up a buttress like a cat burglar and slipped in through the window, emerging with the bells in a sack. But having been gathered in a hurry, the bells swung round and knocked him off balance as he stood on the tower's edge. The Devil fell, making a heel-shaped mark on the stone as before, while the bells clattered off down into a nearby stream. From this point on it's a reprise of the story we already know. Villagers try and fail to recover them – the local witch is called in – four white oxen are yoked – the bells slip out easily – until a child utters one fatal observation, only this time it's nothing to do with devils, but simply, 'Look at the black spot behind that bull's ear,' and as soon as it was known that the oxen were not pure white, the magic was at an end and the bells were irretrievably lost.[29]

This version must have arrived from somewhere independent of Knowlton; the ending depends on a blemish in otherwise perfect oxen, whereas in the Dorset version we are just told they were white, without an explanation of how this fits into the plot. Evidently there were two possible endings to the story, one of them a sub-type in which all is lost because of the unseen black hair, another in which it happens because someone swore. That is how tragedy happens – a single understandable but nevertheless fatal flaw destroys all hope just at the moment of triumph. And although the motif of the white oxen could be combined and recombined with other stories – at Newington it was evidently introduced during the twentieth century – it is, in itself, an old piece of storytelling. The use of oxen for haulage had died out in most of England by 1600, but it lives on in this one episodic fragment, whereas nobody ever talks about a team of pure white horses.

The stories themselves remain resolutely modern, however, and if they owe anything to medieval precedent, it is very well disguised. At Danbury near Chelmsford, the Devil stole the church bell and dropped it in Bell Hill Wood; it landed with such a crash that it made a hollow, soon filled with water, which people used to visit in the hope of glimpsing a lost treasure.[30] We are on familiar ground here, and might even guess that legend has picked on this church because it is near Bell Hill, even though that really gets its name from being shaped like a bell. But we would be wrong. The truth of the matter (if you can describe the impossibly bizarre as true) goes back to the great storm of 25 May 1402, when a fiend dressed as a Friar Minor broke in through the roof of the church, ran up onto the altar and leapt to and fro three times in a sort of jeering dance before smashing out through the chancel wall, leaving a nasty smell of sulphur behind.[31] This apparition was set down in writing by learned monks at St Albans Abbey, which would explain the unusual costume worn by the fiend; there was little love lost between monks and friars. Although the details of this scene were copied more or less faithfully in later

Danbury church.

histories, tradition has ignored them completely and remembered
the incident as yet another day when the Devil stole a bell.

The old chroniclers didn't say that Danbury was visited by
the Devil – just by *a* devil, one of the countless demons of the air
whose power was unleashed in wind and storm. The difference
is not so clear in the original chroniclers, since their Latin had
neither capital letters nor a definite article, but it was typical for
monks to be preoccupied with demons in the plural and not with
a single Author of Evil. Sometimes the text makes this clear.
Eadmer, the eleventh-century biographer of St Dunstan, opens
a scene with his hero working at the forge when there is a tap at
the window and he is asked if he can help someone from outside
– but the stranger is a devil, *daemon unus* (which is not quite good
Latin, but it was Eadmer's third language after Old English and
Norman French, so we can let him off on that one). This devil,
true to the mutable instincts of his kind, has the flickering appearance and tone of a man, a boy, a giddy girl, and Dunstan is not
fooled but he sits out the charade, stirring the fire with his tongs

and waiting . . . until with one swift movement he thrusts the tongs out of the window and grabs hold of her, or him, or it, by the nose. A tussle follows, saint on one side of the window and demon on the other, and not until the accursed thing has broken free and gone screaming through the monastery do the other monks have any inkling of what was going on.[32]

This story had a long life ahead of it. But whereas all the medieval versions talk about one particular demon which paid the price for annoying a saint, all the modern ones make the antagonist into the Devil himself; it is he who tries to tempt Dunstan by appearing in the form of a lovely maiden – not a key feature in the original story – and then reverts to form as the sizzling iron takes hold:

> Her dove-like eyes turn'd to coals of fire
> Her beautiful nose to a horrible snout,
> Her hands to paws, with nasty great claws,
> And her bosom went in, and her tail came out.[33]

This is the Devil of folk tale, and in a more elaborate version he flies desperately through the air, Dunstan keeping a firm grip on the tongs all the while, until they land near Mayfield in Sussex and at last the saint lets go so that his opponent can rush off to the nearest spring and cool that scalded nose: hence the reddish tint and sulphurous taste of the waters at Tunbridge Wells.[34] Given that Tunbridge's spa was not discovered until the seventeenth century, the story must be comparatively modern. In fact it is not recorded before 1900, but it imagines the Devil in archaic style, like some Dreamtime hero, imprinting colour and form on landmarks as he passes through the half-made world.

Here is a paradox: this mythical Devil of local legend only took shape in the last two or three hundred years, while earlier in the Middle Ages, when people believed so many other wonderful and unlikely things, their stories about devils were relatively practical. Eerie though these demons were, supernatural and shape-shifting, they nevertheless made sense once you had accepted that the world really was inhabited by crowds of intangible intellectual beings who hated the human race and sought our spiritual downfall.

It is not as if medieval people knew nothing about the Devil of Scripture. They had the same theological framework as later generations, a web of biblical commentary that identified all the avatars of Satan and Lucifer – the Old Serpent, the Accuser of the Brethren, the Proud Angel, the Tempter in the Wilderness and so on – as one single person. This construction was already in place by the end of antiquity and no one disputed it. It was just that storytellers were not interested. Their saints and hermits battled demons in the plural, just as their knights fought with multiple dragons and giants. At some point in the sixteenth century this multiplicity collapsed, and when people begin to write serious spiritual autobiographies, we find them full of personal struggles with Satan himself, just as the amusing adventures in comic literature were told about the Devil and not some minor spirit. He has become a recognizable folk character, one of the few who can feature in stories told across the length and breadth of the country. Other heroes and villains are local. Hereward and Hickathrift and Guy and Godiva each have a native region to which they belong, but everywhere the Devil is at home. Only Robin Hood and King Arthur come close to this kind of cultural ubiquity, and it makes them a gift to the narrator because they come with characters already fleshed out by tradition; the background is already familiar, we know what Hell and Sherwood and Camelot are like, and this cuts out a great deal of exposition and lets the story move directly to events.

But there must be more to the rise of the Devil as a character than his convenience for storytellers. His singular personality fitted much more reasonably into a world where power and social responsibility were being unified. When sovereign government became a reality under the Tudors, power was portrayed as something that radiated from the monarch and no one else. The majesty of Heaven correspondingly came to focus on God alone, so that God's opponent likewise became not many but one, an individual Devil.

In England this shift took place during the cultural earthquake of the Protestant Reformation, but that may not have been a necessary precondition, since France and Catholic Germany seem to have undergone a similar shift in Devil lore at the same time. It is part of a wider move away from medieval ways of thinking. In the old world, spiritual action had tended to be collective; the founders of abbeys felt that, all things being equal, a monastic convent was better than a single hermitage, and a choir of twenty monks would be better than ten when it came to taking on the black host of demons. The saints themselves were a mighty army on whose help the beleaguered Christian could always call. But Protestantism cut all of this away, and left the believer alone on the cosmic battlefield. Behind him was no one but Christ, and ahead of him only Satan.[35]

4

THERE STOOD THE STRANGER: RASH DEALS AND BINDING PROMISES WITH THE DEVIL

Promises made with the Devil must be kept. Whether a rash tailor has agreed to clothe the mysterious gentleman or a proud black-smith has boasted that he can shoe his horse, they must go through with it, and only the intervention of a friendly clergyman can save them. Support from the minister was needed to save those who had agreed to sit up by a grave when the Devil came to claim his own. Priests were master conjurors and could let a wrestler outmatch the Devil; even when uttered by ordinary people, holy words had the power to make diabolical illusions vanish. They would bring an end to the feasts the Devil laid on for damned souls, in a low-key variation on the international theme of the infernal Sabbat.

Unequal Bargains

Leave the road at Windy Corner, and the next mile of walking will take you through increasingly barren ground. Below, the trees of the plantation thin out to stumps; round about you is heather, dotted in season with cranberries and whorts; and above, thin lines of rock break through the grass in parallel streaks and lead the eye up to the top of the hill, where the crest of the Stiperstones dominates the sky.

Stiper rhymes with viper, and there is something dragonish about this long line of stones, as if it were the serrated crest of a subterranean monster breaching the surface of the earth. More prosaically, they are the exposed edge of a bed of white quartz sandstone and were raised by one of the shiftings of the earth that left all this part of Shropshire channelled into north–south crests and valleys. The stones remain viciously sharp and nothing grows on the barren ridge. Their outline rises and falls in a series of jagged peaks: Cranberry Rock, Diamond and Saddle Rocks, and then Manstone Rock at the highest point, looking out east over England and westwards to Wales.

The grey spine of rock slumps for a few yards, and a thin growth of heather and hair-grass covers the top of the hill. Then the last outcrop strikes up against the sky, a squarish block called the Devil's Chair. Walk on past it, look back down the whole ragged line of tors, and you see it as a low platform with ridges raised on either side like armrests, a throne on which the Devil can sit and gaze towards his kingdom in the north. By day it is an easy climb and you can sit there, snack on a handful of whorts and admire the view. In morning and evening it casts a long shadow and forms the defining point of the crest to the villages below. At night it must be very bleak, but people do not stay on the Stiperstones overnight.

The Devil has been associated with the Stiperstones for longer than almost any other place in England. Already in 1595 the line of rocks was known as the Devil's Bridge. By 1883 there were multiple traditions. According to the mainstream version, the Devil arrived at the hill with his apron filled by a great load of stones brought from Ireland (is this an echo of the Stonehenge story?). He'd already been travelling a long time, it was a hot day and he had just toiled up this steep slope, so he sat down to rest on the tallest rock he could find. As he stood up to resume his journey, the apron-string snapped and out fell the stones, so, uttering the most hellish curses, the Devil went on his way. 'There they lie to this day, scattered on the ground all round the Devil's

The Devil's Chair, Stiperstones.

Chair, and if you go up there in hot weather you may smell the brimstone still, as strong as possible!'[1] It is the old story of the broken string; there is even a twentieth-century variant in which the apron belongs to a giantess, confirming our suspicions about the ultimate origin of this tale-type.[2]

The apron story is pure comedy; it is a pratfall gag, treasured because it shows the Devil losing his dignity. But another story, also collected by Charlotte Burne in the 1880s, casts him in a more sinister light. It was told to her by old Netherley, a lame coal-carrier who came this way to sell coals to the miners. They were a rough lot, underground all day hacking out the ore, and stumbling at night into little squatters' cottages among the fern; but they knew the hill like the back of their hands. Some of them drank hard and fought hard; some had got religion, and they were the ones who prayed hard. It must have been an evangelical who explained that of all countries the Devil hates England most, because her people are Protestants and have the Bible.

Now if ever the Stiperstones sink into the earth, England will be ruined. The devil knows this very well, so he goes whenever he can, and sits in his chair on the top of the hill, in hopes that his weight will flatten it down and thrust it back into the earth, but he hasn't managed it yet, and it is to be hoped he never will.[3]

There was something uncanny about this bare crest of sharp stone. It was here that the ghosts of all Shropshire met on the longest night to choose their king.[4] People looked with foreboding at the rock –

> black, massive, untenanted, yet with a well-worn air. It had the look of a chair from which the occupant has just risen, to which he will shortly return. It was understood that only when vacant could the throne be seen. Whenever rain or driving sleet or mist made a grey shechinah there people said 'There's harm brewing'. 'He's in his chair'.[5]

So wrote Mary Webb, the novelist of Shropshire life, but she liked to lay it on thick, especially when it came to rural superstition, and it is not clear how many local stories she actually knew: all her identifiable folklore comes from Burne. The most that can be said is that the image of the Devil sitting on his chair in the shadow of cloud and rain is accepted nowadays by people who live within sight of the hill, though they do not seem noticeably alarmed by the prospect, and tell the humorous stories with just as much relish. As so often in Devil traditions, terror coexists with laughter.

The one local story of an encounter with the Devil has a comic ring, no doubt because it ends happily, with only a receding prospect of Hell. The hero is Slashrags the tailor, who was as wicked as a tailor can be in his rather limited sphere. He overcharged and underperformed, palming off thin scraps as good stout cloth and putting in only a few perfunctory stitches wherever his work would be out of sight. As might be expected, his clients were few. The country people came to him, having no alternative, but, cut corners as he might, there was not much profit to be had out of their coarse working clothes. So he looked rather enviously on a stranger as he tramped back one night from Shelve through Pennerley. The sun had just dipped below the horizon. On the crest of the hill ahead, the hollow block of stone was beginning to merge with the black horizon, but there was still enough light to see the smart dark suit of the gent on the road. That must have cost a pretty penny, thinks Slashrags. Some people get all the luck.

And then the stranger stops, as if noticing him for the first time. 'I say, you tailor. You make suits, don't you?' Slashrags stammers, 'Yes.' 'You couldn't have one ready for me, could you, in a week's time? It has to be a quick job, I need to be – somewhere else. Don't worry about the money. You'll get everything you deserve.'

Quickly, before the dusk thickens, Slashrags pulls out a measuring tape and is taking down chest, arms, waist, inside leg . . . ah . . . this distinguished stranger is wearing elegant riding boots, but there is something unexpected about one of them. But Slashrags has been doing the Devil's work without noticing it for so many years that he hardly registers the difference now that he is face to face with him. Payment is payment, after all, and he agrees to meet his client in seven days – same place, same time.

It's his wife who realizes that something must be wrong; wiser in sleep than waking, Slashrags has tossed in a returning nightmare. He tries to brazen it out by daylight, but the frightened look in his eyes is more eloquent than words. So she pulls him off to see Parson Brewster, who makes him tell the whole story from beginning to end. 'What did the stranger say – what did you answer – and' (parson looks very serious here) 'did you promise?

Yes? Well, then you must perform what you agreed, and with every stitch perfect, if you value your life.' That was all there was to it.

All the week Slashrags works with a quite unusual level of application, and by the appointed time he has a fine suit ready to take to Whitemedale Gate. There is the gentleman, waiting in the shadow of the hedge, and as the sun sets he steps eagerly forwards, his arms stretched out to grasp – not the suit. Then a spasm of pain distorts those elegant features and the Devil squints aside, like a fox who has heard the distant bay of hounds. The sound of prayer is heard, and out from behind the gate steps Parson Brewster, a great book in his hand, reciting the rolling phrases of divine service. The Devil flees, his suit drops disregarded into the mud, and Slashrags returns home with the parson, a wiser and more honest man.[6]

That is how the story is told in the shadow of the Stiperstones, although this version carries hints of a literary origin: the Reverend Waldegrave Brewster really did live a few miles away, at Middleton-in-Chirbury, where he spent the long years of his incumbency (1872–1901) collecting local folklore.[7] It may have been an in-joke from a colleague to put him into the story, if indeed it was not copied wholesale from a previous version, for there are other stories in which a tailor makes a suit for the Devil. At the coastal village of Cresswell, east of Morpeth, the hero is honest but drunken, and when he is in his cups he makes the fatal boast that he could make a suit even to fit the Devil. Soon he is taken up on his word, and after a sleepless night, as before, he consults the parson. In this version, he is instructed to talk his way out of the predicament, and as quickly as the Devil finds fault with his tailoring, the quick-witted workman has an answer for him; if one sleeve is too short, the other is plenty long enough; one pocket is small, but that's because the other is large enough for two; and eventually he out-talks the Devil, wisely disregards the proffered payment and learns to drink less and work more.[8]

The Cresswell story has a different ending from usual; perhaps the original tale-type was modified by someone who was thinking of a separate tradition, in which a fiend or spirit is met on the road, and will seize the unlucky traveller unless kept from having the last word. More often the Devil's intentions are defeated by the presence of the clergyman close by, although this is modified in a version from St Briavels where the hero is a cobbler and not a tailor. He gets talking to the stranger and is commissioned to make a pair of boots but as he kneels in the road to get the measurements, he realizes whom he has contracted to work for. Here the parson's advice is simply to refuse payment on the return meeting.

> So there stood the stranger, and he gave him the boots. But when the money was offered, the shoemaker he wouldn't take it. And there was a great crash in the hedge, and the stranger rose up in the air and fled away, and there's a great big hole in the hedge to this day. Yes, him did take the boots.[9]

We have already met with cobbler heroes in the Devil's Spadeful stories. Tailors had an equally low status in the folk hierarchy of trades – their sedentary occupation, as well as their preoccupation with fabric, made them look a bit effeminate to men who took pride in the sweat and muscle of field labour. But since their work involved going from house to house, they could always have the last laugh, because their hosts would welcome a new story, and this could easily be reconfigured so that a tailor or cobbler became the hero. When it comes to the tales about a rash promise to the Devil, there has evidently been another shift in emphasis, for many of them structure the plot around the moral shortcomings of the main character: if Slashrags had been more honest, or the Cresswell tailor less of a lush, they would not have needed rescuing by clergymen in the first place. These versions have been modelled by members of the employing class, who felt that they might usefully point a moral or adorn a tale.

That is unusual. If we have found a connecting theme so far in traditions about the Devil, it is that they have very little to say about good and evil and are much more interested in questions of power, law, desire and cunning. There are things that you must not do, to be sure, but they make up a specifically magical morality: a set of arbitrary prohibitions, closer in spirit to not stepping on the cracks in the pavement than to a code of ethics. You must have the last word. You must not swear. You must keep a promise. You must not take tainted money. Of course these rules point to genuine principles of conduct in the real world, but in the story-world they are simply taken as given, with no more moral content than the injunction not to go outdoors after dark.

Before any sermonizing influence got to work on these stories, it was probably not greed or slapdash performance that left men open to the menace of the supernatural, but boasting. Since classical antiquity, saying that you were superlatively talented or lucky had always been received as an affront by the otherworld. Consider another story in this group, from a crossroads in the Quantock Hills. Here was a forge where the smith had such a good opinion of himself that he declared he could satisfy any customer, yes, the Devil himself, if he would like to bring his horse for shoeing. But when there is a thunder of knocks on his door at midnight, and he sees the fire in the eyes of the great black horse and the grim look of its rider, he is not so inclined to talk big. A quick excuse – where's that shoeing hammer? must be down in the village somewhere – and our smith is at the parson's window. He gets the same advice as before – do a good job and don't take the money – and, as before, the clergyman slips behind a hedge to keep an eye on what is going on. At the end the Devil, having quite failed in his attempt to press unlimited money on the

Tarr Steps.

blacksmith, sees his adversary, forgets that he is a gentleman and shouts in broad Somerset, 'Ah, if it weren't for thic old blackbird behind the hedge, I'd 'a made 'ee take the money.' And he vanishes in a burst of flame.[10]

Not far away, some old clapper stones at Tarr Steps were built by the Devil to bridge the River Barle. Because Somerset is so far from the main distribution of Devil's Bridges, the tale-type has been watered down here to the unfortunate death of a cat which crosses the bridge first, followed by a match between the Devil and a parson. 'You're a black crow,' says the Devil in this version, and quickly the clergyman, knowing how important it is to have the last word, answers, 'But not blacker than the Devil!'[11] This is magical thinking with a vengeance: there is nothing holy about the parson and he does not pray or exorcize, but simply knows the right way to defy the old enemy. In fact the exchange suggests a certain equivalence between the two, and if more folk tales had been recorded directly from the lips of the folk, and fewer had passed through clerical intermediaries, we might find this unflattering attitude more often.

When Victorian farm-workers described the Devil, they often said that he looked exactly like a clergyman. Historically, this derived from the sensationalist witchcraft tracts of the seventeenth century, in which the Devil went on the tempt dressed in sleek black clothing; it was the most expensive costume option available at the time, so it presumably hinted at the riches held out so many times to his dupes, and so seldom delivered. But with the passage of time, the dress of the Man in Black began to sound very much like ordinary sombre clerical costume. In Lincolnshire clergymen arriving without warning were liable, quite literally, to be taken for a diabolical apparition.[12]

Skin in the Game

As the scale of the stories contracts, so there is an intensification of menace. We have left behind the bombastic threats of the Devil-giant, with his hill-digging and boulder-throwing. It was not easy to imagine him ever being successful; after all, the towns and churches that he wanted to destroy are visibly still there. But the Devil who wants to crush a single human life is much more plausible. The stories of the rash promise are not entirely fantastic, once you accept that there is a spiritual enemy of humankind and that he is on the lookout to trap us. There is another class of legends which ratchet up the threat, since they represent the Devil as having already acquired one victim and anticipating another.

In St Mary Tavy, on the edge of Dartmoor, the squire of the parish lay dying. Not long before the end, he called a neighbour to his bedside and confessed to a secret double life: there had been things that should not be talked about, dealings with the Devil, and the condition was that the fiend should take his skin. 'Neighbour, would you see that he – that he doesn't take any more than that?' Well, you can't turn down a dying man's request, but when the squire had breathed his last, the neighbour got cold feet and went knocking on the rector's door. (These West Country parsons seem to have tolerated more call-outs than a midwife.) The instruction is, as always, that he must go through with what he promised, but as an added bit of advice the rector tells him to carry a cock with him. On the night after the funeral the neighbour lets himself into the dark church, stumbles his way inside and hides in the parson's pew.

> At twelve o'clock the devil arrived, opened the grave, took the corpse from the coffin and flayed it. When the operation was concluded, he held the skin up before him, and remarked: 'Well! 'twas not worth coming for after all, for it is all full of holes!' As he said this, the cock crew; whereupon the fiend, turning round to the man, exclaimed: 'If it had not been for the bird you have got there under your arm, I would have your skin too'. But, thanks to the cock, the man got home safe again.[13]

That's the story as told on Dartmoor in the 1850s, but its plot, like the skin, is full of holes. What motive for their actions does anyone have – squire, man or Devil? A Gypsy version, told by Gus Gray at Cleethorpes in 1914, makes a little more sense. This time it is a farmer's wife who dies, and she offers anything – free firing, sacks of potatoes, the rent let off – to her tenant on condition that the poor woman watches her grave for three nights. The tenant goes to the parson, who arranges for twelve priests to stand by her, praying. On the third night comes the Devil, who opens up the coffin, skins the body and folds the skin over his arm; but the poor woman, who has come armed with a long hook, uses it to haul the body back into the grave, so that the Devil gets the skin and no more.[14] Here there are reasons for the actions of the rich and poor women, though the Devil still seems rather lacking in motivation.

There's a version told in Monmouthshire which makes the logic of the story much clearer. Again, there is a dying woman, and again she agrees to write off all the money she is owed if the debtor will sit by her grave the first night after burial. As in Devon, he goes to the parson, and in this version is told to sit within a magic ring and not put anything outside it except a hook. At midnight a fierce dog attacks the circle unsuccessfully; then it digs the woman's body out of the grave and eats it, all but the skin. The man takes the opportunity to hook the skin into his circle, around which the dog runs snarling till daybreak, when the man is free. He reports to the parson, who says, 'Ah well, give me the skin, and I'll burn it, for evil spirits use these skins to appear to the relatives of the dead person and frighten them.'[15]

It may seem odd that it is the latest version which makes best sense – it was collected some eighty years after the first – but the English and Welsh variants of this story about the Devil and flayed skin are outliers anyway; like the Devil's Bridge and the church-building troll, this is a mainly Continental story which has only been imitated a few times in these islands. It is most popular in Eastern Europe and Germany, and the plot depends on assumptions that only really make sense in the medieval culture of these regions.

The flayed skin calls out for explanation. It's true that the Devil of folk tale is very physical: he leaves footprints, digs with a spade, carries things in an apron. If you kick him he jumps, and if you grip him with a pair of tongs he can't get away. Conventions like this are necessary if he is to appear in a tale at all, because the idea of an intangible spirit defeats all expectations: there would be no knowing what he would do or what could be done to him. Even so, magical disguise is common enough in legend and fairy tale without going to the gruesome extreme of dressing up in a dead man's skin.

Originally this motif seems not to have been superstitious at all, but highly educated; it derived from the ideas that medieval scholars held about demons. There was a time, at least in Northern and Eastern Europe, when instead of being wispy presences, ghosts were thought of as walking corpses, horrible half-alive things more vampire than phantom. This is what ordinary people believed, anyway, but Church scholars would have none of it: dead was dead as far as they were concerned, and bodies could not rise from the grave. In those days, sceptics did not deny the reality of other people's anomalous experiences, so they had to find some alternative explanation that fitted their theology better. This was that demons were getting into the bodies. You have to remember that the medieval demon, though he was a spirit, wasn't quite supernatural as we would understand it; he was more of a manipulator, a sort of warped, ageless super-scientist.[16] One of his skills was to get into an as yet intact body and use it for his own dark purposes. What the superstitious thought was a dead neighbour come back to haunt them was, the scholars explained, a lifeless body lurching around as the demon inside tried to get a grip on the decomposing controls.

Let the Devil be substituted for a demon, as he has been in so many other traditions, and this scenario, half rationalized, half magical, makes sense of the flayed-skin stories. The Devil cannot haunt in his own person but needs a physical vehicle – taken, presumably, from one of his former votaries. The rest of the story has grown around this initial premise, but if it was ever told by clergymen to explain what they thought was credible rather than superstitious, then that part has withered away, leaving only a feeling that the priest should be consulted before any dangerous dealings with the other world, because he will have a magic that is stronger than anyone else's.

The Wrestler's Grip

Suspicions that a parson might be a master conjuror continued to shape perceptions of the clergy in southwest Britain until well into the nineteenth century. This could be because the peninsula was culturally remote, like other mountainous western districts; perhaps incumbents thought it better to use their own Latin and Hebrew in high occult style than let their parishioners trust in the village wizard; maybe the poor communications of the region forged too many lonely parishes where, in the absence of any social equals to talk to, a university-trained scholar could go quietly mad. Whatever the cause, Devon and Cornwall are the heartland of the conjuror-parsons.

When versions of the rash promise story were told in these parts, they placed a special emphasis on the powers of the clergy-man. At Ladock, midway between Truro and St Austell, there was a champion wrestler who, in the heat of success and the pride of the hour, boasted that he could give anyone a fall, even the Devil. And before long, a black-coated gentleman met him by the light of the moon, and invited him, in a manner that brooked no contradiction, to test his strength next midnight. So Cousin Jacky tells his wife, and his wife tells the parson, as we have come to expect; but in a particularly Cornish twist to the tale, the Reverend Mr Wood offers Jacky more than good advice. He writes mystic signs and words on a slip of parchment and slips it in his waistcoat. When the two contestants meet, it is all up with Jacky until the black wrestler happens to touch hold of his waistcoat pocket and then recoils as if he had been cut or stung. They close again, more carefully this time, and after some tough play the Devil has the worst of it, grumbling just before the third fall that he can do nothing while Parson Wood's eyes are boring into him from the far side of the hedge.[17]

It is the same tale as before, but subtly modified to suit a more independent-minded audience. The parson is not so much a moral exemplar as a source of rival mystic power. Jacky may have let slip an unwise word, but for all that he is still a champion wrestler, and the storyteller is quietly satisfied that Cornishmen can hold their own even against the prince of this world. A story is like a recipe, which may be borrowed by many different countries but always takes on a flavour of the place where it is prepared. In America they tell it about the Devil and the fiddler, not the wrestler: the two compete, tune for tune, and for every piece of music remembered the Devil has an answering passage, so that things are starting to look grim for the champion fiddler until he has a bright idea and starts on a hymn – then away goes the Devil in flames.[18] In America music is the Devil's business, while nothing like this is known in Britain, though corresponding traditions do appear in Ireland and on the Continent.[19] On the other hand, the British find it natural to associate the Devil with sports and pastimes, a theme that carries little resonance in American tradition. As for the parson, usually brought into the story as a member of the governing classes who steps in to save the day for a working man, he has disappeared altogether from democratic America.

A similar denouement, in which the devilish show is brought to an end by holy words rather than a holy man, features in a wrestling story from furthest Cornwall. Between St Just and Penzance is a long stretch of barren ground broken only by the outline of Carn Kenidjack, the Hooting Cairn. Though this region was thickly populated by tin miners and their families, the moor lay waste, regarded with suspicion even in daylight and absolutely avoided at night. A few scraggy horses were turned out to graze; their poor condition was put down, not to the meagre grass, but to the fact that night after night they were ridden by something that hunted down other things that were forever trying desperately to flee, and were always taken in the end.

It was late at night when two miners set out for home, and their only path took them over this moor. Though the night was calm, they could hear the cairn hooting as if a gale were blasting through it, and soon after this came the sounds of a galloping horse. They stepped aside in case they should be run over in the dark, and saw only that the rider was cloaked and hooded. He summoned them upwards to the wrestling, and they had to follow. The horse galloped without hesitation over the broken rock, and as they stumbled after it they saw figures emerging from the granite, first one and then another; big rough men with long hair that straggled around them in place of clothing. These were the audience, and soon the two wrestlers arrived. They were stronger and bigger even than the men of the rocks, patched with hair like the winter coat of an old mine pony, one of them a little taller, the other a little bigger in the chest. The dark rider sat to watch the play, although nothing could be seen of his face but a red glimmer of light from under the hood. Then came the contest. The miners had been to fair and market, and had seen the wrestling of champions, but it was nothing to this. The two shaggy opponents clutched and swayed desperately, and it soon became clear that they were fighting not for a coat or belt, but for dear life itself. At length the stout fellow gathered his strength and gave the long fellow such a throw that he landed on a ridge of rock; they heard his back snap, but still the rider and the rock-men looked on impassively. Well, miners are not always the most gentle of men, but for all that these two were Cornish lads and they knew the meaning of fair play, so they ran up to the fallen brute. He was dying, and the elder of the friends instinctively took off his hat and said, 'God speed you, friend.' All at once the rocks shook, everything went dark and they heard a confused scrabbling all around them. Dawn found the two friends still sheltering under an overhang of rock, alone on the moor.[20]

Naturally they were the only witnesses to their story, but the wild look in their ideas was testimony enough. This was not true for the soloist of Tavistock church choir. Business took him to Horrabridge a few miles away, and the pleasure of good company kept him there until late, so he had to ride his donkey back over Whitchurch Moor. This part of the road had a bad name; it is a long spur of Dartmoor reaching into Tavistock on the eastern side, as bleak and shelterless as the deep moor beyond it. The singer got along well enough, with an occasional kick to his donkey, until halfway along he saw demons dancing in a ring and beckoning him to join in. Summoning all his presence of mind, he cried, 'Stop, Mr Devil, stop! I am a righteous man and a psalm-singer, and I sound the keynote in Tavistock church!' To prove it, he leaned back in the saddle and gave them the first notes of the Old Hundredth, but his donkey was not used to this sort of competition and bucked him off. Next morning the market women found the donkey grazing on some rushes nearby and the singer snoring in a ditch, but when he told his story they just told him to take more water with it next time.[21]

The key phrase is 'righteous man and psalm-singer', always used in these mocking anecdotes. It features in the story told about the sexton at Molland, on the edge of Exmoor; another pompous church official at Watchfield near Swindon; and yet another at Munslow below Wenlock Edge.[22] It is a tribute to the travelling powers of a good joke that people from opposite ends of the country, who most likely couldn't have understood a word of the other's dialect if they'd met in person, should still be telling the same story almost word for word about different local characters. At Wednesbury in the Black Country it is given an added twist by the suspicion that the village sexton is in partnership with a crew of body-snatchers, and the graves are no sooner covered in than they will be opened up again. So the young men of the parish set up an elaborate charade to put the fear of Hell into Old Picks, who falls to his knees and cries, 'Good Mister Devil, do forgive me this once! I've been bell-ringer, psalm-singer and amen-dinger at the old church for forty years! If you'll let me off this time, I'll never rob another stone, nor steal another bone!'[23]

Like most satire, these false-Devil stories caught the popular imagination because they adhered closely to the common knowledge of how things should be. 'Mister Devil' is addressed as a gentleman, which is how he always appears in the stories. As for Old Picks, his supplications to Satan sound very much like the voice of a man pleading to be let off by a stern but not rigorous magistrate – whatever that tells us about class divisions in an early nineteenth-century industrial district. And the self-serving testimonies of all these psalm-singers and bell-ringers bear witness to a principle we have already met with: that the Devil is best defied by sacred sound. This is why he is so active in throwing great rocks at church towers and trying to steal their bells.

Langford Budville revel, held on 1 July, was the highlight of the year for this village between Taunton and Tiverton, with garlanded processions, wrestling and cudgel-playing. Sometimes the excitement was too much for the authorities, and in the 1850s police were sent to break it up. They arrested the king of the revel and put him in irons, but while they were out imposing order the village blacksmith forced his way in and broke the irons off again. It sounds as if the Devil would have been quite at home here, but this was not the case: in fact, the climax of the revel came with clipping the tower, a moment when all the villagers surrounded the church, holding hands and embracing their building as the bells rang out. Then at a signal, they gave a shout that would have echoed to the lowest depths, let go their hands and chased the Devil down Hell Lane, past Bogie Hole and onto Harpford Bridge, at which point he was forced across the River Tone into the neighbouring parish of Thorne St Margaret. People at Thorne would be ringing their bells in order to drive him back again: so, one way or another, the Devil had a hard time of it.[24]

There is something refreshingly rustic about banishing the Devil to Thorne St Margaret. More ambitious exorcists might have tried to cast him out of the world, or at least away from the haunts of men, but as far as Langford people are concerned it was enough to despatch him into the next village, like a beggar in the old days when vagrants without a certificate were whipped over the parish boundary. Like the vagrants, he always came back again.

Another story of inter-village rivalry is played out at Shebbear in North Devon, where a long boulder lies on the patch of grass in the middle of the village. It is not any kind of stone found in the parish; the story, or one story anyway, is that this block was

Langford Budville.

originally brought to act as the foundation stone for a church at Henscott, which is over a mile away on the other side of the Torridge. But every night the stone disappeared, and every morning it was found on the village green at Shebbear. Henscott people would come over and roll it back again, which must have taken them the best part of a day, as the boulder is several hundred-weight. As soon as they had finished their work, it would be getting dark and time for the stone to mysteriously make its way back again. After a while it occurred to them that it might be easier to source their building materials somewhere else, and the Devil's Stone was left to lie where it is now.[25]

But it is not altogether undisturbed: once a year, on the night of 5 November, the bell-ringers of Shebbear take their stand in the belfry to ring a deliberately clamorous and discordant peal, as if challenging something that lies outside in the damp winter air. Then, accompanied by the vicar, they leave the church and pick up the crowbars left stacked ready for them. They station themselves alongside the Devil's stone, pitch the crowbars under it and, on the word of command, flip the whole thing over. The next year they will ring the bells again, lift up the crowbars and turn it back. In this way the power of the Devil is defied and the village of Shebbear is kept safe for another year.

What would happen if the stone were left alone? The crops would fail, they say, with death and poverty striking the village, and the powers of Hell let loose in an unspecified sort of way. One year the stone was left alone because the young men had all been called away to the war, and such disasters ensued that it was never allowed to remain undisturbed again. Which war, First or Second, is a little vague, and this is not surprising because the turning of the Devil's Stone at Shebbear is far from being an ancient custom. It is first mentioned in 1928, the Devil did not come on the scene until 1937, and the event did not really take off until the BBC arrived in 1953. This is a part of Devon that was thick with Victorian folklorists – the great Sabine Baring-Gould lived only 15 miles away – so in the absence of any earlier reports, we can assume that the custom came into being at the beginning of the twentieth century, probably as a diversion for bell-ringers, since Bonfire Night was their traditional date for ringing.[26] Within a few years tradition had become ritual, and ritual called for an explanation, at which point the Devil (well known for his association with large stones) was brought into play to explain why the custom must carry on.

The Devil's Stone lies just opposite the pub, and since heaving over a large conglomerate boulder is thirsty work, landlords may have had their own motives in keeping the custom going. The tradition about Henscott looks like a very diluted version of stories about the Devil disputing the site for a church, and, modern though it may be, the Shebbear back-story fits into patterns with which we are already familiar: the Devil is the ultimate outsider and threat to the village, but resourceful locals will put him in his place.

Feasting at Midnight

Though the stone lies just outside the churchyard, the holy influence of consecrated ground isn't enough to keep the Devil at bay without some support from the bell-ringers' muscle. Graveyards are unchancy places at the best of times. In the Yorkshire Dales, the Devil presides once a year over a meal held in the churchyard of Kirkby Malham. Invitations are not much sought after, but it happened one year that the vicar had gone to the aid of one of his choristers who had got himself in some boyish scrape. It was late when they walked back through the village and they thought there was no one else around, until a black shadow stepped out from the churchyard gate and gave them an imperious summons to the feast. To say no was impossible, and the vicar followed up the familiar pathway, with the boy clinging on behind him. An old table tomb had been spread for dinner, and it really was quite some meal, the dishes planned with taste and beautifully laid out, all of them (naturally) piping hot. Coffins had been pulled up to serve as chairs, and the Devil sat at the head of the table, doing the honours to damned wretches who had been brought out of their graves for the occasion. The vicar decided to go along with it, so he joined this unearthly company, sat down on one of the more solid bits of coffin and started on the soup course. It was nicely garnished but a bit tasteless. 'Excuse me,' he said politely to the crumbling horror that sat beside him, 'but would you mind passing the salt?' And at the word 'salt', the whole company disappeared with a shriek, and the vicar and chorister found themselves alone under the stretching branches of a funereal yew.[27]

That's how they tell it nowadays, but an earlier version of the Kirkby Malham legend plays out without any intervention by the Devil. This account, which saw print in 1827, begins with a careless boy playing football with a skull he has found in the churchyard. (Bones were tougher in those days, and so was child psychology.) He is dared to pick it up and promise to meet the skull's owner for dinner that night; he does just that, and of course he has to follow the summons – 'promises made with the grave are not to be lightly broken' – and, like our tradesmen and sportsmen who make rash deals with the Devil, collects the vicar on the way. They proceed to the churchyard, a table is laid with the ghost facing them over the dishes, and the story ends in the same way with the vicar's request for salt.[28]

There is another, very similar set of stories in which we find the same hesitation by narrators over which antagonists would give the best chill to the story, demons or ghosts. When the Primitive Methodists were first preaching in Warwickshire, one of their best itinerant ministers was Providence; this was not his

Kirkby Malham church.

real name, of course, since that had long since been superseded by a nickname from the word most frequently heard in his sermons. Once on his travels he stopped at an old house a long way from the main road, with only an elderly couple living in it. So he was surprised to find that having retired to his room, he was called down again to supper, and even more taken aback when he checked his watch and found the hour was midnight. But he dressed and went down, to find the dining room full of an elegant and well-dressed company. Providence didn't usually move in circles like that (the Prims were very much a working-class movement), but as he circulated and nodded and smiled, he recognized first one face and then another: they were all the big and little devils that he had exorcized in the course of his ministry, and they had a nasty look on their faces when they thought he wasn't watching, but for the time being everything was quite polite and he was invited to take his place at table. Which he did, and as soon as a plate was put in front of him he said grace – and then all was silent and dark, and there he was alone in the dusty abandoned dining hall.[29]

But in Cornwall and Dorset, exactly the same story is told about a haunted house with no indication that the ghosts are anything but ghosts.[30] The Cornish version has John Wesley himself as hero, and the story seems to have circulated among Methodist preachers, who were mostly men of the people; they were much more open to talk of the supernatural than their counterparts in the Church of England, who had received the sort of education that makes men laugh at such things. If they were too honest to claim the story as their own personal experience, they would at least be open to the possibility that it had happened to one of their colleagues. A version from Calver in the Peak District begins in the usual way with a Methodist minister lodging at an old haunted house, but here the supper is attended by a crowd of beautiful men and women, and the story is framed as 'The Minister and the Fairies'.[31] However, they all disappear at the moment in the grace (evidently a long one) when he says 'devils, fear and fly': so these are fairies of an equivocal sort.

The same ambiguity appears in the earliest version of this story. This appears in a life of St Collen, written in the fifteenth or sixteenth century. The saint invites himself to a feast held by Gwyn ap Nudd on 'the hill of Glastonbury' (no doubt Glastonbury Tor), and at a convenient moment scatters holy water on the fairy host, who disappear shrieking into the night.[32] The hagiographer who wrote this story had his own axe to grind, of course. From the viewpoint of Gwyn's fairy kingdom, Collen was not the ideal dinner guest, but religion forces us to take sides, and saints are on the side of good. Folk tale is more forgiving: in the other examples of the story, the disenchantment was only brought about by accident. This makes a much better turn to the tale, and it is probably its original form, even though it is missing from our one medieval example. We can take this as likely because there is a Turkish version of what is recognizably the same story which opens with a man alone at an inn, where he is joined by some devils who are sharing their gleanings from the human world. Generously, they ask him to join the feast. As he sits down to eat, being a good Muslim, he says 'Bismillah!' The sheytans scatter, and all their leavings – food over which people had carelessly forgotten to say a blessing – turn into cow dung.[33]

Stories can travel the world, of course, but it seems unlikely that this one is a recent import from Warwickshire or Cornwall: the circuits of Primitive Methodist preachers stopped well short of Anatolia. Instead, this version is simply one more link in a chain of stories which tell how a mortal disrupted an otherworldly banquet by an inopportune mention of religion. The setting at the feast is evidently an early feature, repeated with certain narrative inconsistencies in the later English versions: we have a ghostly dinner being served on the stroke of midnight, or in a graveyard, because it has to be fitted into the narrative somehow. Feasting suggests fairies rather than devils. It is one of the pastimes in which they delight, along with music, dancing and the riding of fine horses, the entertainments of aristocrats everywhere. On the other hand, the most elaborate of these tales come from a much more diabolical gathering, the witches' Sabbat.

The Sabbat never quite took off in England; nor did the torture of suspected witches. One absence led to the other, for it was only under the threat of pain that people would admit they had attended these ceremonies knowing that the confession would lead to their own death, and to that of others whom they named as having been present. But so mixed is human nature that alongside the agonized depositions of the witches, consenting to the most horrifying scenes their torturers could suggest, we also have jocular stories about husbands and boyfriends being taken along to a sort of satanic inversion of a Ladies' Night, in which they got to meet their partners' business colleagues and dance to the music of an indifferent band. Here, once again, we meet with the clumsy chap who says 'Thank God the food's arrived,' or 'I could do with a bit of salt,' and plunges everything into darkness. These stories were already being set down in print in 1536.[34]

Other equally cheerful anecdotes hinge on the same plot device of a blunder in good manners at the Sabbat. There is the eerie ride, where everyone mounts the nearest beast and they are steeplechasing over the hedges when the clumsy guest looks down and realizes he is on a bullock. 'God, that was some jump for a bull' – and at once he plummets down to earth. Or the company have slipped, by subtle ways known only to the Devil's servants, into the king's cellars, and are doing justice to the fine wines there when the thoughtless chap mentions some saint's name on the labels. At once the rest have fled and he is alone, to face inevitable capture by angry guards. This group of stories has been told and retold across Europe since the thirteenth century, but they are oddly inconsistent in their setting. In countries with a strong local tradition of the witches' Sabbat, they are told about the Devil and his servants. In countries which, like Ireland, were largely indifferent to the witch mythology, they were told about fairies instead.[35]

So whose perspective should we take in the end, that of Gwyn ap Nudd or that of Collen? Are these fairy traditions that have been demonized, or stories out of demonology which were afterwards reassigned to the fairies? The sources do not offer a clear answer and it is possible that there never was one; the smile is on the face of the storytellers, juggling with the expectations of their audience.

5

OFF IN A SHEET OF FLAME: FIGHTING THE DEVIL AND ESCAPING HIS CLUTCHES

Anyone taking on the Devil could expect a fierce fight. Unless you had mastered the arbitrary rules that governed the supernatural, a grim fate awaited you; as for those who could best the Devil in combat and learn his dark secrets, they were transformed by the experience, and not for the better. Alienation from friends and neighbours was a high price to pay for anyone who wanted to trade on a sinister reputation. Even when he offered to help, the Devil was not to be trusted; his work at harvest brought many risks and no profit, although a popular tale told how he had been deceived by a shrewd partner in the division of crops. Growth was not the Devil's forte: he was a spirit of wild and neglected places.

Overthrown by Night

Coastal Essex is flat, rich land. Long fields of green wheat and barley are broken up by hedges odorous with honeysuckle and elderflower, where the wild roses tumble as pink and white as the plaster on the painted villages. Tolleshunt Knights stands on a spur of land above the fields, but the rectory is a long way from the village and the church is even further from the rectory. Both have passed into the hands of the Orthodox Church, and the blue mosaic tiles and clustered half-domes of the Monastery of St John the Baptist offer unexpected colour, as if one of the

Greek islands had unexpectedly floated ashore, though beyond the fields there is an unmistakeably English glimpse of grey sea.

The church is simple enough, with rubble walls and a bell-cote instead of a tower. A black moth settles on the white plaster and flies off under the oak trees that are scattered around the graveyard. A scramble through the trees returns you to the road, which is steadily downhill now; streams run down towards Salcott through the low damp land, with flashing blue damselflies settling on the marshy vegetation. If you look back, the village has disappeared, all except one long scarp where the houses stand in outline against the sky; at the end of the ridge is the largest and oldest, Barn Hall.

And then, passing over the culverted stream, you see the Devil's Wood ahead, black and four-square. Around it the oak trees have been laced by thorns and elm scrub into an almost impenetrable barrier. Viper's-bugloss grows around the edges, mixed with spiky teasel, buzzards mew overhead, rabbits jump out of the way and something larger than a rabbit can be heard shifting its ground within the wall of the wood.

At one corner the undergrowth clears to reveal a long, stagnant pond. Like many shabby, out-of-the-way places, this one has a glorious second life in the imagination: it was to have been the seat of a noble family, for in those days the Salcott creek was deep water, and it was their dream that the flags and pennons on their towers would be reflected in the bay, so that riches could come to them by sea and land. But this was not to be. They dug a moat and began the walls, but every day's work was undone at night in storm and confusion, and after a long time they were no better off than when they had started.

Then the builder realized he was up against more than he knew, and he watched overnight by the piles of wood and stone to see what might come. He built a fire and sat up late, scratching the heads of the dogs that he had brought to keep him company.

At midnight came the sound of a great wind, though nothing moved, and in the firelight he could see something tall looking down on him from between the trees. A voice rang out: 'Who's there?' 'God and myself and my two spayed bitches,' said the builder, so the Devil passed back through the trees and everything was quiet once more. On the second night it happened again, the grim face in the flickering light calling gruffly, 'Who's there?' and the man answering, 'God and myself and my two spayed bitches.' It was the same on the third night, but this time when the Devil asked, 'Who's there?' the builder said, 'Myself and my two spayed bitches and God.' This was the opportunity the Devil had been waiting for. 'Mine!' he screamed, 'mine by day or night, on land or water, in church or churchyard!', and with one stride he was through the trees. Though the dogs tore and worried at him, he brushed them off as if they had been flies, gripped the builder and clawed his heart out. Then he twisted the great lintel beam of the house out of the pile and hurled it high in the air, shouting

'Wheresoe'er this beam shall fall
There shall ye build Barn Hall.'

The beam came to rest on a hill a mile away, which the noble family wisely accepted as their new home, building the rest of the house around it. It is still there in the cellar, and you can see the marks of the Devil's fingers on it. The beam is black, though not with age; it was whitewashed, time and again, but the coats of paint darkened as soon as they were put on. It has been left alone ever since someone, too inquisitive, tried to trim off a bit of the black surface; the knife slipped and he cut an artery.

As for the builder, he had courted death and it had come for him at last, but the neighbours thought that eternity in the Devil's grasp was a bit much. So they carried his maimed body up to the church at Tolleshunt Knights, and, remembering the Devil's triumphant sneering scream, they were careful to carve out a hollow in the church wall for his burial. There he lies, neither in church nor churchyard, under an old carved slab that shows him with his heart in his hands and the two bitches at his feet.[1]

When storytellers want to bring a legend alive in their own familiar landscape, they usually fix on one particular spot, like the Devil's Bridge. Sometimes, as with the stories about the disputed site for a church, the narrative moves from one place to another, but this Essex story is unusual in the way that it develops the idea of a chosen site to embrace three locations: the Devil's Wood itself, Barn Hall and the church at Tolleshunt Knights. In practice this was a bit much to remember and most versions (this is a tale with many variants) drop one of the three. Whenever the church monument is brought in at the end as material proof of the story, the spayed bitches are a pair, since two dogs featured on the tomb. When the action is evenly split between the wood and the hall, there are three bitches, three being more of a folkloric number, and lucky as well. Not in this case, admittedly, but there was a long-standing tradition that a spayed bitch kept in the house would ward off ghosts and other presences of the night. Because she was female and yet could not bear pups, she was a living contradiction, a little uncanny, however loyal she might be – and so a natural guardian for boundaries between one world and another.

When versions are based at Barn Hall, they tend to make the hero into a builder, or just a nightwatchman who has been taken on specially to guard the site. Those based at the church are more likely to represent him into a warrior, because the monument shows an armed knight. In one account, probably the oldest as it was being told in the 1760s, the encounter with the Devil is not a mere challenge in the darkness but a closely fought engagement, the knight armed with his sword, the Devil with a great club.

After winning the third fight he hurls this into the air, and it is the club and not a piece of builder's timber which forms the unhallowed core of the future hall.

This is unexpected, because the Devil rarely appears in legends with any kind of weapon. It's true that in many of the old mumming plays, performed at Christmas or some other fixed date in the year, the heroes who fight and fall and are brought to life again are joined by various supernumerary characters, whose job is really just to appear in costume, join in the song and dance, and divide up takings afterwards. One of these introduces himself: 'In comes I Beelzebub/ Over my shoulder I carries me club.' But that may just be for the sake of the rhyme. Perhaps the Essex Devil has got mixed up with the Wild Man of medieval romance, who always carried a club, like a prototype caveman, and used it to belabour knights. Or maybe we are catching the last echo of some tradition about the Devil and his magical club. In the 1660s there was a magistrate, a great persecutor of the Quakers, who used to roar at the people he was interrogating: 'What a devil, are you all dumb? Hath the devil cast his club over you and bewitched you?'[2]

A club is a heavy, cumbersome sort of weapon, but, as we have seen, the Devil of folklore is very physical. In Bradley they talked of Gret Dick of Cinder Hill, who would take on any man when he had the ale in him. He had plenty enough of that on the night he met the Devil, who was coming down a lane near Brunshaw, leading (for reasons not explained) a dun cow. Neither would yield to the other, they had words, and soon both were laying their jackets aside on the bank and stepping forwards with fists up. Then:

Dick and t'Devil and dun cow fought
Dick thrashed Devil, and dun cow laughed![3]

Tainted Wisdom

This fight – or the report of it, as the cow seems to have been the only spectator – did Gret Dick's reputation no harm at all, but he did not build on it. Other, more sinister characters made sure it was known that they had mastered the Devil. There was a man who went out at nights from his home at Child's Ercall near Newport; he would step briskly down the lane, well dressed, confident; any neighbour who bid him good evening had only to wait, and shut their ears to the dreadful noise, until he staggered back, his clothing rumpled and torn, but with the light of victory in his eyes. The man with the evil eye (his identity was well remembered by the storytellers, but they chose not to name him) had a mean streak, and used his hard-won uncanny powers to stop travellers on the road, or set them unwillingly back in the direction they had just come from, for no reason at all, just to show folk that he was not to be trifled with. He could call up ghosts; he once made a phantom coach appear, flitting through the hedge to the astonishment of his companion. Every year, on New Year's Eve, he would visit the church at midnight and stand in the shadows of the porch, waiting until he had seen the drifting wraiths of all those who would die in the year ahead. It was not pleasant to be in the pub with him in the early days of January, and watch his eye passing over neighbours, one after another, and dropping with a smile when one of them talked of plans for the future.[4]

Everyone knew there was one night in the year when those who were brave enough to venture into the darkened church could learn this secret, although the particular night varied from region to region. Some said it was New Year's Eve, some Midsummer, some St Mark's Eve on 24 April. In the Welsh Borders it was held to be All Souls' Night or Hallowe'en, and at Dorstone near Hay-on-Wye they told the story of what happened on that night to Jack of France, a man of evil life. We are not told what kind of evil, but the context suggests that he too was a claimant to supernatural knowledge. Jack was walking late through the village and saw a light shining out of the church; he went over, curious to see what was going on, and climbed onto a stone that gave him a good view through the window. There were prayers under way, of a sort; dry twisted bodies sitting here and there in the pews and a tall hooded preacher in the pulpit. Every now and then the preacher would call out a name and one of the wizened forms would answer to it. Jack realized that he was listening to the names of the dead, and he pressed his face as close as he could to the glass so he could hear and memorize who they were. But the next name that he heard was his own, and the preacher was looking up at the window where he stood. He saw two eyes of fire, fell fainting off the stone and remembered nothing more. When morning came he limped home, took to his bed, repented and died.[5]

Other things could be learnt on St Mark's Eve by those who were brave enough to take the challenge. In Lincolnshire, aspirants for secret knowledge would gather the fern-seed that only then falls from its parent fern, all in one instant on the stroke of midnight. Dropping with such violence that it shattered two pewter plates, the seed could be caught in a third, and at that moment the Devil would ride up on a pig. Only the most fearless could hold his gaze, talk to him face to face and learn the lore that would make them into cunning men.[6]

But it was not for curiosity that the gatherers of fern-seed and the church porch watchers set out on these nightmare errands: they were after control over other people's lives. If a man could make other men do his bidding, if he had the power to make them sit or stand or go as he wished, and could tell who was going to live and who was going to die, then that man was in a fair way to being himself the little devil of his neighbourhood. The Devil knew all about power – that was why he was forever dressing as a gentleman – but he did not give it away readily, not without a fight.

In the broad, fertile fields of East Anglia there was a working-class elite who capitalized on this belief: the toadmen. They owed their position, feared and admired in equal measure, to the intensive arable farming of the region. Here all farm work revolved around ploughing and harrowing and carting, so the heavy horse was king, which gave special status to anyone who could keep horses biddable when they were in his hands, or make them run wild under anyone else's. The farmer couldn't give such a man the sack; as for his neighbours, no door was ever closed to him. The power to make a horse stop or go at will lay in the toad's bone. To get hold of this, the aspiring horseman had to catch a live toad and skin it alive, or peg it to an ant-heap until the ants had eaten skin and flesh. Then, on a night when the moon was full, he would go to a rivulet and throw in the bones, which would scream horribly when they touched the water. One and one only would float upstream, and to take hold of it he had to fight the Devil. Once the man's blood had dripped on the ground, he was a fully initiated toadman. But there was a price to be paid for these powers: although he might be respected he was never envied, for after his initiation he could not rest.[7] The toadman at Fordy Gate near Ely would sit and drink of an evening, silent and aloof; no one ever offered to walk back with him past Wicken Fen, for

Mark Thorby never wanted no lantern when he went home of a dark night down that owd black lane with the Fen on one side and the Mere on t'other. He didn't want no light, 'cos the owd davvle walked beside him and lit the path wi' flames![8]

The secrets of the toadman were too dreadful to be revealed. When a man announced that he was thinking of becoming one,

Wicken Fen.

his father pulled a gun down from above the mantelpiece and threatened to shoot him. 'I daren't tell my own son,' said one initiate. 'What I know goes to the churchyard with me.'[9] But of course the secrets were revealed, and not with much reluctance, judging by how many times the toad, the bone, the stream and the brutal moonlit fight appear in the literature, variously combined. Initial reluctance only pushed up the number of drinks that a folklorist had to buy before the silent old chap in the corner of a pub could be persuaded to tell all. In any case, there was nothing to be gained from reticence towards strangers, who lay outside the circle of village life. The mystique of the toadmen gave them power, but only within the world of those who knew and believed.

The toadman fought the Devil until he had won what he wanted, a Jacob wrestling with the dark angel. Others struggled to get free of his demands. In St Leonard's Forest, between Crawley and Horsham, there is a clear avenue of land, about a mile and a half long, called Mike Mills' Race. Mike was a smuggler who worked the Brighton coast; he had a lot on his conscience, for the smuggling trade only exists where people keep silent about it, and silence must be imposed with an unsparing hand. It is a dangerous business, too, and Mike was not prepared to wait for a bullet in the dark or an exciseman's cutlass before he found out how things stood with his soul. So one night, alone under the shadowy trees, he called up the Devil and made him a straight promise, man to demon: they would run a race down the avenue, and if the Devil won, he could have Mike's soul there and then, but if Mike won, then it was quits for good. The Devil lost, so Mike Mills escaped damnation when at last he died; on the other hand, there was no chance of Heaven for a man with his record, so he was left to wander St Leonard's Forest, and he is probably there still.[10]

No doubt the place-name came first and the story was shaped to fit. This was certainly true of another Sussex field, east of Lewes. A gentleman was riding back one winter's night after dining at Laughton Place, and had just come to this spot when the Devil appeared, all flaming red, and chased rider and horse round and round the field. The gentleman eventually got home,

Mike Mills' Race, St Leonard's Forest.

half dead with fright, his horse being covered with foam and blood, and ever since that field has gone by the title of the Devil's Race.'[11] So a later traveller was told, but in fact 'Devil's Race' is a common Sussex field-name, found at eight other places including Eastbourne and Alfriston, and usually describing the steep side of a long valley. Perhaps it means that these downland slopes are so smooth and precipitous that only the Devil could race there, but even if this is the intention, the expression is purely metaphorical and didn't originally imply a story.

But once suggested, it was hard to shake off ideas of the Devil chasing after you. It might seem a childish fear, with the fiend reduced to little more than a bogeyman, but then children, just because they are children, live at the mercy of those larger and stronger than them, and when they imagine an ogre it is simply a shadow of the parent, with our power made absolute and all our good intentions stripped away. There was a story told in Northamptonshire in which the Devil appears very much as a surrogate adult.

It begins with a farm boy being called over by his master and shown a large field dotted with piles of dung here and there, wherever they had dropped off the cart. The master says he will be away for a week, the muck needs spreading, and the boy can get it done by the time he comes back. Yes sir, says the boy, and means it; but a week is a long time when you are young, there are all sorts of distractions, and each day he is sure he can catch up on the next one. So when the week ends, not a bit of the work has been done and the boy throws himself down in the same field where he should have been at work and cries his eyes out. A little old man who happens to be passing by stops and lifts him up in a kindly way to ask what's wrong. 'I ben't done me work, zir.' 'Never mind,' says the old one, 'ca'st thee run?' 'Ees, zir.' 'Then I'll do thy work, and gladly, while all thee needs do is run over to that stile there. But then if I catch thee before thee do reach the gap, thou'll be mine!' Youth is rash, and maybe the boy thought that the muck could never be spread that fast, but having a good idea of who he was dealing with, he didn't stop to look. Not that he needed to; he could hear the dung being flung around in all directions and instantly, as the last pile scattered, his adversary was after him, no longer an old man and no longer kindly. Hard claws reached out just as he gained the stile and were pulling at his smock, but the burning grasp scorched a hole through the fabric and only tore it. That night the farmer came back and complimented the boy on how carefully and evenly he had worked, but the next morning the dung was all back in heaps again, just as it had been before.[12]

A similar story was told at Stansted Mountfitchet in Essex, though here the Devil is brought into the story not by idleness but by unwise words. A shepherd was making a sheepfold but grew weary of the work of dragging out the hurdles and knocking them in, and wished that the Devil would set it up for him. Rashly, he spoke aloud – we are in the realms of magical morality here, where what matters is not what you think or believe, but what you say – and at once the Devil appeared to take up his side of the bargain. As in Northamptonshire, and in landscape stories like the transport of Stonehenge, the work is no sooner imagined than done, and the shepherd is nearly caught. This time it is his boot that is ripped off in the Devil's clutch, and 'for years afterwards the shepherd obtained considerable local notoriety by exhibiting the marks of the Devil's finger and thumb, which showed on his ankle as a brown scar.'[13] That part, at least, sounds as if it really happened and one wonders whether the scar came first and the shepherd found a way of capitalizing on it.

Outrunning the Devil makes for a lively climax, but it lacks subtlety. Typically, it was the tailors who adapted the story; given the nature of their trade, they were unlikely to appear as heroes in any mile-and-a-half sprint, so they came up with a cleverer version. The story, told at Ashton-under-Lyne, has come down to us in one of those bouncy Victorian rhymed versions, opening with the foolish craftsman invoking the Devil, who offers him wealth untold. Prudently the tailor proposes a match instead: each of them is to make a coat, and if he finishes first, he gets the gold, while the Devil on the same terms gets him. The Devil agrees, but then, like most amateurs, finds it hard to thread the needle, so the tailor magnanimously agrees to do it for him:

> A needleful he put him in,
> The tailor did, with pleasure,
> Sound and true,
> To last all through
> A hundred yards by measure.

Now the Devil's lightning speed is of little benefit, for with every stitch he has to flap down to the far end of the room, pull the thread as tight as he can, race back to put the needle in again, then fly off once more, while the tailor calmly minds his work and makes small stitches. He wins and the Devil goes off in a huff, leaving the unfailing sack of gold behind for the benefit of his rival, who becomes a knight and patronizes charities, which was about as grand as imagination could get you in nineteenth-century Ashton-under-Lyne.[14]

A Strong Hand with a Scythe

The industrious storytellers have made their hero outsmart the Devil, which is a common ending in these stories: we saw it earlier in tales of the Devil's Spadeful and Devil's Bridge, and there is a hint of it in versions of the rash promise story where it is vital to win the last word against the Devil. Of course, when the printers of early tracts described the Devil's interventions in daily life, there could be no question of anyone outwitting him. In these godly pamphlets, terror is very much in the ascendant over laughter, though good journalism takes priority over both: sales depended on a memorable story, while readers felt more comfortable about parting with their pennies when it ended in a solid moral as well. So we find the workman Devil transmuted into an exemplary figure in the 1678 tract on 'The Mowing-Devil; or, Strange News out of Hartford-shire'. A farmer had an acre and a half of oats ready for harvest, and a poor man offered to mow them at the standard rate. When he would not be talked down to a lower wage, the farmer raged and swore that he'd rather have the Devil mow it than pay that much. He should have known better than to say such a thing out loud. Or, looking at it another way, he should have known better than to bring in a blackleg, especially one with a cloven foot: in those days the kind of results later reached by collective bargaining were enforced supernaturally. For that very night the oats were seen all in a flame, and yet the next morning they were not burnt, but had been mowed and stacked so neatly 'that no Mortal Man was able to do the like', none of which was of any use to the wicked farmer, who was mysteriously unable even to carry them out of the field.[15]

On the title page, the artist has worked hard to fit all the story into a small space, where the oats are simultaneously blazing into flame, being mown by a small scythe-wielding Devil on his way around the frame and lying in marvellous order. The end result looks rather like a crop circle, though that may be a coincidence; it is a little perverse to use this pamphlet as testimony for crop circles, which have other and simpler explanations, and not as proof of the Devil's intervention to punish pride and injustice, for which there is a much larger supporting literature.

At all events the Devil was known to be a good hand with a scythe, as appears from a story told in the next county to that conveniently vague 'Hartford-shire'. It comes from Ted Allen, who had worked up and down the Essex coast as a shepherd, cattleman and gamekeeper, ending up as looker over the Langenhoe Hall marshes. Next to his house on the long peninsula of the marsh was a field called Hopping Tom's Piece, and in the middle of the field was a pond called the Devil's Drink Bowl. Why? Because:

> They was hay harvestin', twelve men a-swingin' scythes. The master up at the Hall know'd every one on 'em. But when that cum arternoon time there was a thirteenth man slipped in among 'em, a reg'lar mowin' master. He swung a better scythe nor any on 'em. When the rest knocked off work this owd chap went on a-mowin'. He mowed all night by the moon. Cum mornin' time the hay crop was half cut. Some on 'em said he was the Davvle. Next night time they put a lot o' iron bars in the hay what still stood. But this chap come and mowed in the morn again. He sliced through them iron bars like cheese. Cum mornin' the crop was cut. The men goes up to the Hall to draw their pay, this owd chap among 'em. The master looks down at his feet and sees he's got the cloven hoof. So he says 'I 'on't pay you no money. You're old Hoppin' Tom.' With that, the Davvle lets out a shrik an' flew off in a sheet of flame. He hulled his drink bowl into the middle of the field, drowned the whole hay crop, and that's where the pond lays today.[16]

It adds an extra shiver to think of that relentless scythe cutting through iron as if it were straw. But this seems to have been Ted's own spin on an older story; most often the iron bars are introduced, not in testimony to the Devil's unstoppable strength, but as a cunning device that brings him to a halt where everything else has failed.

Dividing the Harvest

A smith lived at St Mabyn, outside Bodmin and not far from Egloshayle; he was a hard worker and a good neighbour, much in demand for all kinds of useful gear, and also celebrated for keeping the Devil in check. No one quite knew how he did it, but there were rumours of fierce fighting late at night in the glow of the dying forge; the smith's strong arms had hammered and beaten all day, and no doubt they struck many a good blow. Eventually the Devil gave up on brute force and instead proposed a wager of skill. There were a couple of acres nearby ready for harvest; who could mow them quickest? The smith agreed readily enough, but the night before the match he rootled through one of those boxes of oddments that you find in every smithy, looking for the tines that he kept for harrows when their teeth dropped out. Quietly he slipped into the field and strode up and down the Devil's acre; every now and then he dropped in a harrow tine and with the heel of his boot trod it halfway into the ground. Morning came, smith and Devil took their places, and off they started. At once the fiend was well ahead, but then there came a snick where he had met one of the half-buried tines. The Devil is no weakling, and he had scythed straight through it, but of course this took the edge off the blade, and he had to stop and whet this back to a cutting edge. Meanwhile the smith carried on, slow but sure. Back to work went the Devil, cutting furiously through the corn, stopped almost at once by another tine, and needing a renewed application of the whetstone. And so it went into the afternoon, until the smith was ready to cut his last sheaf, when the Devil threw a paddy, hurled his whetstone up in the air and disappeared. The stone, turning lazy somersaults in the sky, grew larger and larger as it descended and came down the size of an old menhir or longstone, in which form it stuck deep in the ground and remained as a witness, until an unbelieving farmer pulled it down to make a gatepost.[17]

St Mabyn.

At St Mabyn this scything match is the only contest between man and Devil, but elsewhere it is just one episode in a series. In Monmouthshire and Radnorshire, the Welsh counties that border on the Midlands, the role of the smith is taken by a mysterious character called Davies Sirevan, of whom no one knows anything except that he and the Devil were always sparring and trying to get the better of each other. It was Davies who dropped the harrow tines among the corn, just as it was he who had to race out of the field before the muck-spreading was finished, the Devil getting to him just in time to tear his coat-tails off. Davies got his own back by demanding that the Devil stuff a bed for him; he carried up an old feather-bed mattress onto a hill in a high wind, cut it open and let the feathers fly before insisting that these and these only be put back into the ticking. The Devil had to give him best on that one.[18] But the longest episode of the cycle comes when Davies and his old chum decide to take up farming together.

They're partners, so they agree to go halves on the crop, with Davies generously offering to put in the first year's work ploughing and tilling and planting. He sets some rows of potatoes and on a fine summer day the Devil drops by to see how things are going. 'Fine crop,' he says, a little vaguely – nothing much grows in Hell – 'and I'm thinking I should pick my share.' 'Which would you be wanting,' says Davies, 'tops or bottoms?' The Devil looks at the thick green shoots sprouting along the ridges and the little potato-apples just starting to swell on them. 'Tops,' he says.

Come the autumn, the Devil finds himself raking dry potato haulms off the ridges, while Davies digs up a fine crop of King Edwards. But a bargain is a bargain, and the Prince of Darkness is too much of a gentleman to complain. Only, when next year's crop is being discussed, he demands that this time he gets the bottoms, and in return for playing him such a sneaky trick, Davies can go plough and till and plant all over again. Which he does, and sets a fine crop of wheat. When autumn comes, Davies harvests the grain and the Devil is left with a field of stubble and some dirty roots. So after that they left off farming.[19]

It's a popular story, told in many places: the best versions fuse it with the scything match, so that the human partner wins three times over, first with potatoes (bottoms), then with wheat (tops) and finally with wheat again (side by side). People expect the episodes of a folk tale to cluster in threes – at least, they do if they've grown up with the storytelling conventions of Western Europe – so this triadic structure sits easily in the memory. The antagonist need not be the Devil, and is often a boggart or bogle. Exactly what a boggart might be is left to the listener's imagination, though one narrator from Mumby, just up the coast from Skegness, is more detailed: 'boggard look'd as strong as a six-year-owd hoss, an' his airms was o'must as long as teäkle-powls.'[20] In other traditions the boggart is more of a spook, an ill-defined something that haunts lanes, woods and stiles. If he resembles the Devil, it is only after both have been reduced to a lowest common denominator of menace in the dark. In more developed interpretations he belongs with brownies, hobthrusts and other working spirits, all of them tireless, hairy, ragged beings who do the work of field and farm.

It seems that versions of 'Tops and Bottoms' with a boggart as the antagonist are closer to the original than those that feature the Devil. Ideas have clearly been swapped to and fro between versions in comparatively recent times, leaving traces even at the level of wording – always the most superficial aspect of a story. When Davies takes on the Devil at mowing, the fiend wants to 'whittle-whattle' his blunted scythe; in a Northamptonshire version, the bogle calls plaintively 'when do we wiffle-waffle, mate?' and gives up when he finds he can't do this till noon.[21] Wiffle-waffle is an onomatopoeic word for the sharpening of scythes, from the sound that the strickle makes as it rustles up and down the blade, and it must have been borrowed by one story from the other.

In an early version, beautifully told by Rabelais, the antagonist is a devil; this was written in 1552, at a time when (as we saw from Camden and the other antiquaries) devils in the plural were beginning to give way in landscape legend to the Devil himself. Here the order of the Davies story is inverted, with wheat coming first, followed by turnips (not potatoes, as those were unknown then). Rabelais presents us with a very little, pre-school devil, whose training in malice has not yet stretched much beyond putting a frost on the cabbages, and his injured dignity every time he is outwitted adds to the charm of the story.

That is a key feature of this story: the Devil, devil, boggart or bogle is not tricked by truly superior cunning but through basic ignorance of life. Compare this with the deceit in the Devil's Bridge, a story in which the fiend knows what he is about, and is in a fair way to succeed until the human party finds a way to get round him. By contrast, the plot of 'Tops and Bottoms' implies a spirit who simply doesn't know what wheat is, or potatoes, or turnips. This is a curious idea, though clearly one with international appeal as the story is widely told. It is strange, knowing what we do now about the transmission of tale-types, to step into the shoes of a Victorian folklorist like Thomas Keightley as he realizes, translating the story from Danish ('A Farmer Tricks a Troll'), not just that it was already in Rabelais, but that it had recently been taken down from storytellers at Laghman in Afghanistan.[22]

But how old is the story? In several versions, including that first one in Rabelais, the boggart-devil claims a prior right in the soil, which is why the crops are to be divided between him and the interloping human. It is as if we are present at an encounter between the first farmer and a hunter-gatherer who has never seen cereals before. Of course we don't need to reduce this to the level of plodding literalism and look for remnant Mesolithic colonies in Victorian Northamptonshire; storytellers could imagine a what-if scenario just as well as we can. But it is curious to find them playing around with ideas of primitive culture.

There is a hint of this in the Devil's aversion to horseshoes. Like many ubiquitous customs, the practice of hanging these up is so widespread that it is not easy to pin down its origins. When it is first mentioned in 1584, it serves to keep witches out of the house, and there were many other magical protections current at the time for the same purpose – bottles buried under the threshold, secret things concealed in chimneys, special marks scratched on beams and windowsills. Later in the nineteenth century, the Devil took over from witches as the spirit of motiveless malignancy, and a back-story was invented about how he was so traumatized by his encounter with St Dunstan that he never again dared to approach an emblem of the smith's craft.[23]

Behind the superstition, at least as practised in the nineteenth century, there is symbolic logic: the Devil keeps well away from something made of iron, the defining material of human craft, and which belongs to the horse, who at cart and plough is the motive force of the agriculture that sustains human life. This is a curious inversion of the role the Devil played in the toadman stories, as a guarantor of craft knowledge; here he stands at the opposite pole, a spirit of the wild opposed to cultivated human existence.

Spirit of the Wilderness

It is not surprising to find that in the place-names that were coined around this time, 'Devil's' is shorthand for wilderness, especially the sort that is caused by neglect.[24] Woods named after the Devil are not, as you might expect, regions of old shadowed forest; instead they are little squares set among the fields, presumably land that had got out of control and was then allowed to disappear under scrub growth. The Devil's Kitchen in Wrotham is a hollow at the meeting of Labour-in-Vain Road and London Road; the Devil's Green at Dilwyn is a bit of land at a triangular road junction.[25] The Devil's Garden at Kington, a sheltered spot concealed at the top of the Stanner Rocks, might be famous for its profusion of wild flowers, but not for any more useful horticultural qualities.[26] 'Devil' here is almost a negative qualifier: it's his garden because it is not a real cultivated garden at all.

Sometimes this negative allocation was taken a step further. Around Frieston, to the north of Grantham, triangular clumps of trees were allowed to grow in the corners of the fields; these were known as the Devil's Holts and they were left for the Devil to play in so he didn't roam abroad and spoil the crops.[27] That was the story, at least, and it recalls the old Aberdeenshire tradition of the Guidman's Faulds, pieces of land that were left 'long time unlabourit', like one at Belscamphie which the Kirk Session heard about in 1649. They immediately gave orders that it should be cultivated in defiance of the Devil.[28]

The Devil's Kitchen, Wrotham.

So he was evicted from his little wild patch, just as he was in Cornwall, Lincolnshire and Northamptonshire, though it is more satisfying to imagine the Devil losing a competition (even if a rigged one) rather than being turned out on the orders of the godly. There is a hint of exorcism even in tales of the ploughing match; in broken-down forms, such as the tradition about Thomas Dunston of Bedfield Hall near Framlingham, the last thing to be remembered is that the cunning human interrupted the corn with iron rods, as if the metal itself had some apotropaic power.[29]

For all their hints of archaic magic, these stories of the mowing match cannot be very old, at least not in the English versions, where the plot depends on comparatively modern agricultural practice. Two competitors, both at work with scythes, cutting a crop of wheat: that couldn't have been imagined before the eighteenth century, because until then cereal crops were cut by small handheld sickles. A scythe cuts its swathe at ground level – which is where the harrow tines are planted, and why the Devil doesn't see them – whereas sickles were for cutting off ears of corn at waist height. In the Continental versions, which are technically more primitive and therefore probably older, the man agrees to reap the middle half of the field with his sickle, leaving the outer half to his adversary, who exhausts himself going round and round in circles. There may be a hint of this behind the 'Mowing Devil', but the folk stories seem to have reworked his episode at some time after 1700 to make it more realistic under new working conditions.

If so, it is curious that the working men who updated the story didn't necessarily make its hero a labourer like themselves. Thomas Dunston was the master of Bedfield Hall, while another version is told about Sir Barney Brograve of Waxham Hall on the Norfolk coast. In this case, the storyteller has ingeniously set the Devil and Sir Barney to cutting beans, not corn; by harvest time, the beanstalks are dry and black, so naturally the Devil doesn't notice the dark iron rods with which his opponent has staked out the patch.[30] Since there is no shortage of land on the Waxham Hall estate, the two contestants are vying not for the harvest of this small beanfield, but for the much higher stake of Sir Barney's soul. He wins, of course, as the hero always does in these contests with the Devil.

There was a real Berney Brograve – the name, in true aristo-cratic fashion, is pronounced differently from how it is spelled – and he went to his rest, or at any rate died, in 1797. He must have been a larger-than-life figure, for stories about him were still being told in the 1910s; it helped that he was the last of the Brograves, and like many of his kind – hard drinkers, ready fighters and fatherers of bastards throughout their little domains – he had a rakish reputation to live up to. So perhaps Sir Barney really did challenge the sweep who overcharged for cleaning Waxham Hall's chimneys, and call off the fight after three rounds, so choked with soot that he had to wash away the taste with whisky. It is unlikely that his hair turned white in a single night after he had rashly laid covers for dinner and invited every

Brograve who had died by violence to return to the Hall for a night. Six pale ancestors duly arrived, still bearing scars from Agincourt and Marston Moor, but Barney braved it out and matched them drink for drink, to be carried off to bed at last when he was found at daybreak slumped alone over the table. But he certainly did not sell his soul to the Devil, though local opinion had him clutching the contract post-mortem and arriving of his own accord at Hell's gate, for a gentleman always keeps his word.

> But the Devil saa, 'I've been looking trew your account and it fare to me, if I hev you in here 'twon't be a sennight afore yew'll be top dog and I'll hev to play second fiddle, so there's your writing back and now be off', and Sir Barney, he say 'Where am I to go tew?', and the owd Devil he forgot hisself and saa 'Go to Hell', and Sir Barney had no idea of wandering all about nowhere, so he tuk him at his word.[31]

It may not be everyone's idea of a happy ending, but evidently Sir Barney was much happier in Hell than he would have been in a more tepid environment.

6

NEITHER INSIDE NOR OUTSIDE: RAISING THE DEVIL AND LAYING HIM AFTERWARDS

Making friends with the Devil may sound a high-risk strategy, but he could be good company – for a while. Working together, he and a magician channel rivers and create new highways. But just as often they fall into competitive bickering, with cycles of stories telling how the ingenious mortal gets one over on his uncanny friend. At the end, when relations are about to turn nasty, the magician springs a final trick of liminal burial that saves him from damnation. Others, less skilled, find that when they have raised the Devil they cannot be rid of him; he must be given tasks that are beyond his powers or he will wreak a terrible vengeance. Once set three tasks, the Devil will always succeed in the first two, and it taxed the imagination of storytellers to come up with a third that was beyond him.

Magicians at Work

Morpeth is a Goldilocks town, just large enough to have everything and small enough to be friendly. You can set out from the Clock Tower, walk through the market and within a few minutes you've passed the shops and the Bagpipe Museum and are standing on Bridge Street, where you can look over the low yellow sandstone parapet of the bridge and see the rolling Wansbeck. Turn left at St George's Church, follow the road out of town and before long the view is all trees and water. The

Wansbeck, which runs through a steep-sided wooded valley, is a low stream that continually breaks into ripples over a riverbed of flat slabs. A path runs along it until you get to Bothal, where it broadens out; after a short detour by road you are back by the stream at Sheepwash Bridge.

This is a plain bit of engineering with latticed ironwork painted dark green on either side, and it marks the point where the Wansbeck becomes tidal. But things might have been quite otherwise, according to the story. There was a time when the councillors of Morpeth were jealous of the other towns to their south; they could see the great ships coming to rest in the Wear and Tyne, and wanted a piece of the action for themselves. There was no human art that could turn their little Wansbeck into a harbour for seagoing vessels, but they were ambitious and pre-pared to go beyond what was permitted to men, so they sent for the wizard Mitchell Scott. He gladly offered to help, so long as no questions were asked about his methods and complete confi-dence was placed in whatever he should command. The Morpeth people agreed, and Mitchell went to work. He called for the fastest runner in the town and sent him down to the seashore, where the thin stream, as it then was, trickled into the sea at Cambois. At a certain hour, and not before, the runner was to sprint as fast as he could from sea to town. Mitchell locked himself up, to all appearances alone, but certainly not in good company; he performed certain rites; and at the stated hour, the runner took to his feet, going faster and faster as strange sounds echoed behind him. In terror he heard the roar of rising waters, the angry hiss of a galloping tide, until at last, convinced that his life was in danger, he glanced back at the wave that seemed about to overwhelm him – to see nothing; nothing but a tranquil stretch of tidal water downstream of the point where he stood, and upstream nothing but the chuckling beck. The sea had come as far as Sheepwash and stopped dead at the point where he lost

The Wansbeck, Morpeth.

confidence, so Morpeth never had a chance to eclipse Newcastle and Sunderland.[1]

Others say that Mitchell promised to carry out the same feat at Durham and was again defeated through the terror of the man he sent to guide the tide. It is hard to imagine how the Wear could be made navigable that far without drowning miles of farmland, so on the scale of probability (sometimes, though not always, a good way to judge stories) the Morpeth version may have priority. In any case the earliest recorded version comes not from either of these places, but from the other side of the Pennines, where Mitchell, under the name Michael Scot, was commissioned to improve the trade of Carlisle. The demands of the townsfolk seem to have been more ambitious here – no less than to make their home into a port, by reshaping the estuary of the Eden into a bay. In this version, set down in about 1675, there is no runner: Michael himself is riding the Devil's horse, and the sea follows him until at Boustead Hill, 8 miles short of his destination, he loses his nerve and glances back.[2]

Normally Michael showed more sense. On one occasion he had to cross the sea, and called on the Devil to carry him piggy-back. They were far out from land with the ocean waves rippling below them, chatting of this and that, when the Devil said casually, 'And what is it that the good wives say first thing in the morning?' 'Mount, Devil, and flee!' snapped Michael. If he'd given the true answer – 'God bless us a' this morning' – he would have been plunged into the sea and drowned.[3] This curious little story is an outlier, the only English story (or rather British, for Michael Scot is just as well known in Scotland) to feature someone riding on the Devil's back; in other folk-tale traditions, like the Russian, it is a regular motif. The story has a knowing relationship with the legends of the clumsy man riding to the Sabbath who blurts out the name of God and at once drops from his aerial steed. You have to understand that this is what usually happens to appreciate Michael's shrewdness in giving a safer answer.

A medieval origin would not be surprising for this story, since the historical Michael Scot (1175–1232) was one of the leading intellectuals at the turn of the thirteenth century. Even at the time, popular anecdotes about quick-witted answers were being fathered on him; he must have been a larger-than-life character, but then he was court philosopher to the Holy Roman Emperor, the kind of job in which it pays to be memorable. We could see him in purely intellectual terms, a figurehead for that surge of translation which brought the learning of the eastern Mediterranean to the limits of Europe, but he also wrote a practical treatise on magic for his emperor, which suggests that he had learnt more in Toledo than Arabic grammar, and Dante found a place for him among the masters of divination in the eighth circle of Hell.

Medieval magic, of the sort taught in the Sworn Book and other forbidden works, was a two-part process. You prepared yourself ritually – the books are full of intricate details, but popular imagination remembered only one of them, the circle – so that you could conjure up a demon. Then, while still magically protected, you bound him to work for you. It was the second part which entered popular lore, and many centuries afterwards, when the magician's demon has been upgraded in the usual way to the Devil himself, we find him engineering works on a scale that would have surprised the original necromancers. It was not just the creation of navigable harbours: in Northumbrian tradition, the Devil drove roads through hills and across marshes at Michael's command. In one night he built a Roman road, Mitchell Scott's Causeway; in two weeks he constructed what we know as Hadrian's Wall.

These stories are very like the Devil's Ditches and Causeways that we have already encountered, except that there the fiend is acting for his own purposes, whereas in the Michael Scot cycle he is compelled to perform these great works. Sometimes the stories hint that he must be kept employed, that if not occupied with one grandiose project after another the Devil will find work for his own idle hands and turn on the magician. Medieval anecdotes about ceremonial magic usually follow one of two storylines: either the magician makes a mistake with his conjurations and is torn to pieces horribly, or he successfully controls a demon and the point of the story then lies in their subsequent conversation. In the later traditions this plot line is extended: Michael is continually asserting his mastery over the Devil, while never quite safe from being mastered by him.

Over time, storytellers lost interest in the original framing device of these narratives, the circles and conjurations by which diabolical power was called up. These elements were not forgotten entirely. In the chapbooks about Dr Faustus, the magician par excellence, the scene of invocation still provides an opening to the story, and these cheap publications were copied and copied again into the nineteenth century, with Faustus eventually transformed into a mysterious Dr Foster. But indigenous magicians are presented quite differently. Their relationship with the Devil is taken as read, and at the point where the stories begin man and fiend are already working as a team.

William of Lindholme lived in the Isle of Axholme, on the Lincolnshire outskirts of Doncaster. He first appears as St William, which adds some support to the speculations of eighteenth-century antiquaries who thought he had once been a hermit; certainly Lindholme, a small gravel bank among the marshes north of Wroot, had harboured a real-life hermit's cell. So William may be another medieval cleric endowed posthumously with magical powers, until by 1727 'he was by the common people taken for a cunning man or conjuror.'[4]

No stories were supplied in support of William's reputation then, or if they were the antiquaries brushed them off, but a hundred years later some found their way into print. One of these unites two traditions found separately in Michael Scot's cycle, the river and the road. William has been asked to provide a causeway, something much needed in this low-lying fenland country. He sends a rider galloping on a fast horse, the rider disobeys and looks behind to see hundreds of little devils throwing up stones and gravel to form the bank, and in a moment of terror and confusion he cries 'God bless the work' with the inevitable consequence, his failure of nerve monumentalized for all time by the stub of a causeway petering out in the marshes.

William's magical career began early. When he was a boy, his parents went to Wroot for the annual fair but left him behind, saying the fields were near harvest and someone had to keep sparrows from nibbling at the grain. Bird-scaring was a regular introduction to paid work for farm lads in the nineteenth century, so this part of the story is realistic enough, and so is the strop which William threw at missing out on the delights of Wroot Feast; but, since everything is on a heroic scale in these stories, the pebble he hurled indignantly after them takes the form of a boulder, lobbed 5 miles into a field on the far side of the village. William then headed for the fair and, when chided by his parents for having left the fields at the mercy of the birds, answered that he had thought of that, and that they were all out of harm's way in the barn. When the family return home, they open the doors of the barn and find it full of the sparrows that have been locked up by William's dreadful powers, most of them dead, while the plumage of the rest has turned white with fright. In later years those who were sceptical about this incident could be silenced by pointing to white sparrows that nested around Lindholme, evidently the progeny of those terrified survivors.[5]

Stories of magicians usually begin later in life, because the protagonist has to grow up and go to the Black School before he can acquire his powers. William's childhood escapade is closer to the traditional lives of mighty men or of saints, both of whom are shown demonstrating their marvellous powers right from birth. In fact the two wonders credited here to diabolical magicians were previously reported of saints: the leading of the waters is told of St Enswith at Folkestone, and the incarcerated birds feature in the life of St Werburgh at Chester.

By the end of the nineteenth century, the story about the birds in the barn was being told of another mysterious figure, Jack of Kent. The original Jack, John or Siôn seems once again to have been a medieval clergyman, possibly a vicar at Kentchurch on the Welsh border halfway between Hereford and Abergavenny. In legend he has lost any trace of a clerical vocation and wanders from village to village, so it is natural that he should help a farmer out with a little bird-scaring: crows this time, and the wonder is increased because the barn in which they are confined has no roof. 'Their master, "the Old 'Un", was sitting on a cross-beam, keeping them in order till Jack came back. He was like a big old crow, was their master, and every now and then he said "Crawk, Crawk".'[6]

Pulling a Fast One

The same story was told of Davies Sirevan; he and Jack are the heroes of very similar cycles of stories, told in the same regions of the Welsh border, one a little north of the other. Jack wins out over the Devil in a 'Tops and Bottoms' story; he triumphantly beats him in a mowing contest; he sets him to build a bridge over the Monnow; he even wins at buying pigs, the Devil's favourite live-stock ever since he appropriated the Gadarene swine. It was a Saturday, which is market day in Chepstow, and the two friends had pooled their resources bidding for porkers. They agreed, as they usually did, to split the takings half and half. What could possibly go wrong? Well, the weather, for one thing: the rain came down in torrents as they drove the herd back home, and neither of them cared to stand out in the drizzle counting pigs; besides, it was get-ting dark. After a glance at the damp, despondent beasts, the Devil proposes a simple criterion: when they meet again in the morning, he'll have all the pigs with straight tails, and Jack can have those with curly ones. Jack, like a true friend, makes no objections; then, like a shrewd one, he waits until his colleague has left for some-where warm with a fire, and then drives all the pigs bar one into a snug dry barn, provided with dry straw and everything that is agreeable to pigs. There they spend the night, indifferent to the squeals of their miserable brother out in the rain, and in the morn-ing the Devil finds the tails well curled up on all the pigs but one. The next time they go to market, he announces firmly that this time he will be having the curly-tailed pigs, but Jack has been careful to choose another day of inclement weather for their pur-chases, and that night all the pigs are left out in the rain except for one who gets the five-star treatment, so when the Devil turns up next morning to claim the curly tails, he finds he has lost again.[7]

Here the Devil has been fooled once more; he may not be as much of a simpleton as in 'Tops and Bottoms', but he is still ignorant of facts about the care of pigs which, when the stories were first told, must have been common knowledge among farm workers. Jack, on the other hand, knows how to manage livestock, just as he is good at bird-scaring, muck-spreading, threshing and mowing. All these cycles have an agricultural setting, which is probably what made them memorable; they seem to have reached their present form through competitive storytelling sessions, when two or more raconteurs searched for fresh variations on the theme of how Jack (or Davies, or William) won yet again.

Jack is one of us – which, for the original audience, meant a farmworker and not (despite his original history) someone as remote and gentrified as a priest. We root for him, however close he has placed himself to the powers of Hell, and this is surprising when many peasant societies elsewhere believed that success, in the farmyard or out hunting in the woods or in business and manufacture, could only be explained by the help of the Devil. This gave a kind of moral licence to hate the successful; people in these communities are deeply envious of anyone who does better than their mates and call on imagery of the Devil to

Blackingstone Rock.

express this. But in England there is very little folklore of envy. English country people seem to have been surprisingly relaxed about one of their number doing well, and when Jack gets a crop or a field or a barn full of pigs by outwitting the Devil, he is fondly remembered as a clever businessman.

Of course, Jack of Kent was safely in the past, when all sorts of wonderful things could happen. Like William of Lindholme, he can effortlessly lob great stones for miles: in one episode of the cycle, he and his dark mate are idling on the heath of Tidenham Chase when talk turns to who is the best athlete. Competitive as ever,

> The Devil, intent on the best of throws,
> Pulled up a stone, and lifted it high,
> Then, as he tauntingly cried, 'Here it goes!'
> Over the valley he made it fly.
> Away went the stone, and far off, at Stroat,
> Down at the Severn by Horse Pill fell:
> Then Jack in his turn pulled off his coat,
> And muttered, 'I think I can do as well.'
> Jack twirled his long slab over his head,
> As if it were merely the twig of a tree;
> Then off from his grasp the missile fled,
> And lighted far down by Thornbury.[8]

You could see these two competitors as successors to the giants of old, who were forever hurling great rocks around. But their contest is rooted as much in real life as mythology: quoits was a favourite pastime for young men until the nineteenth century since, like the long jump and wrestling, it didn't require any sports equipment and was a useful outlet for physical assertion.

To join in these competitions, the Devil needs an opposite number. It need not be one of the legendary magicians: in

Somerset he was pitching stones in company with Sir John Hautville, the local hero of Axbridge, and lost by about 400 yards.[9] On the eastern slopes of Dartmoor they go one better and match him against King Arthur. Taking their stand on the two hills of Blackingstone Rock and Heltor, the king and fiend spent hours aiming at each other with boulders, most of which fell short in the space between them and still litter the ground. Finally each contestant hurled the largest mass he could find, and these form the tors on the opposing hills. After that they gave it up as a bad job.[10]

More often, the Devil is matched against a giant.[11] After all, giants were the traditional protagonists in these stone-throwing stories, and the Devil with his hill-moving and ditch-digging powers should have been their equal; unlike the stories where the Devil loses out to the local hero, these giant traditions rarely make it clear who won, only that their contest left a lot of rocks cumbering good agricultural land. By contrast, the legend of Great Rock in the Calder Valley makes much out of the Devil's discomfiture as he tries to stride across from Stoodley Pike, ignominiously loses his footing and slips all the way down. But this time his opponent was God himself, and the two of them had been making bets as to who should get the future town of Hebden Bridge, so the Devil's defeat caused much rejoicing in the neighbourhood – at least among those who favoured the other side.[12] This is the only English story to feature God and the Devil, although other countries such as Estonia have whole cycles telling how they wandered the earth together, in the days when they were still on reasonably good terms, and how God was always doing wonders and the Devil kept cocking them up. Their tense, competitive friendship is just like that between the magician and Devil in the Jack stories, although the narrative plot lines are quite different.

The Last Trick

Always in the English stories, behind the jovial trickery with pigs and potatoes, we know that the magician is playing with fire and that his buddy may just be waiting to win the last trick – the one that has eternal consequences. The history of magic, or rather of magical theory, suggests as much. Theologians taught that the business of conjuration – all those sigils and suffumigations and circles – had no real effect on the spiritual world: they were simply eyewash. But the demons were real. This is the guiding principle of medieval thought about the supernatural, as we saw before: that you didn't dispute what people reported but simply reinterpreted it. So yes, a demon would appear, and sit in the space allotted to him, flinching at the dread seal of Solomon or whatever you prodded him with, but he was simply stringing you along, and far from being coerced by mighty words of power, he did the things you commanded because he wanted to you to think of anything but God, until the time came at last when he could reap the benefit of his long charade.

Obviously this line of thought is far distant from nineteenth-century legends, but it survived subliminally in a suspicion that the Devil, stupid as he seemed, might suddenly at the end stop fooling and claim a magician for his own. And that is why there is a sudden turn towards the serious in the final tale of Jack of Kent. When he knew that he was dying, he called the people to his bedside and confessed that he had sailed pretty near the wind in his day, and now it was not at all certain which way he should go; if they wanted to know how things stood with his soul, there was one certain augury, and that was to wait until he was dead and then cut out his liver and lights, climb up the church tower and pin them onto iron spikes. A raven would come from one direction and a dove from another, and they would fight over the flesh. If the dove won it was a sign that his

Stoodley Pike and Heptonstall.

soul had been saved, but if it was the raven, then things were otherwise.[13]

They say the dove won, after a fierce fight. It is an eerie scene, quite different in character from the earlier stories; the same mysterious conflict ends the parallel cycle about Davies Sirevan, except that his liver and lungs were not pinned onto the church tower but thrown out onto the dunghill.[14] Davies was supposed to have been buried at Llanfair Waterdine, where the grave of the real Andrew Davies (d. 1780) has carvings of two birds, so that at first sight the tradition looks like iconotropy, the reworking of a misunderstood picture or sculptural feature to make a good story. But this 1780 grave was simply a lucky coincidence, for a contest between the raven and the dove was the last tale told of Michael Scot, and the same duality of white birds and black can be found further afield in the legends of Icelandic magicians. Herefordshire simply happens to be the furthest penetration southwards of an international motif.

It's true that funerary art has often provided the visual kernel around which a legend can grow. We have already seen how the emblematic heart on an aristocratic tomb at Tolleshunt Knights was transformed into the grisly relic of a combat with the fiend. The other story told about this effigy, that its owner escaped the attentions of the Devil by being buried neither within the church nor without it, is told of many other local heroes. Since medieval tombs were regularly set in a recess in the wall, there is no shortage of visual prompts for the tradition that someone was buried neither in nor out.

In the magician cycles, this arrangement is presented as a final proof of the cunning man's cleverness:

Davies had made one last compact with the Devil. If his body was carried through a door, or along a road, if it was buried either inside or outside a church, then the Devil was to have his soul. Accordingly when he was dead, Davies was let down through a window, and carried over hedges and ditches. He was buried under the church wall, and was thus neither inside nor outside of it.[15]

This is a more elaborate development of the motif, and seems to owe something to real funeral practices, for dead bodies were often carried out through special openings in the house and taken to church by field paths, as if carrying them along the ordinary way might set a precedent which the living would soon unwillingly follow. The obsequies of Jack of Kent were less elaborate: he simply defeated the Devil by being buried neither in nor out of the church, though there is some uncertainty among storytellers as to whether this meant along the line of the wall, or with his head sticking into the church and his feet in the graveyard, like someone trying to sleep in a too-short tent.[16] Here the motif seems to have been disengaged from any particular tomb.

But at Aldworth, in the valley of the Thames near Reading, the tombs are unmistakeable, a set of ten memorials to the de la

Beche family. For the first two hundred years after they were carved in the fourteenth century, a more or less reliable history of the family could be read in the church; then the parchment was taken off to show to Queen Elizabeth, who never returned it, so that henceforward the storytellers had a free hand. The erstwhile de la Beches were now all known as John (like Jack, a good name for the anonymous everyman) and particular statues were identified as John Long, John Strong, John Never-Afraid and John Ever-Afraid. The last of these got his name because 'he gaue his soule to ye Diuel if euer he was buried either in Churche or in Churchyard.' So they told the antiquary Richard Symonds in 1644, and rounded off the story by saying that 'he was buried under the Church Wall under an Arche.'[17]

We are once again in the realms of magical morality: it does not matter how you lived or what you did, as long as you are smart enough to get yourself buried in a place which is outside judgement, neither in church nor churchyard, neither one thing nor the other. The imagination is easily swayed by these borderline situations, especially when they take on physical form and the storyteller can triumphantly point to the half-hidden tomb. This is what makes these vernacular traditions about conjurors so different from the high magic of the occultists: in legends, power is always to be found in things and places, not in words and texts. The learned grimoires are in love with language; they promise that if you recite the angelic invocations and divine names perfectly and in proper order, then the demonic empire will be at your command. But magic in folk stories is always something physical and local, a lore of crossroads and thresholds, rings and staffs and bottles. When writing does feature in folk tales, it is presented as the illiterate see it: not books but the Book, an object made all the more frightening by its ability to speak in the hands of the learned.

A Novice at the Black Art

There was a magician in Yorkshire who had a Book. It was bound in black and cased with iron at the corners, and it had to be chained down to a desk, with the desk bolted to the floor. The Book was closed by a heavy clasp that locked with an iron key, and when the magician did his work, he shut himself in his study and opened the Book, which told him everything. This magician had one pupil, or rather a servant boy, since he hadn't advanced very far in the magic arts and was kept mostly to run errands and sweep the house, though he didn't sweep the study because that was out of bounds. Of course, being a boy, he was all the more eager to get in because he was kept out, and he had his chance one morning when the magician left for the day and forgot to close the door. Hardly daring to open it more than a crack, the boy slipped in and marvelled at everything on the shelves: the alembics full of strange stuff, black or iridescent or golden; the mirror that sucked in your reflection and showed only inky space; one fading flower from no earthly garden; shells and horns full of confused sound. Fancying himself halfway to Magister already, the lad walked up and down the room, but none of the tools of the craft would speak to him or bend themselves to his will. Then he looked at the desk, where the Book lay, and saw that it was lying unlocked. So he sat at the desk and opened a page.

It was difficult to read, because most of the letters were unfamiliar, and those he did know kept changing when he wasn't looking at them, but he spelled one line out loud. All at once the room shook and everything went dark. At first the boy could see nothing but black mist, until two red lights appeared in the darkness, and slowly he could see that they were eyes, eyes set in a terrible face. 'Set me a task!' said the face, in a voice like the roar of an iron furnace. The boy sat rigid, silent. The face spoke again. 'Set me a task, or I shall strangle thee!'

Not until the mist took form and stretched out a hand to burn his throat did the boy recover the use of his voice, and then he gasped 'Water the flower!' It was the first thing that occurred to him, but he was pleased enough to see the Devil disappear for a moment. Back he came with a can and watered the flower as he had been told. Then he came again, with a bucket of water, and poured that out. Then with a barrel, and another, and another. Water washed around the boy's feet as he realized that he had commanded the Devil to work but had no idea how to make him stop. More and more water splashed around him, a rising tide that reached first his chest and then his neck. He was beginning to splutter when he heard the sound of an opening door: the magician had come home. After a moment's heart-chilling pause his strong voice chanted a Spell of Dismissal. The dreadful tide ebbed away, leaving not a patch of damp behind, the Book slammed shut of its own accord, and the boy cowered by its heavy desk. But his master felt he had been punished enough already.[18]

'The Sorcerer's Apprentice' is a story found in many countries. In its fuller versions, with the location left conveniently vague and the plot nicely rounded off, this is a story told for entertainment, not the sort of local legend that is supposed to have some truth in it. But the idea of frightful risks centred on a book was so memorable that it crossed genres and can be found in traditions about historical characters. The story of the black book is often told of conjuror-parsons. At Bratton Fleming, between Barnstaple and Lynton, William Gimmingham was rector from 1818 to 1838; like many other West Country incumbents, he was the focus and probably the promoter of supernatural stories. Thieves who took firewood from his copses would be instantly found out when he looked in his book; a man who tried to steal cabbages from the rectory garden was subjected to a spell that left him motionless for half an hour, unable to stir from his crime. And,

Once while the parson was at church, the two maidens
got one of the Books in the kitchen, and they began reading it. And two Things like chickens came in while the
door was shut, and one of the maidens ran off to the
church to fetch the parson, and when he came, there was
the place full of the Things. As soon as he came in they
all disappeared. And he told the maiden it was a good job
she had sent for him, or the Things would have pinched
her up a bit.[19]

The same story is told of Thomas Favel the vicar of Mullion near
Helston, who died in 1682; he was leading a service when he
suddenly stopped, told the congregation to go home and ran to
the vicarage, where a servant girl had opened his book. Her flesh
had already been crushed black and blue by the clustering spirits
before the Reverend Favel could speak the words that laid them.[20]
It is as if, to the illiterate imagination, it is not necessary actually
to read a spell from the book; merely opening its terrible pages
is enough to unleash consequences. You can see why a bookish
clergyman, with piles of paper on every shelf of the vicarage study,
might use superstition as the best way to keep prying fingers from
his manuscripts.

Reading and writing were so much the Devil's business that
schoolmasters as well as priests were credited with unholy knowledge. After all, the learned clerks of the Middle Ages, magicians
among them, had taught as well as preached; until well into the
nineteenth century it was assumed that ghost-laying could only
be successfully performed by an Oxford scholar. At a humbler
level, the legends suppose that words to command the Devil can
be composed, with a little difficulty, by every master of a
village school.

Banishing Rituals

So we hear stories of the 'Sorcerer's Apprentice' type in a school setting. At Burnley Grammar School, an old foundation next to the parish church, the boys found an old book of spells and, greatly daring, waited until the masters were away. The boldest began to recite, and when he had got as far as saying the Lord's Prayer backwards, a flagstone shifted under his feet and the Devil began to rise into the light. The sequel is unexpected: instead of shivering in horror, the boys crowded around the threatening head, hammering away at it, hitting it with the fire tongs and, for want of anything better, taking off their clogs and battering down on the horns. It was too much even for the dark lord, and after a few minutes of assault he sank back down into his own place. The black mark he left behind was pointed out to visitors for years afterwards.[21]

It is an endearing tribute to Lancashire grit, though you suspect that this particular variant originated with someone who remembered how the story began but needed to improvise after

Burnley Grammar School.

forgetting the ending. The story told in Bury is more orthodox. When it was told in the 1820s it must already have been a long-standing tradition, since it begins with that old-fashioned item, a wooden trencher, used where later generations would set out a plate. This particular trencher was supporting the lunch of Mr Hodgson, Master of the Grammar School, and when it began to spin round of its own accord, he knew that something was wrong. He pushed back his chair and set off at a trot for the schoolhouse, where he found, as suspected, that the boys had said the Lord's Prayer backwards and raised the Devil, and were at a loss how to lay him again.

Now there is a law in these things, as Hodgson knew: the Devil will carry out whatever commands you give him, one, two and three, but once his final task is done he will be at liberty, which can be very unpleasant for all concerned. Your only chance is to set him some work that he cannot perform. Hodgson stared down the fiend and sent him off to count the blades of grass that grew in the Castle Croft; surely he could not do that. But no, the Devil returned instantly with an answer. The schoolmaster frowned and sent him off to the hill at Sand Brow, to say how many grains of sand were there. That took a little longer, but it proved not to be impossible. Back came the Devil with his answer, smug as a prize pupil; the schoolboys ducked behind the writing desks; the master looked grave, for he had only one task left. But the momentary absence of the old enemy had given him time to think. 'Count me,' he began – the Devil smiled, broad as a cat – 'count me the letters in the great church Bible.' At once there was uproar as the fiend realized he had been worsted, and he disappeared in darkness, noise and stink, leaving a large crack on the hearthstone through which he returned to the nether regions.[22]

It is a neat turn, to give the Devil a task he cannot perform, not because it is beyond his strength or knowledge, but because he cannot touch holy things. It brings our characters to a happy conclusion without breaking the conditions of the plot that had put them at risk in the first place. But where did that framing device come from? Why must the Devil be given a command that he cannot fulfil? There is nothing to suggest this in the books of the medieval magicians. All their art focused on raising demons and getting them to do things; certainly a fallen angel was dangerous unless brought under the magician's power, but there is no suggestion that simply telling him to perform a task made him any less dangerous.

Instead, the plot device of the impossible task is much closer to the rituals of exorcism. Like the magician, the exorcist commanded things of the unseen world, but to send them away, not to summon them up. 'Away' is too weak a notion for the practical, physical imagery of folk tradition: instead, the spirit must be sent to an identified place, and as it will doubtless set out instantly to return, something must be thought of to keep it occupied there. Even if you regard exorcism as nothing more than ritual theatre conducted for the benefit of the living, it makes sense for the minister to put into their minds a concept more concrete than mere absence; as long as they are imagining the ghost, hobgoblin or whatever bailing out the Red Sea with a sieve, they aren't thinking of it back home causing trouble on the farm.

These fused motifs are found in another Lancashire legend, this time from Cockerham on the coast. I don't know why all these stories come from Lancashire; it may simply reflect local transmission, with features like the black crack in the flagstones of the floor being imitated from one school to another. Bungled Devil-raising is a storytelling convention in this part of the world, as conjuror-parsons are in the West Country, and it may not be a coincidence that both regions were at the furthest ends of the chain of authority from London. Lancashire in particular was so remote that it missed out on much of the Reformation, with a substantial Catholic community retaining the old faith. Perhaps that left them more open to ideas about ritual control of the Devil, a power that came more naturally to the old Catholic priests than to new Anglican ministers. Certainly in all these stories the initiative is taken not by the Church of England vicar, as in the Stiperstones and Quantock stories, but by the village schoolmaster, whose sectarian allegiance might have been quite different.

At Cockerham the story has two versions. One begins as usual with the foolish schoolboys and the cracked flagstone, but in the other we plunge straight into the action, with the Devil rampaging around the neighbourhood and the schoolmaster called to deal with him as if this were part of his regular duties. Drawing a protective circle around himself, the master summoned the fiend, but lost his nerve when he saw the dreadful majesty of Hell, and weakly agreed to the usual deal with the three commands. 'Count the raindrops,' he said – you can take the master out of the classroom, but you can't take these classroom habits out of the master – 'count the raindrops on the hedgerows from here to Ellel.' 'Thirteen,' sneered the Devil, 'the blast of my coming dried up all the rest.' One down, two to go. 'Count the ears of corn in the great West Field.' The Devil returned a prompt answer which sounded realistic, and anyway there was no means of contradicting him. Desperately, the master gave up arithmetic and proposed something much simpler. 'Twist a rope of sand and wash it in the river without losing a single grain.' Off sets his enemy and soon returns with a golden rope slung over his shoulder, fused by who knows what diabolical alchemy. 'But you haven't washed it yet,' the schoolmaster insists. 'A mere formality,' says the Devil, 'come down with me to the riverside and I'll show you how it's done.' Too wary for that, the schoolmaster keeps inside his circle. Reluctantly the Devil goes down to the River Cocker and begins to feed out his rope, but pure water undoes the tortured spell, and its illusory threads disintegrate in a shower of trickling sand. Howling with his frustrated hunger for souls, the

Devil bounds to the top of Cockerham church steeple and takes one gigantic step from there to the bridge at Pilling. Travellers still point out the hoofprint of the accursed one on the parapet. Another 7-mile stride would have taken him to Blackpool, or maybe Hell; out of the story, anyway.[23]

The same story is told at Clitheroe, ending again in frustration with a rope of sand, although here the impossible task is not to wash it but to tie it in a knot.[24] A version from Hotherstall forgets the school setting and makes it a straight contest in ingenuity between Devil and magician:

> The Devil and mate went to the strand,
> In a jiffy they twisted a rope of fine sand,
> But when they brought the rope to be washed
> To atoms it went, and the rope was all smashed.[25]

Despite these brave efforts, the waterproof sand rope remains an unaccomplished dream. But the motif of its manufacture is not confined to these stories of cowering schoolboys and brave masters. It is just one of the innumerable endless tasks that were imposed on exorcized spirits, along with making sand beams or bundles, carrying water in a sieve and picking a hill free of grass a blade at a time.[26] The Devil, as so often, has stepped into a role originally sketched out for spirits of a quite different cast.

Substituting Satan for the village spook is not just a careless aberration by the storytellers: they were deliberately shifting the legend into a different emotional key by heightening the stakes for which contestants play. Though traditional ghosts were bad enough, the Devil is infinitely worse. However chatty and comical the story in which he is embedded, he will always be the spirit of damnation.

When following the schoolmaster stories, we accept the fiction of magical morality by which a failed third question will hand over the poor teacher to eternal torment. But if the stories introduce the theme of a pact with the Devil, their morality is no longer magical or fictional, but real. If there is a Heaven and a Hell at all, if there is a God and a Devil, then rejecting one and submitting to the other will have serious consequences.

Not that the stories always end seriously. Near Ormskirk there lived a tailor, well-off as tailors go, healthy and industrious, but miserable: he had an unhappy marriage. It was very comical for the neighbours to hear the tailor and his wife scold and quarrel and curse, but it wasn't so funny for the couple themselves. They could still remember what it had been like to be young and in love; neither of them could think what had gone sour, and each blamed the other. On a midwinter night, after his spouse had stormed off to bed, the tailor sat alone by a cold fire, reading a curious old book that he had picked up at market. He came to a page that described certain forbidden things, and with a flash of determination he snapped the book shut and left the house. It was shortly before midnight.

The tailor walked on, a dark outline against the winter blanket of white, until he came deep into the woods where an old yew tree stood. He picked up a stick, scratched a circle in the frozen snow, clapped his hands as the book had instructed, and cried out, 'Come here, James.' There was a whisper in the trees, a murmured cry of 'Here, tailor, here,' and then all around him whirled a shapeless mass of heads, eyes, hoofs and tails, deep black mouths and lolling tongues. 'Take a shape, that I may know you,' said the desperate tailor, and at once the fantastic show was at an end, and out from behind the tree stepped a spry little attorney, a pen behind his ear, a ledger book in his hand. 'You are aware of the conditions?' said the old gentleman. 'You may call on my service for three things, after which ... *you* will serve *me*. Non-performance by either party invalidates the contract. Sign at the foot, please, in the red fluid. I have a pocket-knife if you require assistance.'

The ledger was very old and contained a surprising variety of names, some obscure, some well known, many of which you could never have imagined would be there at all. But the tailor had not come out of curiosity. Flinching a little, he made the necessary arrangements and signed. The Devil blew on the page and shut his book.

'And your first requirement?'

'Make my wife love me.' The enemy of man gave him an old-fashioned look and said 'That's not what we usually do. Lust, yes. Different girls, unusual positions, can I interest you?' But the tailor just said, 'I want her to love me again.'

'Very well. It may sound like virtue but it's still part of the contract. And second?'

What the tailor wanted for his second wish will be forever a mystery, but his third – he wasn't really bothered by then – was an exaggerated version of one of his boyhood feats: to raise a wall as high as a man across Aughton Moss, to build it without mortar and to do it in the hour before sunrise. 'And so,' said the tailor resignedly, 'I shall see you in seven years' time.'

'Hours,' said the Devil. '*Hours!*' shrieked the tailor. 'Seven hours. Never sign a contract without checking the detail.' Legal advice, like Scripture, is something that the Devil can quote for his own purposes. 'Your first two commands are fulfilled, and I am at your service . . . until we meet at Aughton Moss. Enjoy!'

Unsteadily the tailor clambered out of the wood, and as soon as he came in sight of home, his wife ran out barefoot into the snow to hug him and dragged him inside for warm towels and hot toddy. For one mad moment he had hoped his night was a dream, but no, here was the proof – and he told her everything. Her face fell. She would gladly have died for him, but you can't be damned by proxy. However, she soon rallied and insisted that they call on the priest. The old man heard the story through and told them to wait outside, then appeared a few minutes later dressed warmly with a mysterious lumpy blanket under his arm, and they all set off for the Moss. Eastwards over Beacon Hill the sky was growing pale.

Punctually, an hour before sunrise, the Devil appeared, this time looking like a wizened old stonemason – paper cap, dusty apron and all. 'Release his soul, Satan!' cried the priest. 'Here there are neither stones nor mortar. How canst thou hope to build a wall?' But the Devil ignored this well-meant distraction and ripped the hillside open like someone looking for things lost at the bottom of a drawer. Stones scattered to right and left, and quickly he laid them into the first course. Then he spread black wings and shot off seawards. The tailor groaned: he had forgotten that you can set stones in sand. There was a brief interruption when the tatty apron broke its strings, and the three mortals almost recovered hope, but the Devil scooped up most of the pile from Shirley Hill and carried on working. The wall was as high as a man now, light had filled the sky, and he was timing it so the last course would be laid just, agonizingly, in time. Why throw away the first fruits of eternal despair?

But as he held the last stone in his hand, he heard the sunrise sound of cockcrow and spun around, to see the priest trying to shake the last feathers out of his blanket, and the bird of dawn strutting beside him. The Devil hurled a missile that flattened the unfortunate cockerel with one throw – but that was his last stone. He raced after it, but the man of God stood between him and his prize. And as they faced off, the first golden edge of the true sun appeared above the hills.

So the fiend went back to his own place, and the priest returned to his fireside, and the tailor and his wife held hands and went home. Gradually, as time passed, the Devil's magic wore off, but they pretended it hadn't, and were happy.[27]

7

WOMAN'S WIT IS BETTER THAN MAN'S: MAIDENS AND MOTHERS BEAT THE DEVIL

Women were no weaklings when dealing with the Devil; their resilience and inventiveness often saved the day when fathers and husbands had failed. Even witches sometimes got the upper hand in their partnership with the dark lord. Old wives could make Hell too hot to hold them when handed over to the Devil, while their younger sisters could rely on women's secrets to outwit him. In one branch of tradition, the Devil is a sterile fiend, baffled and repelled by the female body, but he appears in another as a sleek and persuasive suitor. The wise girl will parry his love-talk and turn down his offer of eternal union, but the foolish adulteress is carried off to a terrible fate.

Witches in Pursuit

For a roam over the heaths below Farnham you can start by following the River Wey downstream of the town, duck across the Shepherd and Flock roundabout, and from there step at once into the well-heeled Surrey countryside of rhododendrons and racehorses, heading towards the eighteenth-century grounds of Moor Park. Like most gardens of the period, these have a grotto, which can be seen towards the end of the riverside walk. Although rounded off with a picturesque arch of irregular stonework, it is modest as grottos go, just a hemispherical scrape in the hillside with a rill of water trickling across the sandy floor and a neglected sign telling you that you are at Mother Ludlam's Hole. There used to be benches inside where ladies could rest out of the sunshine; now the Victorian screen is locked to keep the bats safe inside and local youth safely out.

It is not far from here to the ruins of Waverley Abbey, reduced to a set of low walls and stone arches, but still represented in John Aubrey's time by standing buildings. In the lay refectory he saw a roundel of stained glass that had survived the vicissitudes of the Reformation and still showed 'St Dunstan holding the Devil by the Nose, with his Pincers'.[1] No sign of it now, so following the river you cross two old bridges into Tilford, where they still play cricket on the village green. Here the southern branch of the Wey joins the main stream and leads you out of the woods to the café at Frensham Little Pond.

In June, the ridge between the Great and Little Ponds is dry and shadeless walking; broom pods snap in the summer heat, and the paths are all dusty. South of Kettlebury Hill, you pass the Sandy Lane Museum, a modest display in an old phone box which tells you that you are approaching the Devil's Jumps. And there

The Devil's Jumps, Frensham.

they are, studding the skyline towards Churt and Hindhead: Stoney Jump on the east, then Middle Jump and High Jump. The scraggy branches of a dead pine frame the path up Stoney Jump, which is capped by streaked bands of ironstone, scorched at the highest point by fire. Have we arrived just too late for some frightful scene, the stifled victim dragged upwards under the scorching sun, cruel hands holding resinous torches to ignite the heaped brushwood? Probably not in rural Surrey, next to a gastro-pub and down the road from the sculpture park; the nearby barbecue dish suggests a simpler explanation. Once you've scrambled back down the hill, it's another hour's walk to see Frensham church and by then the day is getting late.

In Frensham church there is a copper cauldron large enough to cook dinner for a neighbourhood party or an extended family gathering, if late medieval open-hearth cookery is your thing. This is not the sort of equipment you normally expect to find in the north aisle of a church, but it has to be kept on sacred ground, because it is the cauldron of Mother Ludlam, and its first home was the arched cave we passed earlier, overlooking the river in the grounds of Moor Park. Mother Ludlam's Hole is on the small side as residences go, but old people were less fussy in those days, and anyway most of her time was spent in the realms of the supernatural, with only the cauldron remaining visible by the trickling stream as testimony that its owner would be back soon. Mother Ludlam was a kindly soul and would always help out those in need; even when she was away on her travels, they only had to drop a coin in the cauldron, and then their unspoken wish would be fulfilled. So the cave became quite a calling-place for the neighbourhood.

One afternoon, when the old lady had just returned to physical form and was sitting on the bench by the wall, getting some circulation back into her limbs, a shadow fell across the floor and she looked up to see the latest visitor outlined against the entrance of the cave. Something about him seemed familiar, but then there were lots of people in the village who dropped in time and again with their little problems. Only he didn't sound like a villager: he was ever so well-bred, asking if this was the cave with the famous cauldron. Pity she hadn't swept out lately; there was loose sand all over the floor. She glanced at the ground and saw that the stranger had left footprints. One of them was the outline of a hoof.

Like many old ladies, Mother Ludlam had been a bit of a wild girl in her youth, when she had done things and gone to places that you don't bring up in ordinary conversation. So as soon as she realized this was the Devil, the memories came flooding back. She'd grown old and stiff, but look at him, he hadn't changed a bit, fit as ever: which he showed by suddenly snatching up her cauldron and darting out of the cave with it. Now Mother Ludlam wasn't going to take this lying down, so she flew after him – literally. The Devil couldn't match that, but he was a champion at the long jump and with one leap he was away to Tilford Reeds. She followed him through the air, shaking her fists and shouting, but the Devil bounced away over Rushmoor. The cauldron was weighing him down, though, and he was starting to get out of puff, while Mother Ludlam was getting nearer and angrier. His last three leaps were nowhere near as vigorous as the first, and at Stoney Jump he gave it up as a bad job, tossed his burden aside and took a dive southwards into the Devil's Punchbowl. The cauldron was found eventually on Kettlebury Hill, but as it seemed likely that the Devil would return for a second attempt, it was carried off for safety to Frensham church.[2]

This is how the story is told now, its plot more or less fixed by a version recorded in 1869. But with that convenient motif of flight over the landscape, the legend fuses two locations that were originally quite separate: Mother Ludlam's Hole and the Devil's Jumps. The Jumps were a place-name calling out for a story, just like the corresponding hills in Dorset, and now they have one, although for the first hundred years after the name was first recorded, it was simply a way of noting that there were three distinct hills. We know that the Mother Ludlam story existed in an earlier version without the Devil because Frederick Grose, who saw the Hole in 1785, tells us that before it was done up as a grotto, it was the scene of a strange ritual. People would arrive at midnight, turn three times round, and say three times: 'Pray, good Mother Ludlam, lend me' – whatever it was that they needed – 'and I will return it within two days.' In this way the cave supplied the neighbourhood with all sorts of useful items on short loan, until one careless visitor, having asked for the use of a cauldron, failed to return it within the stipulated two days. In vain did they return it a day late: Mother Ludlam was offended, and nothing ever came from her cave again.

You'll notice how in this version, the presiding genius of the cave is dematerialized: she doesn't appear onstage, so to speak, and nobody sees her. This is hardly surprising, because Ludlam, too, began as a place-name. According to the annals of Waverley Abbey, fresh water was provided to the monastic buildings from a spring called Ludwell, which began to fail in 1216. One Brother Symon dug out fresh sources for the Ludwell conduit, and because Waverley was a Cistercian house, with a special devotion to the Virgin, his fellow monks gratefully dedicated the main spring as St Mary's Well.[3] So before the grotto was a garden feature, it had been an enchanted cave, and before that it was a holy well. Though religion had turned into magic, people never quite forgot that this stream had something to do with a kind and generous supernatural lady.

But that's not the end of it, because the 1785 story was itself an import to Ludwell/Ludlam's Hole. Aubrey, writing a hundred years earlier, tells exactly the same tale about a stone on Borough Hill, where villagers would knock and ask to be lent some household goods, stating when they would return them, until the sad day when the borrower of the cauldron failed to keep their side of the bargain and the good times came to an end. Although Aubrey simply refers to 'a Voice', there is no doubt that the mysterious lending was being done by fairies, who are credited with the same conditional generosity elsewhere. Borough Hill has disappeared off the map, and so has the great stone, but it was probably somewhere on Frensham Common. When the original landmark was lost the story needed a new home, which it found in the cave near Moor Park.

In the later versions of the story, where the mysterious Mother has become a witch, it seemed natural for storytellers to match her up with the Devil. Tradition deals in broad-brush, instantly recognizable figures, and here you get two for the price of one, just as you do at Court Moor on the hills overlooking Guisborough. Time was when the Devil and his minions would visit these hills, to go hunting in Kildale Woods; he could have been worse employed, but it was still poaching for all that, and Stephen Howe the forester (forgetting who he had to deal with) threatened publicly to chastise the villain who was taking his game. Next day a carriage pulled up at Stephen's door, and as its coal-black horses tugged at the reins, out jumped the fiend with his fists up, ready to show who was the better man. Stephen fled, but Nanny his wife was not so timid, and made such good use of her broom that the Devil was forced to call it quits. Still he insisted that, having come such a long way, he was not ready to return without company. Fortunately Nanny had taken a bit of a shine to him, and, abandoning her pusillanimous husband, she vaulted up beside the dark fighter on the passenger seat of his coach, and they set off in grand style for Hell. She still returns from time to time to terrify the locals with midnight broomstick flights over the barrow named in her honour, Nanny Howe.[4]

Such is the Yorkshire tale, or rather fantasy, for it has no real shape as a tale: like Ludlam's Hole it has been worked up from a place-name, in this case a barrow, which in the local dialect is called a howe, but with a qualifying Nanny, which suggested a woman rather than an earthwork. Perhaps the proximity of another earthwork called the Devil's Court suggested this association, which is not common, for witches in folklore generally have little to do with the Devil.

At first this seems absurd. How can two such familiar Halloween figures *not* be connected? But witchcraft is a complex topic, with its own history, and by the nineteenth century it was ascribed to three quite different kinds of people. There was the white witch, a female counterpart of the cunning men and magicians, who used her occult skills, like a doctor, for good – or if, like a lawyer, she used them against someone, it was done without spite and in the interests of her client. Then there was the witch of rumour, usually a village woman who in reality had nothing supernatural about her at all but was suspected of malevolently overlooking her neighbours. And then there was the witch of legend, who, unlike the other two, was not a contemporary but had lived a generation before the storyteller's time. As she was not around to contradict anything, she could safely be said to have floated down the lanes on a hurdle, to have turned herself into a hare and darted into her cottage ahead of the pursuing dogs, and to have taken over a cart and made it stop in the road, only to be evicted when a slash with a whip made the wheels bleed.

But none of these three types was associated with the Devil. The white witch had no dealings with him; often illiterate, she certainly knew nothing of the occult books which even the more ambitious cunning men tended to keep for show rather than use. The witch of rumour was simply unpopular rather than evil. As for the witch of legend, none of the stock stories with which she was credited suggest any dealings with the Devil. Her powers were supposed to come from some inexhaustible inner fund of malice and not by permission of the Prince of Darkness. Occasionally the Devil comes in at the end of the story to carry off her soul, proof conclusive of her wickedness during life, but that is their only point of contact. The demonology of sixteenth- and seventeenth-century witchcraft trials seems to have left very little imprint on the popular imagination, and in England even the demonologists lagged a long way behind their colleagues in the rest of Europe. Scotland, by contrast, yielded little in the ferocity of its witch-hunts to the worst of the Continent, and Scottish legends continued to draw on themes of the Sabbat and the diabolical pact until well into the nineteenth century.

Too Hot for Hell to Hold Her

In England we hear of the occasional termagant witch like Nanny Howe, but these are simply variations on that ever-popular character, the fierce old woman who cannot be subdued by anything in this world or the next. This is the image that propels the popular ballad of 'The Devil and the Farmer's Wife'. One version opens:

> There was an old farmer in Sussex did dwell
> And he had a bad wife as many knew well.

It doesn't have to be Sussex, of course: this kind of song can be adjusted or updated as the audience requires. Ballads are not like local legends, which can only work if they are pinned to the right kind of landmark, or folk tales, which require a style of performance that was rarely cultivated in England. By contrast, everyone knew a few songs, and some a great many: Henry Burstow, the godless old bell-ringer of Horsham, could remember 420.[5] 'The Devil and the Farmer's Wife' came in as no. 405, so it obviously wasn't called for much, but since it is found in over fifty variations it must have tickled something in the singers' fancy.

With a song like this we can be confident, more so than with the rarer story-types, that it reflects the expectations of performers.

Or at least of the men among them: the song comes very much from the husband's perspective. There he is, managing the team at plough, and as if hard work wasn't bad enough, up comes the Devil in search of a victim. Fortunately, however, he doesn't want the eldest son and is quite content with the old wife, so, sighing with relief, the farmer hands her over, like a parcel that is best got rid of. The Devil puts her into a sack, throws it over his shoulders and sets off for the infernal gates. But once they have swung open and she is among the everlasting terrors – then all Hell breaks loose.

> Oh, then she did kick the young imps about,
> Says one to the other, 'Let's try and turn her out!'
> She spied thirteen imps all dancing in chains,
> She up with her pattens and beat out their brains.
> She knocked old Satan against the wall –
> 'Let's try and turn her out or she'll murder us all!'

So the Devil picks up the sack, stuffs her inside and carries his struggling burden back up to Sussex, where he hands her back to her surprised husband and tells him to lump it.

> I have been a tormentor the whole of my life
> But I never was tormented till I met with your wife.[6]

All right, this song is unlikely ever to be anthologized by someone looking for forthright traditions of fearless women. But as so often with folk genres, it's all in the way you tell them: you can put the stress on that ruthlessly patriarchal farmer (in some versions he's happy to lose his wife as long as he gets to keep the horses) but you can also emphasize the insuppressible resourcefulness of a wife who makes Hell too hot to hold her. The earliest version, printed in 1630 and much more verbose, explicitly speaks for both sexes:

> Then widdowes, wives and maides, give eare, as well as men,
> And by this woman learne to gull the world agen:
> You may by this turne artists, or masters of your art;
> And when the Devill comes for you, you need not care
>   a fart.[7]

Sympathy for the Devil was in short supply when these songs first circulated. They were composed in jolly counterpoint to the much more gruesome godly ballads in which sinners have their necks broken and their bodies hauled away by the vengeful fiend. In an age when Satan was an ever-present spiritual threat, it was good to relax sometimes and tell how he made a mistake and got beaten up, and if the beating was done by women, so much the funnier. He is helpless in the face of London's fish-wives in a seventeenth-century encounter.[8] Two hundred years later he is no better off when he gets lost in a London peculiar and drops into a laundry somewhere in the neighbourhood of Islington. The Devil has dressed himself up in the height of fashion, from a top hat to the latest thing in cavalry boots, but the laundrywomen are not fooled:

> They said they'd give him a scrub,
> Then seized him by the neck and heels
> And pitched him into the tub.

Mother Jones scrubs away at his horns, Mother Brown at his feet, and Mother Higgs rubs the blue bag into his face, while Mother White gleefully pulls off his tail (or was it his tail?). Any resistance is met by repeated blows of the copper posser, while fresh supplies of water reach scalding heat. Eventually the Devil gets out of it by offering gin all round, and makes his escape, less like a spirit of evil than a young gentleman who has extracted himself from an undignified piece of class revenge.[9]

Mothers Jones, Brown, Higgs and White are not just working women but independent ones who earn their own money and drink their own gin. In traditions like these, the older woman is allowed to take on the Devil; she is, for most purposes, interchangeable with a man. You'll remember how in the Devil's Bridge stories, the protagonist was sometimes an old lady and sometimes the local shepherd, so evidently the storytellers did not mind much either way. But when it comes to young women – those of courting, marriageable or childbearing age – the rules are very different. Yes, they can take on the Devil and win, but only when they do it on behalf of their menfolk, and only when all other attempts have failed.

The Task That No One Can Do

'The Devil once called on a farmer and exed 'im if he could give him a job,' said a thresher in a barn on the slopes of Bredon Hill near Evesham. It's the same situation that we saw at Langenhoe and St Mabyn. Not recognizing his new recruit, the farmer asks him what he can do – 'Oh! Anything about a farm,' says the Devil – and since there is a stack of wheat to thresh, they head down to the barn. The day starts with the farmer throwing down the sheaves and the Devil threshing, but there is no keeping up with the new workman: before a sheaf has landed, he's slapped it with the flail, knocked the corn into a heap and tossed the straw out of the door all in a bundle. 'You'm a queer sort of thresherman,' says the sweating farmer, 'do you come up and throw out.' So the farmer climbs stiffly down, while the Devil poises himself on a pitchfork and in one move has bounded up.

Bredon Hill.

With a single sweep of the fork he has thrown down enough sheaves to cover the barn floor, and as the farmer wearily threshes the last of these, swish, down comes another floorful. So with one up and one down, they have got through the whole stack long before dark, and the farmer politely bids goodnight to his new hired man. Then he goes to find the cunning man (not the vicar, notice, but a village wizard: this is the working man's version). ''Tis the Devil,' says the cunning man, not unexpectedly, 'an' seeing as you exed him in, you oon't get shut of him without you give him a job as he can't do.'

So another day dawns, and with it comes the new workman, eager for fresh tasks. The farmer says thoughtfully that he's not sure they threshed enough wheat yesterday, and could the new hand count how many grains there are? Within minutes he is back with an answer. 'Bist sure thee's counted 'em all?' 'Every corn, master.' So next the Devil is sent off to fill the water barrel with a sieve, but that doesn't cause him any difficulties either. Every task that is set him, he performs instantly, and the farmer doesn't like to be in the company of his new man, not a bit.

Even when he resorts to the mowing contest, and makes sure the ground is well seeded with harrow tines, it's no use: the Devil scythes through them regardless, gaily calling out across the field, 'Seems 'tis *another* burdock, master!' So after that they knock off early.

Come evening, the farmer is sitting outside the front door looking glumly into the future, when who should come stumping up the path but an old Gypsy woman. 'You got troubles,' she says wisely, as if it wasn't obvious, and the farmer tells her everything that has happened. ''Tis the *Beng* you has in your house,' she says, 'an' you can't get him out without you give him something to do as he can't manage.' 'Tell I what I don't know already!', says the farmer, 'haven't I a-tried everything?' 'No, that you ain't,' says the Gypsy, 'now do you call your wife down, and when I talks wi' her, mind you turn your back on we.' The farmer does as he's told, and as soon as he's facing away, the Gypsy says to the wife, 'Now, my lady, here's a pretty pair of tweezers, and do you just lift up they skirts and petticoats, and pull something out for the old Gypsy woman.' So the wife complies. 'You can turn round, now,' says the Gypsy to the farmer, and carefully hands over the black hair. 'Give this to your man, an' send him up to the blacksmith's shop, to make it straight on the anvil. Straight's a sunbeam, mind, and you 'on't settle for nothing less.'

When the Devil returns in the morning, it's the third day, and he has a smile on his face. 'What's to do, master?', he asks, and the farmer says casually that there's some work ahead, but first can he do a little job for the missus? Not much, just a hair that needs to be hammered straight. Down to the smithy with it, and don't be back until the job's well done. Off runs the Devil and lays the hair out on the anvil. He hammers until he is in a sweat, and then he sweats more as he hammers, but with every blow he strikes that hair gets more curled and crooked and awkward, until at last he throws hammer and anvil up through the forge roof yelling something awful, and away he goes and never comes back again.[10]

This is an elaborated version of a popular story; the anonymous thresher must have known several different Devil traditions and brought them all into a single narrative, perhaps to spin out the working day. The earliest English variant, 'The Wonder; or, The Devil Outwitted', published in 1736, is much simpler in plot but more sophisticated in presentation, versifying the story for a different social milieu. The poet's audience are familiar with the convention by which a gallant young gentleman lays siege to a girl's honour, in this case with the assistance of a demon whose only requirement is that he be kept in constant employment –

> Of one Thing only let me warn ye,
> Which somewhat nearly may concern ye;
> As soon as e'er one Work is done
> Straight name a new one, and so on
> Let each to other quick succeed
> Or else . . . you know how 'tis agreed . . .

A bailiff dunning his distinguished creditor could not have put it more tactfully. Of course the girl succumbs, but after a night of passion, while the two of them are still snug in bed, the young gallant is roused from slumber by his sponsor demon, demanding employment. Instead of threshing and so on, the labours are suitably aristocratic, but with the same result; great mansions instantly built, wealth accumulated from the furthest corners of the earth, and still the black thing calls for more. The young man's cries of dismay wake the girl, who is no sooner acquainted with the facts than she thinks of the solution, and plucking 'a tendril of the Cyprian vine' sends him off to give his fiend-tormentor one last order:

This Line thus curve, and this orbicular
Render direct and perpendicular.

Which of course he can't do, and young love wins the day.[11]

These tales are a scurrilous counterpart to the demon-laying traditions that we met with earlier from Bury and Cockerham. Their plot works because the audience already know the rules of the standard narrative, understanding that the Devil, once invoked, cannot be banished until he is given a task that is beyond his powers; the twist then comes in substituting a curly hair for the rope of sand or letters in the church Bible.

Undignified Exposure

In the same way, English-speaking versions of a widespread tale-type, 'The Devil and the Feathery Wife', take it for granted that we know about the dreadful pact by which the Devil will bargain for a man's soul and then come to claim his due unless he can somehow be outwitted. Throughout Europe, where it appears as a folk tale, this story is a simple combat of wits between man and ogre-demon, but in England and Scotland it is performed as a ballad, and opens instead with the diabolical contract.

There was a labourer who had a hard life: work to find, rent to pay and bread to put on a table for his wife and seven girls. It was a surprise that he had any spare time at all, but one day he took a break from toil and went to indulge sad thoughts in a nearby forest. 'You want money,' said a voice behind him, and turning round he saw a dark stranger emerging from the thicket. They say the Devil is a liar but this time he seemed to have hit the nail on the head. Though the labourer was in a poor bargaining position, that didn't seem to put off his new friend at all, and soon they came to an agreement: his cattle and crops were to thrive and grow for seven years and at the end he was just to bring down this woodland ride an animal that the Devil could not name – that was all. Hell would be waiting for him if he failed.

The food and plenty were unfailing, the starved looks of the seven daughters soon filled out and as for the wife, she had nothing to complain about. It was all very different from the old penny-pinching days. But as the expiry date came near, the labourer's face turned thin and drawn once more, and it was not until the final day that his wife was able to worm the secret out of him. 'Is that all?', she said:

> Go get you gone you silly old man,
> Your cattle go and feed.
> For a woman's wit is better than man's
> If used in time of need.

'Now I need everything ready,' she says, 'so get out that tub of birdlime out of store, and spread it out thin over the floor.' The labourer does as he's told, and when he looks round again, she has stripped right off and is rolling over and over naked on the floor until she is coated in birdlime. 'Now get the best feather mattress,' says the wife, 'haul it down the stairs and rip it open, quick!' He does as he's told and she throws herself into the feathers until they stick all over her. 'Now get the long dog-leash,' says an indistinct voice from somewhere in the middle of the feathers, 'and tie that round me, round my hips mind, because I'm going to be walking on all fours, and backwards.' So for the last time he does as she tells him. And off they set for the forest glade where the Devil is waiting on a tree stump. He almost falls off when he sees what's coming, because it's certainly not like any creature he's ever seen before. 'Well,' says the labourer, 'aren't you going to say hello?' The Devil nervously approaches the end nearest to him. 'It's got rather large cheeks, hasn't it?' 'Gets a lot of exercise,' says the man. 'It's only got one eye!' squeaks the Devil.

'Don't do much looking with it,' says the man. 'Where's its mouth?', says the Devil. 'Under the eye,' says the man, 'where did you expect?' The Devil has a closer look and jumps back in fright. 'And is this the only one in the world?' 'Course not,' says the man, 'I've got another seven at home, all different sizes. I'm bringing them here tomorrow.' 'Suit yourself,' says the Devil, 'but I'm off to Hell: goodbye.'[12]

Unlike 'The Devil and the Farmer's Wife', this was probably not a song for mixed company; neither is 'The Gelding of the Devil', which begins with 'a baker of Mansfield town' who is riding to market when he meets with the Devil. 'Nice horse you've got there,' says the fiend, and compliments him on the animal's sleek hide and plump condition. The baker patiently explains that that's how horses get when they're gelded. 'Ooh, that does sound wonderful,' says the Devil, 'and could you geld *me*?' Nothing loth, the baker pulls out a bread-knife and starts the operation; by the time the Devil has realized this may be more uncomfortable than he thought, it's too late. Clutching himself between the legs, he snarls that on the following market day it will be his turn to geld

Mansfield Forest.

the baker, and so the two go their separate ways, to Nottingham and to Hell. Of course the baker tells his wife, and of course she has a plan. When market day next comes round, she dresses up in her husband's clothes, with the bread trays by her side, and on her way she meets the Devil, armed with a sharp knife and keen to get operating. 'Too late,' says the wife, 'I was done yesterday.' 'Don't believe a word of it,' says the Devil. 'Look for yourself,' says the wife. And when he sees that the place isn't even closed up after the operation, the Devil turns quite sympathetic, lets the clever wife go on her way and never interferes with the couple again.[13]

These are surely men's songs: you can imagine them being roared out before closing time at the pub. And because they are songs to be sung when men are away from women, they speak with two voices about the wives who are waiting for when they get back home. On the surface the ballads go out of their way to celebrate the clever wife: 'women's wit is better than man's,' says 'Feathery Wife', and 'Here's a health to all such wives/ Who can cheat the Devil so,' ends 'Gelding of the Devil'. But both stories make the wife show her wit (and a lot else besides) in a way that is not very dignified, and if we weren't being reassured that it's all being done to save the family, it would look less like triumph than humiliation. The Feathery Wife may take charge of the situation, but she does it by effectively tarring and feathering herself, after which she is treated by her husband as an animal on a leash. Even the gentler denouement of the Bredon Hill story ends with a fuss about what women have under their skirts, which, when you think about it, is not necessary: why couldn't the farmer have pulled out one of his own pubic hairs?

That's one way of seeing it. Yet if we concentrate not on the power dynamics of the couple themselves but on their adversary, the Devil, these ballads take their place in the wider cycle of stories where he is baffled by the most ordinary aspects of human life. Just as he didn't know in 'Tops and Bottoms' that potatoes grew underground, so now he is ignorant of how animals are gelded, and very surprised to learn that it hurts when your balls are cut off. This Devil is something of an innocent and definitely a bachelor. The birdlime and feathers seem almost redundant: all that is needed to send him running is a view of naked female flesh.

This is a very different personality from the horned master of the revels who presided over witch-orgies in the fevered imaginings of the demonologists. Somewhere between the seventeenth and eighteenth centuries, the image of the Devil has been given a makeover. True, the character of the folk Devil is never consistent, since his profile has been patched together out of stories that originally belonged to other, older beings – ogres and giants and ghosts and fairies. And there was always more to the Devil than these stories let on; people never forgot what they had been told in church about Satan, even when they were getting a laugh out of the thought of that hideous strength being rendered literally impotent by a sturdy baker on his market route. But this folk Devil – silly, combative, vengeful and vain – has a character all of his own, which includes a wide-eyed bafflement about young women. He is a sterile spirit; he does not have a place in their world, and they don't belong in his.

In another ballad the Devil comes to tempt a girl, not knowing that she is pregnant; as soon as he realizes, he jumps back in fright, saying:

> Until that you delivered are
> I cannot touch one single hair
> From off your head.[14]

Here, as usual in stories, symbolic incompatibility is presented in narrative terms as a kind of magical clash. The same contradiction between fertility and iniquity appears in a tradition about Parson

Ladock church.

Wood of Ladock, whom we met earlier giving advice to the wrestler who had rashly offered to best the fiend. The parson was famous for his ebony stick, its silver head carved with planetary signs and strange figures; he also had a hunting whip, with which he belaboured the spirits until they screamed and fled; in short, there was little in this world or the next that could trouble Parson Wood. But he was once bested by the Devil and had to call in help from an unexpected quarter. This is how it happened.

When the bell-ropes in Ladock church became frayed, they were taken down until new ones could be brought from up country. So for some weeks the bells were silent, and it was then that a strange bird took up residence in the tower. The bird was black with glittering eyes, much larger than any rook or crow. It made a mess, and stank; suddenly during the hymns it would screech out, confusing the clerk and the singers. Like a jackdaw, it had the power of mimicry, and would interrupt the vicar's sermons with the sound of a barking dog or squealing pig, a rattling carriage or a creaking gate, so that all the congregation were on edge wondering what sound it would make next, and there was little attention paid to the sermon itself. Of course Parson Woods had a good idea what black sky this accursed thing had flown in from, but there was nothing he could do: he could not draw a circle round the empty air, and it took care to perch and cackle out of range of his hunting whip.

Now there were a great many babies waiting for baptism in Ladock, which was a growing parish where people liked to save up the great event for feast day, when all the family could gather and the pubs were open late. But they would do anything for their parson, and they agreed to bring their children's vows forwards by a few weeks. Within a day he had marshalled nine mothers, with another three from the last feast day brought in to make up the numbers. As they processed to church with the godfathers and godmothers, all dressed in Sunday best, it was a lovely sight. But the black fiend hid himself and saw nothing. The twelve mothers stood in ranks while Parson Wood walked before them, cutting the air in figures with his ebony staff, but still nothing happened. No doubt the young people would have stuck to the spot until their parson was done, but babies are not so patient, and within a few minutes first one and then the other began to whimper. At last the biggest of the babies started to bawl outright, and that set off all the others, twelve of them at once, with such a noise that even the devil-bird could no longer ignore it and peeked out from behind a gargoyle to see what was going on. The sight of twelve innocent tear-stained faces was too much for him: off he went in a streak of flame towards the secret parts of the north, and the parish was rid of him. After that they wasted no time in getting the bells back in working order.[15]

Do Not Trust Him, Gentle Maiden

If the folk Devil is uneasy about young women and babies, it is a trait he shares with the gauche ogres and giants of earlier tradition. But there is another quite different convention in which the Devil makes himself agreeable to the girls, a sleek and persuasive suitor. Behind these stories lies the medieval lore of the amorous demon, behind those were tales of fairy lovers, and so it goes back for generation after generation, for it has always been tempting to see encounters between this world and the other through the prism of relations between men and women. The Devil in these stories is tempting in more ways than one, and it takes holy power to defeat him.

In a cottage at Bridgerule, where the Tamar divides North Devon from Cornwall, lived an old woman with just the one daughter. Young Polly had been busy round the house all day when, as dusk fell, a carriage and four passed by. She thought they must have lost their way, and stepped out to direct them to the Bude road. To her surprise a young gentleman jumped out and apologized profusely for keeping her from her work. They got talking, and he seemed really nice, not like some of the carriage-folk. The next evening this coach called again, and the young man asked if he might stop for a while; he didn't say as much, but was obviously rather taken with her. And on the evening of the third day he called, and stepped into the house, and came straight to the point: would she be his forever? The carriage would be ready and waiting. 'Say yes, only say yes!' And she did.

Well, the girl was all in a dream about what the future held, but her old mother had outlived too many dreams to be convinced, and that night she stumped over to the parson's house and asked him what he thought. He thought none of it was for the good, and told her as much, giving her some solid advice, which she passed on to her daughter. Next evening, the handsome stranger drove to the door, all in a hurry, he was so passionate for his girl; she must come, she must, hadn't she promised? 'Well, yes,' said Polly, 'but not in my working clothes. Let me get into something better.' 'Precious soul,' breathed the young man, 'you girls take forever with your dressing up, I am impatient for you!' 'Well,' she says, 'at least give me until that candle is burnt out. Say yes!' And he did.

But the moment he spoke, Polly's mother stepped into the parlour and blew out the candle. Off she went, by hollow ways and hidden ways, until she was safe inside Bridgerule church. The Devil looked but couldn't see any sign of her, and as for Polly, he had promised to leave her alone, so he leapt back on the seat of his carriage, cracked up the horses with a black whip, and off they galloped until they came to the great marsh at the heart of Affaland Moor, into which he drove, horses, carriage and all. Blue flames flickered as they went down, the bog gulped, and all was quiet once again.[16]

So the story was told by an old lady from nearby Luffincott, but this was not an isolated local tradition; Gus Gray, the Gypsy storyteller of Lincolnshire, knew a version that was almost the same.[17] The migrating story must have been built up around its central element, 'not until that candle burns out,' which is found in other tales, usually as a way of putting off death rather than marriage; long before there were such things as candles, the theme of a life that will last until the final burning of a firebrand was used in the Greek legend of Meleager. These little atoms of motifs endure for thousands of years while more elaborate stories crystallize and melt around them. In its latest form, the legend of the Devil, the girl and the candle would not have been plausible until early modern times, when cottagers could afford candles.

Many a girl must have been glad to find a way of putting off an importunate suitor, whether he was the Devil or not. This inspired the oldest of the ballads about a girl and a disturbing stranger, the one known variously as 'The Devil's Riddles' or 'The Riddling Knight'. As this suggests, it is found in multiple versions, some little more than a riddle contest in which he and she test each other's wit and repartee, others set in a much darker frame.

'There was a knight came to the gate,' begins one version, romantically enough. We are in the world of the classic ballads where everyone is noble: there is no hint of the Bridgerule lesson that gentlemen who flatter village girls may have predatory motives. Instead the knight goes about his wooing quite innocently, at least in the main ballad verses, but the refrain reveals the true state of things:

If thou canst not answer me three times three,
In ten thousand pieces I'll tear thee.[18]

What is whiter than milk? Snow. What is softer than silk? Feather-down. We are back in the realm of magical morality, where it is essential to promptly answer the questions of a spirit, lest a moment's hesitation should put you in its power. So the dialogue that follows is not just an exercise in cleverness but a fight for life. Men contend with the Devil in wrestling, in bare-knuckle, in the hurling of great stones; it is women who battle him with their wits. To end the debate, the girl succeeds in twisting two of the riddle-questions to a theme more serious than snow or feathers. What is higher than a tree? Heaven. And what is deeper than the sea? *Hell.* The Devil's true identity is unmasked:

He clapped his wings, and aloud did cry,
And a flame of fire he flew away.

These Heaven and Hell answers appear in the oldest version of the ballad, found in an early fifteenth-century manuscript, although they lose some of their dramatic force by being placed in the middle of the dialogue. Otherwise this version of 'Devil Meets Girl' (*Inter diabolus et virgo* is the Latin title, although the text itself is Middle English) does not differ much from the versions recorded in modern times. The imagery has a mysterious feel to it, something not often found in medieval stories of the supernatural; in those days, when Catholic teachings encompassed everything in this world and the next, a devil was on much the same level of reality as a bear or a bandit, frightening rather than uncanny. But the antagonist of *Inter diabolus et virgo* is a truly eerie compound of lover and fiend; he offers the girl 'all the wyssedom off the world' if she will accept his embraces, though at the same time he hints that she may have no choice in the matter if she cannot reply to his demands. The girl, it seems, has no need of his tainted wisdom and can answer the enigmas of Hell quite satisfactorily with her own wit. It is as if the fiend knew she would be tempted, not with sex or pride or a desire for unbridled power, but with longing for knowledge: which was not a very common thought about women in the fifteenth century, or for many years afterwards.

As a rule, the ballad-singers had no interest in female education: a girl's business was to fall in love; and, having fallen in love, to get married; and, having got married, to stand by her man. Failure to keep that last part of the bargain is punished more swiftly and certainly than any other infringement of the moral code, even when there are extenuating circumstances. A popular ballad begins abruptly, as these songs so often do, with the return of an old lover for the girl he left behind; he has riches of great store, he has turned down a king's daughter in the lands far beyond the sea, all to come home and marry his girl. Yet she turns him down, because she's already married to a ship's carpenter, and they have a baby son. That's how things are, and let's not talk about what might have been. But when he shows her his gallant ship, with a chair of gold awaiting her on deck, she is tempted, embarks, and is soon far from land.

At this point, the song tradition splits into three. One version, the most recent, is quite businesslike: the adulterous wife sails off with her ex-boyfriend, they come to a bad end, and serve them right. In another tradition we find that the mysterious sailor has returned from the grave to claim his beloved – his ship, with its golden mast and silken sails, is a phantasm, as are its four-and-twenty singing mariners, and the ghost is taking her not out to sea but to death. In the third version, the tempter is the Devil. Hence the ballad is known variously as 'The Ship's Carpenter' and 'The Demon Lover'. In the first known version, a rather plodding text of 1657, the tempted wife is identified as a Mrs Jane Reynolds of Plymouth, and her former admirer was a comely proper youth by the name of James Harris, who is now a ghost. The broadsheet printer evidently thought these details greatly improved the story, but they have at least given it a third alternative title of 'James Harris'. This ghost-story broadside is the earliest account we have, which suggests that a dead lover featured in the original story.[19]

So here we have yet another instance of the Devil taking the place of what was previously a different supernatural actor. The change seems to have been made in Scotland, where the Devil was much more of a moral agent than he was in England, although the influence of these Scottish versions is found among singers all the way to Devon and Dorset. The demon lover has, we assume, adopted the form of the late James (or whoever) in order to test the constancy of the wife, and she fails the test. It does her no good to sink on the deck and weep for her betrayed husband and abandoned baby. It is too late.

'O what a bright bright hill is yon,
That shines so clear to see?'
'It is the hill of Heaven,' he said
'Where you shall never be.'
'Oh what a black, dark hill is yon,
That looks so dark to me?'

'O it is the hill of Hell,' he said
'Where you and I shall be.'

And as she turns round, she sees him grow taller and taller, higher than the tops of the ship, reaching out to the mast and snapping it with one hand, and with the other breaking the ship in two, so that they go down, down into the dark waters.

Of all the Devil tales and legends and ballads, this is the most pitiless in its morality: the wife is not a bad person but only made a single slip, and now she is racked by guilt for it, while her hopes of salvation slip away on the starboard bow. But neither tricks nor magic nor kindly supernatural advisors are at hand to help her: she has sinned, and she must die. English traditions about the Devil are not usually so stern.

8

AMID THE SHRIEKING OF THE STORM: THE DEVIL APPEARS TO CARRY OFF SINNERS

The Devil descended in tempests to shatter churches and visit death on their congregations; although the lightning which struck these buildings was real enough, legend turned it into demonic rage against the sacred, and the accidental victims were transformed by tradition into exemplary sinners meeting the punishment they deserved. Wild tempests were expected at the deaths of the wicked, and even when the weather was clear, Hell's flames could suddenly erupt to carry off the rash blasphemer. Unbelief was imagined by storytellers in strong, clear colours: games on Sunday, or even picking blackberries after Michaelmas, would put you in the Devil's power. For the young and heedless, he came to rebuke rather than destroy, with sessions of Sunday card-playing broken up as soon as the dark stranger showed his cloven hoof.

Rider on the Storm

It is pleasant on a summer day to take the bus from Newton Abbot to Widecombe-in-the-Moor and wander around the village. Of course your pleasure must include the company of two hundred other people who will have had the same idea on the same morning. To visit Widecombe is to be part of a crowd, arriving together to see the same things, all of you obediently buying fudge and postcards printed with a stanza of 'Widecombe Fair', and wondering whether to roll the r's just a bit when you order a pint of Proper Job at the Rugglestone. St Benedict thought that monks should never be alone, because when they were solitary they were more at risk from the assaults of the Devil. Anyone who lives in Widecombe must be in a fair way to being saved, then.

In any case, Widecombe has things that are worth seeing, however many people are looking at them along with you. There is the Church House, solid sixteenth-century work with a front loggia resting on granite slabs, and great open-hearthed fireplaces still holding the pot-hooks where cauldrons bubbled for the parish revel. And, on the far side of the churchyard, St Pancras itself, the Cathedral of the Moor, with its 130-foot tower needling the sky; the interior is bright and clear, the ceiling is painted white between the ribs of the wagon roof, and light grey columns laboriously hewn out of moorstone form the north and south arcades.

The older tombstones in the churchyard, the ones carved only with hand tools, mostly keep themselves to a name and a date in large clear letters, as if the masons felt by the time they got to the

Widecombe-in-the-Moor.

year's last digit any further struggle with the obdurate stone would push them under the turf themselves. This intractability of granite affords quiet satisfaction to the locals: it does not wear away, as the summer crowds do after August Bank Holiday; like the moormen, it takes both storm and sunshine; it is there forever. The tors that looked down on Widecombe at the end of the Bronze Age still look on it today.

Much of the village is built out of granite, too. The houses have thick walls, not just because of a ready supply – why choose thin blocks rather than thick when the whole hillside is made of the stuff? – but to give a better barrier against the damp. However hard the stone may be in itself, damp seeps easily around the blocks and under the mortar of a traditionally built house. This is the land the Atlantic rainclouds hit first when they reach the western shores of Britain. Even churches, unless kept specially dry, soon develop a patina of green algae inside as well as outside; it only takes one storm to push the water through. And it was in a storm that the Devil first came to Widecombe.

It all began in calm weather on a dull, humid October day. The landlady at the Postgate Inn was standing at the door, hoping that some workmen or a miner would call for lunchtime entertainment, when she saw a stranger riding up the track. A gentleman, from the look of him, so he should pay well. And he must be ready for a drink, wearing those stiff black clothes and all.

He called out for cider and she ran forwards to serve him. The stranger did not dismount but sat on his tall black horse; though the tankard was full, he drained it at a draught. It was then that she noticed two curious things. One was the way the cider hissed when it ran down his throat, as no good liquor should do; and the other was the odd-shaped boot that held his foot in the stirrup. Leaning down, the gentleman handed back the tankard with a courtly bow. 'I'm bound for Widecombe,' he said. 'Will you be my guide?' But the landlady had seen enough, and with a few confused excuses she ducked back into the pub. The Devil had to find his own way.

Given the lack of signposts in those days, and the mud that got deeper and deeper just as you were sure you'd reached the solid ground, and the tendency of Devon roads to twist in every direction other than the one that they first seem to be heading in, it is not surprising that the Devil was in a temper by the time he got to Widecombe. Muttering like thunder, he reined in his horse on Hameldown and looked over the village. There was the church; and there, just visible through the lowest lights of the window, was his destined prey.

When Jan Reynolds made his bargain with the Devil, he was shrewder or better advised than most. Jan did not opt for a fixed term of years or to meet some almost impossible demand, but for a simple condition: Satan could take his soul when he caught him asleep in church. For many years, Jan had been last in and first out of Sunday service, a nervous auditor perched on the edge of his seat. With only the props of the illiterate to keep him active in these long dull hours of piety, he had taken to playing long card games against himself. But single-handed games are not very interesting, and with a sigh he dropped the pack on the pew beside him. The afternoon was hot. For a moment, his head nodded down on his chest.

Lightning crackled around the Devil as he spurred his horse onto the summit of the tower. Suddenly the church was enveloped in black clouds and a rising wind lashed rain against the windows, while the horse snorted and kicked, knocking down a pinnacle. It crashed through the roof and there, helplessly exposed to vengeful skies, sat the hapless Jan. The Devil descended in a ball of flame and caught his victim by the hair, smashing his head casually against a pillar and dragging the miserable sinner away to undergo worse things in Hell.[1]

Such is the legend of Widecombe, and unlike many other tales of the marvellous, its origins are not in doubt: they were real events, and they happened on Sunday 21 October 1638. About three hundred people were at afternoon service when suddenly the church grew dark. The cloud came over, 'the darkness increasing yet more, till they could not see one another'; there was a crack of thunder, and lightning struck the church tower on the north side. The shock forced its way down the stair turret and then, meeting an obstacle, broke through the west window. It struck against the north wall of the church as if it were a cannon-ball, and passed up the aisle, killing a man who was leaning against the woodwork. 'The brains fell backward, entire and whole, into the next seat behind him, and two pieces of his skull.' The stream of lightning divided in two: one flash of the electric current broke out of the east wall of the aisle, while the other tore into the chancel. Four people were killed and 62 injured.[2]

Here is the original seed of the Devil's sudden appearance on the church tower and the dreadful fate of Widecombe Jan. The description of 1638 is so accurate that we can see not just what happened, but why. The pinnacles of St Pancras' Church were the highest point of the village, and the nearest to the thundercloud's electrical charge. The actual lightning strike would have taken place quicker than the eye can see, but it is the return stroke that makes the flash and the explosion. The electric current runs through a building as far as it can before earthing itself in the ground, and in an ordinary church, that means a path from the tower down the nave or aisles and into the chancel. Stone is a poor conductor of electricity, so the charge tends to short-circuit along the lines of mortar, especially if they are damp. The expansion of superheated water then hurls the stones out of their bedding.

Remember that storm at Danbury church in 1402: the Devil broke in through the roof, ran down to the altar and smashed out through the chancel wall, leaving behind a smell of sulphur – or, smelling much the same, the ozone released in electrified air. All of this is compatible with a lightning strike. The actual events could be mythologized very fast, even in the testimony of those who were there when it happened. At Shrewsbury, those who remembered the Devil's appearance in the storm of January 1533 said:

> as he passyd throughe the churche he mountyd up the steeple in the sayde churche teringe the wyer of the sayde clocke and put the prynt of his clawes uppon the iiijth bell and tooke one of the pynnacles awaye with hym and for the tyme stayed all the bells in the churches within the sayd towne that they could neyther toll nor rynge.[3]

What is this, the physical effect of electric discharge on bell-metal or the spiritual antipathy of the Devil to bells? It is both: facts are reported by people who are already thinking in terms of legend. And if legend was slow to develop, it could always be given a helping hand. At Great Chart in Kent a storm broke out on the day after Boxing Day 1612, 'and a thing in the middle aisle of the church burned, as one might perceive it, but yet it was like unto a black cloud and smoked'.[4] So wrote the minister, who had bravely stepped out of the pulpit to comfort his people while the afterglow of the lightning strike still burned on his retina. In a pamphlet written soon afterwards for the London market, the shadow has become 'a most ugly shape out of the ayer like unto a broadeyd bul', which dashes the minister's book out of his hand before turning on the crowd.[5] The fiendish creatures said to have cavorted through these storm-blasted churches – black dogs, pigs, dragons – owe much to creative reporting by journalists and chroniclers.

Eventually it was the journalists who called time on the Devil, at least as an explanation of structural damage to churches during storms. That Sunday afternoon at Widecombe had been so dramatic that it was written up almost before the smell of ozone had cleared from the air, once in prose and once in verse, but in both versions it appears as an example of God's visible judgements, with no mention of any interference by his old enemy. By the 1630s it had become conventional, even in popular tracts, for all checks and setbacks to be ascribed to God alone, punishing sinners and testing the faithful. In practice, if not in doctrine, Protestant writers rejected the numberless demons that had provided their medieval precursors with such varied explanations of bad weather; they were also disinclined to attribute disasters to Satan himself, as this would abrogate from the sovereignty of God. The consequence was that, apart from its observations on the providential fates of those who died and survived, the Widecombe tract comes across as a sober account of natural phenomena, the sort of thing that would be published a generation later by the Royal Society. As for the diabolical interpretation, that was left to the oral world of the illiterate, where it continued to flourish until the nineteenth century.

Whenever lightning flickered in the sky, country people had the satisfaction of knowing that the Devil was active – somewhere else. It was a piece of small talk in Wiltshire and Devon, when a storm was heard far off, to say that conjuring was going on in that direction.[6] On such a wild tempestuous night the Devil came to the moors between Foxstones and Crow Holes in Cliviger near Burnley. All decent citizens were in bed, heavy shutters sheltering their windows from the blast, but Johnny o' th' Pasture was waiting on the hill, and when a black dog with flaming eyes appeared out of the storm, he knew he had met the master he sought. Whatever terms they agreed on, Johnny became a celebrated local wizard. When he died, local opinion about his dealings with the Devil was confirmed, for as the old man breathed his last a storm blew up, so violent that houses were unroofed and trees torn out by the roots.[7]

The Fate of the Wicked

In stories like this, the Devil confines himself to picking off the exemplarily wicked, though this was exactly the view that Puritan preachers had tried to root out from the popular mindset. They wanted their parishioners to feel, as they did, the fallen nature of all humanity, our hopeless bondage to the prince of this world; everyone except a handful of the elect was in a chain gang marching to Hell, and lightning should by rights flicker over all funerals and not just that of the village wizard. But the people in the pews insisted on a brighter outlook. As far as they were concerned, reasonable levels of neighbourliness were good enough for Heaven and nobody would be consigned to the Devil unless they had shown grossly antisocial behaviour.[8]

True, the definition of antisociability had a class bias. In a society where all authority was in the hands of the landed elite, masters who departed from the traditional script of benevolent concern and decent behaviour could not be punished in this world, but after death they were fair game. When Frederick Hancock, the rector of Selworthy on Exmoor, heard about the last hours of a local squire, notorious for his evil ways, the news was that:

> A great thunderstorm, though it was mid-winter, came up and shook the ancient house, levelling the great oaks of centuries' growth; and amidst the shrieking of the storm, strange wild voices and unearthly laughter resounded about the place, as, struggling as though with a deadly foe, with wild curses upon his lips, the squire passed away.[9]

Whatever would cause an unseasonal storm like that?, wondered the Reverend Hancock; to which the laconic answer was, Something you parsons know all about.

In tales like this, the storm is not just weather: it is testimony, proof of a wickedness so terrible it breaks the membrane between the human and supernatural worlds and lets the Devil lunge through. The squire, the wizard and the maker of the dreadful pact all thought they could go to the grave hiding the secret of their sin, but wickedness will out, and streaks of lightning blazon to the country who they really were. Accept this, and stories of fiery damnation become very persuasive as propaganda.

In the coastal Dorset town of Lyme Regis, there lived a lawyer, Robert Jones. By the early 1700s he had built up a small attorney's practice in the area, his talents having first been recognized some fifteen years earlier when he helped a judge who was on the Western Circuit. His home at Chatham House was the rendez-vous of wit and fashion; dignity tapped its snuffbox in the salon, loveliness rustled in silk down the staircase. Time passed, and Lawyer Jones retired for the last time to the lonely magnificence of an ornate deathbed. Outside, the weather was on the turn, with sudden winds howling down the chimneys and puffing soot and ash out onto the patterned carpets. Jones died, and at once the

Lyme Regis harbour.

sky split with thunder, there was a great flash in the air, and the gable of Chatham House ripped apart from the building.

Now see what follows. Lyme was quite a port in those days, with vessels trading up and down the Atlantic coast and into the Mediterranean. One ship had finished the Levantine run from Smyrna and was coming back through the Strait of Messina when the sun grew pale and sea-haze obscured the view. Through the mist, the master of the vessel could see another ship approaching, lit fore and aft by red streaks, bright as lanterns, though they were not lanterns. The crew were dark little fellows, like no seafarers he had ever seen before, and he had been in most ports. They ran and scrambled over the rigging like cats, and as the strange vessel came closer he could see their chattering bestial faces and the fire in their eyes. They were devils. Still, the sea has its rules, and a master must hail an oncoming vessel, whether it be crewed by demons or men, so he shouted out to them, asking what port they sailed from, and where they were heading. 'Out of Lyme, bound for Mount Etna with Jones,' screamed the devils, and sailed on towards the growling volcano.[10]

Lawyer Jones was not the first to be carried to this fate. If we are to trust some profoundly untrustworthy literature, locals living near Etna, Vesuvius and Stromboli got so used to the transport of damned souls that they treated it as little more than traffic noise. The earliest story, telling how the soul of Theodoric the Great was thrown into the volcano in 526 by men he had unjustly killed, already contains the seeds of later narratives: the recognition of the victim, the careful recording of the time at which he is seen and the discovery afterwards (in days when news travelled slower than it does now) that this was the exact moment at which he had died.

All these stories are political, circulated by one party to prove the wickedness of another, and this is certainly the case at Lyme. For the occasion on which Jones had made himself so helpful was the Bloody Assizes of 1685, and the judge was Jeffreys, who had come to the West to find and kill all those who a year before had been in arms for the Monmouth Rising. It was on the beach at Lyme Regis that the Duke of Monmouth had landed in his bid for the English throne, and on that same beach, twelve months later, a silent, chastened crowd gathered to watch their former companions lined up for hanging, disembowelling and burning. Jones had betrayed them, and so for all his early Georgian respectability, he met the fate reserved for those who make a pact with the Devil – or with Jeffreys. Same difference, as far as Dorset people were concerned.

The seventeenth and eighteenth centuries saw the last flowering of judgement tales, those chapbooks and ballads in which the Devil came to take a sinner when they finally committed some last flagrant act of wickedness. Occasionally Satan manifests in person, an ugly black shape knocking out his victim's brains and flying away through the window. More often the dreadful fate involves being consumed by fire, or swallowed up by the ground, or falling down lifeless before your astonished friends. If we had matching factual reports, as we do at Widecombe, I suppose we would find that some of these were real people dying in some way known to orthodox medicine, but all we have is pious productions in which the facts, if any, have been subordinated to the moral. The young man (he is usually young, and a man) runs up a bill at the pub, and tells the landlord he can't pay without going to Hell for it; if more drink is forthcoming, he will begin on the most horrid blasphemies; he attempts to debauch a maiden, and sneers at her talk of virtue; if reprimanded, he is prepared to sell his soul to be revenged on his mum and dad; he denies God, and dismisses all talk of the Devil. Little does he know!

These tracts are in tune with popular ideas – they would never have sold in such large numbers if they were not. Taking the Devil's money is never a good idea, as we have seen, and the hero of *A Terrible and Seasonable Warning to Young Men* survives only because he has sense enough to reject it. When the Devil appears in human form, woodcuts show him in traditional shape, a rich gentleman's rig modified only by a black boot ingeniously split for his cloven hoof.[11] The judgement tales are certainly a kind of folklore, drawing on popular assumptions about the supernatural, told in a very stereotyped way and copied informally from one hack writer to another. But they never made it into oral tradition. All the chapbooks have a moral message and usually a gory end, but in the oral folk tales, we have seen, the Devil is usually baffled of his prey. In any case, you are more likely to fall into his power by boasting about your skill, listening to the love-talk of a polite stranger or simply collecting the bones of a dead toad than by presenting any theatrical displays of wickedness.

But because the chapbooks are still so close to the oral world – they are meant to be read aloud, just as the broadside ballads were meant to be sung – evil is painted in the simplest black-and-white tones. The young man must be seen to do wicked in the most obvious and dramatic way, so never mind what he is like inwardly, what matters are his loud boasts: he didn't believe in the Devil, and/or he was prepared to go to him for another drink. Perdition, if you understand the story in the most literal way, consisted only in saying the wrong thing out loud, and this brings us back to ideas of magical morality, at which point we are definitely in the realm of folk tale again.

Between Bristol and the Mendips lies Stanton Drew, a Somerset village that would be unremarkable except that it has one of the largest stone circles in Northern Europe in the fields between the church and the River Chew. Two smaller circles can be seen close up by anyone who doesn't mind putting a pound in the honesty box and dodging the cowpats, while the garden of the Druids Arms includes a cove or three-stone setting, like the Devil's Brand Irons at Avebury. But the unmissable thing is the Great Circle.

Stanton Drew stone circle.

Archaeologists date it to the Neolithic era, but tradition assigns it a more recent origin – before living memory, of course, but long after the village was settled and the church had been built. One Saturday there was a wedding, and when the service was over the couple and their guests spilled out of the church into the adjoining meadow. Everyone had a delightful time and as a fiddler had been hired to make music, they danced the afternoon away. The bride loved dancing – not ballroom, which wasn't known then, or even country dances, but the real old-fashioned circle dancing. It was a summer night, they were young and full of energy, and though at last the light had faded from the sky, they lit some torches and carried on. The bells on the church clock rang out for ten, and then eleven, and when they finally struck twelve the musician lifted his bow and tucked his fiddle under his arm. 'Well, young 'uns,' he said, 'you've had your fun and it's Sunday now.' The bride pouted; it was, or had been, her special day and she didn't like to be crossed. Wouldn't he play just another round? No. The guests muttered, but the piper stuck to his principles and retired for the night under a hedge.

'Hell!', said the bride, 'isn't there anywhere we can get a fid-dler?' And just as she spoke those words, an elderly gentleman came walking up from the riverside, bowed low to her and offered to help. He stood in the centre of the ring, pulled out an antique fiddle and began a slow and dignified air. 'Pep it up a bit, grandad,' shouted one of the dancers, 'we're not tired yet.' 'Not yet,' said the old gentleman, and at once he began to play a tune so lively and compelling that all the guests leapt into action, dancing and spinning around. He carried on elaborating that strange air, and they danced to it compulsively, as if they could not help themselves, until first one and then another realized that they *couldn't* help themselves: like it or not, they must carry on dancing. Round and round their bodies jerked against their will, drained of strength and finally of life itself, and yet still moving, until first light began to glimmer in the east. The real fiddler, hidden in the shelter of the hedge, saw it all, his eyes wide with horror. He saw the old gentleman end his tune, smile and address the dancers once more. 'Stop! You can stop now – forever.' But they did not hear him, because the moment the bow was lifted from the strings, they had turned into stone, and stone they remain to this day.[12]

This is the Victorian version, but it seems that at Stanton Drew, as in so many other places, the Devil has stepped into a story that did not originally feature him. When William Stukeley visited in 1723, he was told that the stones of the Great Circle had been the dancing company and those near the northeastern circle the fiddlers, or band of music, while the three stones of the cove were the parson, bride and bridegroom. Earlier, in 1664, John Aubrey, who first brought Stanton Drew to the notice of a wider world, was shown the bride, the parson and, unexpectedly, the cook.[13] At this stage in the growth of the legend, villagers knew nothing of the bride's fatal announcement that she would accept a fiddler even from Hell, of the diabolical fiddler who arrives on cue, or of the original godly one who hides to one side of the main event and later confirms the story with eyewitness testimony. In the original version, everybody was petrified – fiddlers, cook and all – because they had danced on a Sunday.

But how original is original? This Somerset village is the only place in England with a legend about a petrified wedding. Throughout the southwest there are traditions about girls petrified for dancing on the Sabbath, and at St Buryan and St Columb Major, people pointed to a stone circle as the dancers, and out-lying stones as the fiddlers or pipers, the same layout that was pointed out to Stukeley at Stanton Drew. None of these stories make any reference to the Devil, and the overall impression is that sin will be punished by some inevitable, impersonal force of retribution: dance on Sunday and, click, you turn into a craggy boulder. And none mention a wedding; this is a detail that seems to have been imitated from France, for there are six monuments in Brittany called Noce de Pierre, and two more in the Pas de Calais called Danse des Neuches, just as the Stanton Drew stones were called the Wedding. On the Continent, the wedding guests are petrified for disrespect to the sacrament, not for breaking the Sabbath, but that was a detail which would be lost in translation to Protestant England.[14]

Never on a Sunday

Stories of people being punished for profaning a holy day go back to the Middle Ages and earlier; if there is less variety in nineteenth-century English legend, that was because every other date apart from Sunday had lost its sacredness. As Sabbath observance became the one remaining ritual in an otherwise secularized calendar, the Devil was brought in to enforce it. Sometimes this could get confusing, as when another megalithic monument in Oxfordshire, known without explanation for over two hundred years as the Devil's Quoits, acquired a legend in 1902:

'the Devil was playing quoits on a Sunday, and, in a rage at being told that it was wrong, threw the three quoits to Stanton Harcourt.'[15] It sheds a new light on the Devil's character to find him embarrassed about breaking the Fourth Commandment.

He wasn't the only one to take Sunday seriously. At Ash near Yeovil a woman was scrubbing the floor on Saturday night and thoughtlessly carried on after midnight. As she threw the dirty water out of the door, she saw the Devil in the darkness: she always swore to this, and no one would doubt her word, since she came from a very religious family.[16] Just as in the legend of the stone wedding, she had inadvisedly continued doing something after midnight on Saturday, and though it was an unconscious mistake, that didn't make any difference: it still put her in the Devil's power. Victorian England was choked with rules about what you could not do on a Sunday – go into a pub, buy food, take a train – and mostly these were imposed by middle-class legislators on the poor, who would rather have been having a good time on their one day off. But there were many who imposed this regulation on themselves. Self-discipline gave you an inner strength, as well as the authority to discipline other people. The Devil – much more moral here than usual, and more frightening – was called in to enforce these rules.

'When I was a boy at Pitton,' wrote Ralph Whitlock, the twentieth-century authority on Wiltshire folk life, 'I heard of some boys who, many years earlier, went "scuggy-hunting" (squirrel-hunting) in Clarendon Woods on Sunday afternoon and had been frightened by the Devil. No one would think of gardening, sewing or knitting on a Sunday, and only religious papers were permitted in most houses.'[17] No doubt there were some who found other things to do on the Lord's Day, but that just showed they came from an unbelieving underclass, and stories were told of how they met with a deserved fate. That is what stories are for.

At Minchinhampton there was a man who went to gather hazelnuts on Sundays. Down Half-Mile Lane the bushes grew thick, with sweet clusters of nuts hanging down over the road. He reached out to pick the heaviest bunch of nuts and said quietly, 'Here goes one!' Even that wasn't the best, because next to it hung a fine handful, so he chuckled and murmured, 'Here goes two!' And then a black hand reached out from the other side of the hedge, and it reached for the man and grabbed him, saying in a terrible voice, '*Here goes three!*' So he died, and they buried him in the Devil's Churchyard: where else?[18]

Sometimes it was said that if you went nutting on a Sunday, the Devil would pull down the branches for you. That sounds rather convenient, but once you caught a closer glimpse of your assistant, and saw his cloven foot, there was nothing for it but to go home and die.[19] Since it was usually girls who went picking nuts, this considerate stranger has a hint of the demon lover about him. It was convenient to take a young man with you when you went nutting; he could reach the higher branches, he didn't mind spoiling his clothes and it was an opportunity for a little light flirtation. Rustic moralists thought it went a lot further than that, but this may say more about their desire to police young women's leisure than about real seductions. A much less doom-laden story comes from near Eastbourne in 1814, when the Berkshire militia were quartered nearby: they were local recruits for the most part, though their drummer had come from the Caribbean to help old England in her hour of need. Five young women met up one Sunday to pick nuts in Tilehurst Wood and, after waiting to see if their husbands or boyfriends would catch up – no sign of them – they got on with the work by themselves, piling up the nuts in an open clearing. It was all going fine until they returned to the clearing and saw ... well, they could hardly bring themselves to say what they had seen squatting on their ill-gotten hazelnuts, but he was dark, darker than any human being had a right to be, with terrible white smiling teeth and red flames shooting round his legs. They screamed and ran back to the village, where no one believed a word of it until the next day, when Satan returned the bag of stolen nuts. He had of course been Dan the drummer, who was walking in the woods when he saw their Sunday work, and decided to play a trick on them by stripping off and sitting down with his scarlet tunic over his legs.[20]

This is, I think, the only English story in which the Devil – forever described as the dark lord, a man in black and so on – is identified with a real Black man. And the joke is very much on the girls, who must have had a bad conscience about their Sunday outing or they would have recognized Dan, who was evidently something of a local character.

Stories are told more often about nutting than any other work you might be tempted to do on the Sabbath; possibly because it was easier to imagine appearances of the Devil out in the woods than nearer home, though perhaps also because a belief that was not originally about Sunday at all has been twisted into a new shape by the kaleidoscope of tradition. John Clare, the Northamptonshire peasant poet, wrote:

> On Holy rood day it is faithfully & confidently believed both by old & young that the Devil goes a nutting on that day. I have heard a many people thought it a tale till they ventured to the woods on that day when they smelt such a strong smell of brimstone as nearly stifled them.[21]

Naming a festival date (Holy Rood Day was 14 September) sounds old-fashioned; perhaps this was the original form of the belief, afterwards assimilated to Sunday. Clare also knew that on Michaelmas, 29 September, the Devil poisoned all the blackberries. Some people identified the fatal day as Old Michaelmas – the date on which the feast would have fallen if it hadn't been for calendar reform in 1752. This suggests that the belief was current before that date, and as early as 1727 a botanist reports the common saying that 'after Michaelmas the D—l casts his club over them.'[22] That mysterious club again, you notice, as in the midnight battle at Tolleshunt Knights.

While the dangers of Sunday nutting seem to be purely spiritual, blackberries picked after Michaelmas really are bad to eat. The fruits furthest up the stem will have ripened when the days are short, so that the fruit is smaller and harder, while autumn frosts make it mushy and more likely to get flyblown and breed moulds. So the superstition was actually quite useful, because it substitutes a powerful supernatural motive (I mustn't pick blackberries after today, or I'll be eating the Devil's own fruit) for a merely rational one (I mustn't carry on picking blackberries after the frosts begin, because they might make me sick). But functional explanations of this kind fail to do justice to the depth of people's feeling: we are not looking at a useful aide-memoire for the date when blackberries start to go off, but an absolute taboo. A charwoman from Arundel, casually asked if she could pick some the day after Old Michaelmas, was horrified. 'If any person were to eat one on the eleventh they or someone belonging to them would die or fall into great trouble before the year was out. No, nothing should persuade me to let any child of mine go blackberrying on the 11th of October.'[23]

The sense of revulsion is clear when people explain exactly how the Devil spoils the blackberries. He breathes on them, puts his paw on them, passes his cloven hoof over them, drags his tail over them or he spits on them. One or two sources say he pisses on them, which sounds even nastier, but spitting is the usual version and it is recorded by too many folklorists (not all of them blushing violets, by any means) to have been a euphemism.[24]

When the Fun Stops

In all these stories, the Devil's role is to prevent you from doing something that you might otherwise want to do. Sometimes he underwrites practical rules, like not eating blackberries out of season or stealing a march on the supply of hazelnuts, and sometimes he enforces moral constraints, like those guarding the sacred quality of Sunday: far from tempting people to further acts of wickedness, the Devil will step in firmly to break up the fun, like a supernatural policeman. But many of these traditions go back to the time before the 1860s when there were no policemen in the countryside, and the man in black had to do the work of the boys in blue. As one anecdote succeeds another, you notice how many of them involve young people in high spirits getting together for some activity – dancing, going nutting in the woods, playing games on the green – which is brought to an end by an unchallengeable older power. Move along, now.

At North Leigh, between Witney and Woodstock, while everyone else was observing Sunday two or three young men crept off to hunt badgers. Once they had succeeded in catching one, the top of the sack was tied up securely so they could bring it home. But when they untied the bag, there was nothing in it but a smell of brimstone. In the same village, the lads were playing cricket on the village green one Sunday. A batsman was in for the other side, a stranger to the village but a really outstanding player, and while the bowler was trying to figure out who he was and where he came from, the stranger disappeared in smoke.[25] At Crawshawbooth near Burnley, it was football that the young men were playing on Sunday when an unexpectedly powerful player joined the game. One shot at the ball and it disappeared into the sky in a flash of fire, along with the strange player, and that was the end of the game.[26]

North Leigh.

When passed down by tradition or remembered long after the event, these stories follow a smooth narrative line, but as we get closer to the actual event, reports are more contradictory. On the Wiltshire Downs there used to be an annual gathering at Longbridge Deverill on Palm Sunday. This was a regular day for a holiday, usually involving the young people getting together on some hillside where they could see and be seen, but the gatherings at Longbridge Cowdown came to a sudden end when the Devil appeared, possibly in the form of a dog, or maybe someone just said that the dog was the Devil. 'Sum'at was there, anyhow,' everyone ran away, and after that there were no more gatherings.[27] At Chideock on the West Dorset coast, old Eli Bartlett reported with grim fascination:

> They seed the old Gentleman up to Gabriel's last week. He was like a great black crow! Some lads was up by the gravel pit on Sunday morning a-playing pitch a' toss – they went there 'cause they didn't want no one to see 'em: and as they was a-playing, down come a great black

bird right into the middle of 'em and carried off the ha'pence. Oh, they was frightened and runned off; they didn't stop to pick up the ha'pence; they thought Satan'd have they too; an' aathey says as they'll never go to play there no more.[28]

You can see what is happening. Young people have got together somewhere isolated, they all have a conscience about whatever it is they are doing that Sunday morning, and it only takes the slightest trigger to set them running. At a time when they were more relaxed, the dog would have been just a dog, the bird a bird. But instead it becomes the Devil, and also an opportunity to break up the gathering without anyone having to come over as a spoilsport and say to the rest that they really shouldn't be doing this.

A Trick at Cards

If that was true of comparatively innocuous pastimes such as cricket or dancing on the green, it was much more so when the company had assembled for gambling. Stories where the Devil appears among a company of card-players are found more often than any other traditions about interrupted sports. They are also a shade darker than the rest, for the Devil appears not to break up the event, but as a tempter. He joins in, confirming the players in their wicked ways and perhaps leading them on to worse; only a lucky chance frustrates his ambitions.

At Shaftesbury there used to be a regular card school in an old barn down French Mill Lane, where young men would sneak in, one at a time, on Sundays. Then one weekend, after they had all started their game, a dignified old gentleman showed his head round the door, and although this put them into a bit of a flurry, the stranger soon turned out to be excellent company. Someone dusted down a chair and he joined them at the table, looking at the cards – and the company – with a practised eye; soon he was playing a winning hand. All the other players were getting a bit flustered, and the lad sitting opposite the strange gentleman dropped one of his cards and had to get down under the table to look for it. He found the card easily enough, but he also found that the gentleman was wearing a fine pair of black boots, and that one of those boots was shaped for no human foot. Standing up, he blurted out what he had seen. There was a general run for the door, and that was the end of Sunday gambling down French Mill Lane.[29]

Such is the tale, told at many places across the country with nothing altered but the locale; it is also popular in Ireland, Denmark and Finland.[30] Sometimes tellers will introduce aberrant motifs or, to be more blunt about it, get the story wrong. In Manchester the detail that reveals the stranger's identity is a club foot, not a cloven one; at Topsham on the Devon coast, the story proceeds on the regular lines down to the point where a player stoops to pick up his card, and then the Devil tries to seize him; at Woodcutts, another Dorset village not far from Shaftesbury, the story has got fused with the Longbridge Deverill type, and the card-players are disturbed at their game by a monstrous black greyhound with eyes as large as saucers, which runs across the room and vanishes on the other side.[31]

The Woodcutts boys had met at the Old Priory, a derelict place well away from suspicious eyes. These stories are often set in some spooky or seedy building, down the alleys that more reputable citizens avoid. The Devil walks in the fringelands: houses on the verge of ruin, pubs on the edge of the law, places where no one goes unless their motives are questionable. Mills, for some reason, seem to have had a shady reputation. At Shaftesbury, the card-players had chosen the lane leading to French Mill; in Eskdale, the story is set at Cock Mill, a secluded haven for drinking, cockfighting and worse; at Botallack, near St Just, workers at the nearby mine met for gambling in an old tin-stamping mill above a cleft in the rocks known as Stamps an Jowl Zawn. *Zawn* is Cornish for a chasm, and 'Stamps an Jowl' means 'tin-stamps of the Devil', so the story must go back to a time when Cornish was still generally understood, which even in this western region of Penwith would have been before 1700.[32]

Whereas the Devil who interrupts nut-gatherers and blackberry-pickers is all too visibly an evil spirit, in these card-player stories he makes an appearance in friendly shape and is unmasked only accidentally. In fact all Devil traditions fall into two classes: those in which he enters the story frankly as himself, whether he is building bridges, throwing stones, or being summoned or laid by more or less skilful magicians; and those in which he comes on stage disguised as a labourer, a lover or a gentleman. The straightforward Devil belongs with traditions of giants, ogres and dreadful phantoms, but when the Devil is in disguise, he acts more like a fairy or a ghost: these stories are all about something from outside the human world being taken for human, up until the moment of discovery. For these stories to work, the teller must introduce, and the audience must be primed to recognize, a sign that reveals the outsider's true identity. The phantom hitchhiker shivers and complains of perpetual cold, the fairy slips out of church before service is concluded, the werewolf laughs and shows his teeth, and the Devil reveals a cloven foot.[33]

Hang on, you might think; is that the only thing that marks him out? It's not as if the Devil has been overlooked in the history of Western art, and even if we stick to representations made after about 1600, the period when our cycles of folk tales about the Devil took on their present character, we can be pretty confident that he's got horns and a tail. I suppose a long riding coat would cover the tail, but what about the Devil's head? He's sitting opposite the other card-players, they're watching his every facial expression with the trained eye of expert gamblers, and they don't notice that their new friend is sporting a pair of horns?

As so often, asking a silly question can unlock important answers. First, there are some tales in which the Devil is identified, in what is called the criterion motif, by his horns: these are not straightforward legends but what we have called false-Devil stories. At Mugginton near Belper there lived a hard-drinking farmer, a brute of a man who cared nothing for his wife or his family or his duties to God, provided only that his cup was kept full. One night when he was already pretty well tanked up, the drink ran out, and though he stormed and raged, not a drop more was to be found in the house. 'Saddle the horse,' he shouted, 'I'll be off somewhere where they know better how to entertain a man.' 'Oh, do not go,' pleads his wife, 'the night is dark, the storm will break, our old horse is sick and cannot run.' 'Damn the horse!' cries the man, 'I shall ride if it means bridling the Devil himself!', and he stumbles into the rain, a halter in his hand. Out in the yard, a black shape is waiting near the door. He grabs it by the neck and throws the bridle over it, and just at that moment a flash of lightning breaks across the sky and reveals – horns. Sobered by the shock, possibly also by the rain, the farmer staggers back into the house, slumps in a chair and thinks about what the lightning showed, sees what he has become mirrored in his terrified wife's eyes. He turned his life around and made a vow to leave off drink and take up prayer, and nothing changed his mind, not even the discovery next morning of their milk cow standing in the yard with a bridle dangling crooked off her horns. After he died the farmhouse became a chapel, and Halter Devil Chapel it remains to this day.[34]

So yes, there are circumstances in which the Devil can be told by his horns. But stories have structures, even as simple a moral story as the Devil and the card-players, and it is the structure that determines the plot. Think back to the pivotal moment at which the player opposite drops his card. Above the table, everything is going fine: the strange arrival is a gentleman. Below the table line, truth is revealed: the apparent gentleman is a beast. There is an above-and-below patterning here, just as in the stories about building a bridge there was a here-and-beyond patterning. Split anything into an upper and lower half, and we will link the up with reason and control, the down with passion and appetite. However clever the Devil may seem above board when he is playing a hand of cards, his real lower motives are hunger and lust for souls. It's the bit below his trousers that betrays him.

9

TO CHASE FOREVER: THE DEVIL IS A HUNTSMAN, AND SOULS ARE HIS PREY

On bleak and barren landscapes, night-wanderers feared to meet the Devil with his pack of hounds; or at least they said they did, although stories of the demon huntsman were told much more readily after the moorlands had been opened up to tourism. Wicked souls on the run sheltered from the demonic pack in ruined chapels, while beleaguered travellers escaped the hunt by falling to their knees in prayer. At the root of these local stories lay a much wider belief in spectral dogs who filled the air with their ominous howling, but this was worked up into a cycle about the Devil by adaptions from other times and cultures – medieval sermon stories and the Germanic lore of the Wild Huntsman. It was a gift to storytellers, this symbolic unease called up by the idea of a supernatural hunt, and if they were more creative than traditional in exploiting it, the results have nevertheless become part of today's Devil lore.

Black Shadows on the Moor

The village of Roche sprawls at the foot of a metalliferous ridge that brought prosperity in the days when mines were everywhere and every second Cornishman was a miner. It is still big enough to have outskirts, and as you walk south through them you come to the oldest part, where the church of St Gomonda is ringed by a wall of granite blocks. Facing it stands the war memorial, a Celtic cross of native granite, and down the road a pyramid of granite raised in order to mark the millennium and show that local masons had not lost their art. This is stone country.

Past the Rock Inn you walk beside the playground of the Rock School, opposite Cornish hedges splashed red with fox-gloves, and on the edge of town a kissing gate turns off the road and takes you to the chief sight of the place. A great beetling block of granite, Roche Rock stands out even in this land of rocks. Its jagged outline culminates in the peaked roof of a chapel that was built on the crest to be dedicated to St Michael, in days when every craggy summit was a potential shrine to the archangel. We are about halfway between St Michael's Mount in the bay of Penzance and Brentor on the edge of Dartmoor, another outcrop where, as we saw, the construction of St Michael's Church pitted its patron against his old adversary the fallen angel.

Approaching, you pass great upright slabs, like sentries with nothing to guard, where families picnic in the grassy lap between boulders. The teenagers, keen to get away from tame options, have clambered onto the crest itself. Originally the chapel hermit must have scrambled up here, one handhold at a time; perhaps he never came down until relieved from duty by the heavenly call. Now you can ascend and descend by a metal ladder, climbing up into the one-room cell that he wedged between the peaks. A doorway still frames the steps he cut in the living rock, every crack stuffed with herb robert and fern, leading up to the chapel over the cell. From the highest ground you look out over the road and the village, green fields and, dark on the furthest northeast horizon, the wastelands of Bodmin Moor.

If you were to edge suicidally round the gable wall of the chapel, you would see the last remains of tracery where the east window stood, and below it the hole where the spirit of John Tregeagle found refuge when he was being pursued by the demon

Roche Rock.

hunt. They were gaining on him as he raced across the moor, and this one solitary building was his only refuge: it was a holy place and the infernal pack would never be able to harm him there. Thunder boomed in the sky, louder than the crack of the Devil's whip, while sheets of icy rain swept across the ground, but Tregeagle sprinted to the chapel with the desperation of the damned. Frantically he clambered round until he found a gap below the window and thrust himself in. The gap was small while Tregeagle was a well-built ghost, and only his head and shoulders would fit through, but they at least were safe. Meanwhile his hinder parts were exposed to the storm and to the hounds of Hell, which being spirit dogs could rip into his spirit flesh, and did so with gusto. Tregeagle screamed in agony, roaring so loud that the people of Roche woke frightened from their slumbers and wondered what horrors were being perpetrated on the lonely moor.[1] And there for the moment we must leave him, for a long back-story needs to be explained.

John Tregeagle – the name is pronounced, and sometimes spelt, Tregagle – lived at the old house of Trevorder on the edge of hills above the River Camel, south of Egloshayle. Like many of the lesser Cornish gentry, he managed his own estate while acting as steward for richer neighbours, gathering rents and seeing to legal business. This was a job that called for probity, trust-worthiness and a reputation for honest dealing, none of which were found in Tregeagle. In fact his dealings were so crooked that he was rumoured to have entered into a contract with the Devil by which all his wishes would be gratified for a certain number of years, in return for the usual price.

Tregeagle's wicked stewardship did not come to an end with his death. There was some legal business – it involved deeds or debts or sureties, the storytellers cannot agree which – which he had left in such deliberate obscurity that it occasioned a long lawsuit between the parties. At length the litigants came into court in Bodmin, where their suit was heard at length but without success, the wily old steward having been careful never to hand over money before witnesses, in case he should later want to deny what he had done. The dispute was so intricate that the counsel for the defence stamped his foot and cried, 'If no-one but Tregeagle saw the money paid, then let Tregeagle appear and declare it in court!'

> By the time the words were well out of his mouth, the enraged spirit stood before 'im, sayin' – 'Thee has found it easy to bring me here, but thee wilst find it harder to put me away agen'; and the enraged Tregeagle wud ha' torn the lawyer limb from limb, if he hadn't snatched a little child from a woman's arms and held it in his own.[2]

Like the Devil, Tregeagle cannot touch an innocent child. He is a strange compound of damned soul and demon, though this did not seem unnatural to the storytellers who assumed that, like migrants to another country, souls would soon take on the character of the community where they dwelt. The dead in Heaven were to all intents and purposes angels, while a soul from Hell 'was just the same as a devil, from bein' with them so long'.

So the lawyer found himself in great peril, but, brandishing that sinless babe in front of him, he drove Tregeagle's ghost from row to row until he had finally got him trapped in a corner. Everyone else had fled the court, apart from the judge, who couldn't get down from the bench, and the young mother, who wanted her baby back. The silence was broken when a set of parsons broke in, having heard what was going on and eager to be at their spiritual work, binding Tregeagle to some task at which he might labour endlessly and never come to an end. Finally they agreed to send him to Dozmary Pool in the heart of Bodmin Moor, and there he remains, fruitlessly trying to empty out its waters using only a limpet shell, and that with a hole in the middle.

This was probably the core of the Tregeagle story. The events take place in a small circuit of country: Bodmin, the market town, is a few miles from Trevorder, and Dozmary, although it lies on the distant moor, was familiar as the kind of wild, lonely place where a ghost might be sent away from human contact. Baffled by his lack of success, he could howl as much as he liked and not be heard by anyone except a few travellers in the waste. 'To roar like Tregeagle' was proverbial, and the phrase did more than reinforce the original story: once it was accepted that any fierce natural noise could be interpreted as Tregeagle's cries, his sufferings would be repeated wherever the background sound effects were appropriate. The wailing of the wind around the outcrop at Roche probably acted as a stimulus for a new episode in which he escapes from Dozmary Pool. This is stitched into the story by a slight alteration in the purpose of exorcism: it seems that when they bound him to labour there, the parsons had meant not just to get him out of the way, but to save him from Hell. So long as he remained in suspense, trying to achieve what could never be done, he was safe from the final judgement. The Devil prowled the moor, his pack forever on the leash, hoping that Tregeagle would down tools and run away from his unfulfilled, in-between state. One foul night of sleet and storm, he did just that, with the consequences we saw above.

Often the proverbial roar of Tregeagle was identified with the sound of the sea. Old men in the Land's End district would stroll out last thing at night to check the weather, and come back saying, 'Tregeagle is roaring, we shall have northerly wind tomorrow.' The expression helped anchor a new version of the legend, telling how, after being rescued from his discomfort at Roche Rock, Tregeagle was set to weave ropes of sand on Gwenvor beach, where still he screams in frustration every time a north wind blows down to scatter the half-finished work.[3] In the longest version of his cycle, the ghost is exorcized from Roche to Padstow, from Padstow to Helston, and finally from Helston to Land's End. No longer confined to one local legend, he has become a pan-Cornish spectre, his stormy bellowing heard everywhere along the coast.[4]

Only in one episode, the flight to Roche, is Tregeagle pursued by the Devil with a pack of hounds; everywhere else he was kept to his tasks by nothing more dreadful than prayer. As described by native storytellers, this was a very practical business; it sounds more like service magic than holy exorcism when the vicar of St Breward claims £300 for laying the ghost (he was charging extra, as this was a particularly fiendish one). Folklorists with literary aspirations ignored the hint of cash in hand, and had him banished instead by figures from local history such as St Petroc. When the Devil makes his appearance, he seems to have been brought in from another set of beliefs altogether. But that was not surprising, since Dozmary Pool was on Bodmin Moor, and everyone knew that the moor was haunted by a demon huntsman.

Pursued by the Hounds of Hell

In the mid-nineteenth century there were stories of men who had met the Devil and his dandy dogs on this wasteland. I do not know what a dandy dog might be, although lexically he fits into a pattern of diabolical alliteration. Midnight is the Devil's dancing hour, and any unnaturally flat field his dancing ground; a shady wood can be the Devil's dressing room; dragonflies are the Devil's darning needles.[5] We have already met with Devil's Dykes and Devil's Dens.

Whatever breed they may have been, the dandy dogs were not a welcome sight. 'They are most commonly seen by those who are out at night on wicked errands, and woe betide the wretch who crosses their path.' It was on such a night of storm and wind that a man battled up the slopes of the Bodmin Moor, anxious to get home by the straightest route. By lining up the tors on the horizon he could tell that he was about halfway when, faintly at first, he heard behind him the baying of hounds. Home was still 3 or 4 miles away, with no other shelter visible on the barren waste. He wrapped his coat tight around him and walked faster, but he could hear the drawn-out yelps of the hounds clearly now, and something else that put a chill in his heart, the call of the huntsman whooping them on. Then there came a pause in the calling of that terrible voice, followed almost at once by the clear tones of the halloo, the cry of a master who has his quarry in sight. There was no escaping them, nowhere to run to. Turning round, the man saw the hounds cresting the slopes of the hill behind him. They had spread out over the dark surface of the moor, each dog a jet-black outline with pinpoints of fire where its head should be, yelping and calling to each other as if they had intelligence. Behind them, tall and indistinct in the blackness, he could see the red eyes of the hunter beneath an angry horned brow. This was the end, then. The man sank to his knees – if these were to

Bodmin Moor.

be his last moments he would spend them well – and he poured out a strange mixture of everything he had ever heard in church or chapel. The yelping of the hounds turned to a long-drawn-out, dismal howl; they stood at bay, keeping their distance from the kneeling man; and the hunter came slowly to the fore, rested for a moment on his long hunting pole, and said in a dry, rasping voice '*Bo shrove!*' And at once he and the demon dogs swept away to chase further over the moor, leaving the man behind.[6]

Bo shrove, says the storyteller, are words from the old language which mean 'the boy prays'. Was this 'old language' meant to be Cornish? It isn't: it's an attempt at Middle English, not surprising since the story was told in Polperro in the eastern part of Cornwall, where English had been dominant since about 1400. This detail must have been picked up from some display of learning, perhaps a Lenten sermon explaining the meaning of the phrase Shrove Tuesday. As so often, a local legend has come to us through the voice of an intermediary who gave it an erudite gloss.

But it was a real migratory legend, with parallels elsewhere. A Welsh story of the *cwn Annwn*, the hounds of Hell, is an almost exact match, if we replace the bleak slopes of Bodmin Moor with the ridge of Cefn Caer Euni running northeast from Bala. As before, the hounds appear to someone who has been out on no good business; as before, the sound of dogs is heard getting gradually nearer, they are seen to be accompanied by a black horned huntsman, the hounds are about to rush on their wretched prey, and he is saved at the last moment – in the Welsh tradition, by pulling a cross from his pocket and showing it to the pack, which scatters in all directions.[7]

There is something medieval about that cross; you would expect a Protestant recension to emphasize the power of the Word, as the Cornish version does, and not the apotropaic power of a sacred object. Luckily we have some first-hand evidence of medieval devils engaged in hunting, which comes, like the Bala story, from Wales. In the twelfth century Meilyr of Caerleon had a reputation as a prophet, gained the hard way. One spring he had been out walking in the countryside when he saw a girl whom he had long had an eye on. Now that they had a chance to meet, one thing led to another and then – then, just before the critical moment, she changed into a frightful thing of the woods, rough and hairy all over. Meilyr looked down at her face, or snout, and completely lost his wits. Eventually he was taken to St David's, where the quiet and prayer brought him back to his senses, but he didn't forget his companions in the other world and used to chat with them when they called by, asking if they knew anything that was going to happen soon. There is something of the fairy about these spirits, and you wonder whether Meilyr's story, in other hands, would have come closer to that of Thomas the Rhymer, who had a similar unsettling experience with the queen of Elfland, and was gifted with the tongue that could never lie. The spirits that appeared at St David's, however, were definitely supposed to be demons, and 'they would appear in the form of huntsmen, with horns hanging round their necks, but it was human souls which they were pursuing, not animals or wild beasts.'[8]

There is a fine demon huntsman in the margins of the fourteenth-century Taymouth Hours. He is running lightly over the waste, wings spread wide, with two stocky greyhounds bounding before him; they pursue three naked, stumbling souls who look as if they have been chased over that terrible moor where 'the whinnies shall prick thee to the bare bane.' In the next scene, the souls have fallen and the dogs are rending them.[9] But this is not, even in the imagination, a picture of what you might see in this world. The souls are in Hell, where the endless chase is one of their torments, as it is in Dante, where squanderers are pulled down by black bitches in the Wood of the Suicides.[10]

As a rule devils do not appear as hunters in medieval art – or in medieval life, either, apart from one celebrated episode in 1127 when the deer park of Peterborough was haunted by black riders. They were tall in the saddle, very fierce to see, some of them on horseback and others riding goats; their hounds were black, too, all but their eyes, which shone bright and wild. The monks of Peterborough Abbey could not sleep at night for the noise of those black things, which whooped and cried and blew loud blasts on their horns.[11] The hunt first rode on 6 February, when the unpopular Henry of Poitou was appointed abbot, and it continued, night after night, all through Lent. Though their sleep was disturbed, the monks clearly felt that these black riders had their heart in the right place, and would soon sling their new abbot over a billy goat's saddle and carry him off to his rightful place. No such luck: the damnable Henry remained in office for a further five years.

These demon huntsmen had their place in visions and sermon stories but they were not typical of medieval devils. It seems improbable that such a minor tradition should have survived down to the nineteenth century in Wales and Cornwall. More likely, the black huntsman of Bodmin Moor was a fresh imaginative construction out of a much more widespread belief – that phantom dogs, sounding just like a pack of hounds, could be heard at night, a presage of death or ill-fortune.

This was how most Welsh people thought about the *cwn Annwn*. Annwn is an ambiguous word, in some contexts clearly referring to Hell but just as often indicating a morally ambivalent otherworld. So the dogs may in fact be fairy dogs, and at their earliest appearance, in the First Branch of the Mabinogi, they are simply a pack of nobleman's hounds, chasing a stag in the woods, except that they belong to the otherworldly prince Arawn and have the fairy coloration of white with red ears. By the eighteenth century they had acquired a much more ghostly character, and their terrible howling preceded someone's death. They were heard passing through the fields, usually predicting the route that a funeral would follow. From their alternative name of *cwn wybir*, dogs of the sky, they were evidently thought to be chasing overhead and not at ground level.[12]

Beliefs about sky hounds are also found in England, where the pack are usually known as Gabriel ratchets or Gabriel hounds. Although the name is sometimes corrupted to gabble-ratchet, the forms in 'Gabriel' are older, first appearing in a fifteenth-century wordbook, where the phrase is bizarrely translated as 'chameleon'. This sounds like the end result of a string of misunderstandings and we shall probably never know what was originally meant. By the seventeenth century they were definitely thought to be spiritual creatures passing overhead with a baying cry. The Victorians recorded variations on the theme in Durham, the West Riding, Lancashire, Derbyshire and Staffordshire: roughly the length of the Pennine chain.[13] There seems to be some connection between these beliefs and mountainous country.

Some people spoke of them literally as dogs, yelping like a litter of puppies; some as a supernatural bird which made an ominous gabbling sound; others as a natural phenomenon, wild geese or swans calling to each other in their flight. There were more exotic explanations. In Durham they were monstrous human-headed dogs, and in the district around Leeds they were supposed to be the souls of unbaptized babies, who were not fit for Heaven but could not in all charity be consigned to Hell. Like Tregeagle and Mike Mills they were lost forever in a crack between the worlds, neither saved nor damned.

There were similar beliefs in Devon, although here the unbaptized souls were sometimes the quarry instead of the dogs themselves.[14] In the north part of the county, the pack were known as the hounds of the heath, Yeth Hounds in Devon pronunciation; in the south, as Wish Hounds, from the dialect word *wisht*, earlier *ill-wished*, which from its original meaning of 'cursed by a witch and wasting away' had developed senses that ranged from 'lean and grotesque' to 'spooky'. Like the *cwn wybir* and the Gabriel ratchets, the Wish/Yeth hounds were typically heard overhead baying or yelping, but this was not all that was audible to the believing ear. At Mary Tavy on the western edge of Dartmoor, Roger Burn was working in the fields in 1850 when he heard the baying of hounds accompanied by the shouts of the huntsman, the blowing of a horn and the crack of a whip. 'How could I be mistaken?', he said afterwards. 'Why, I heard the very smacking of his whip.'[15] Where there is a hunt, people will imagine a huntsman: and if the hunt pursues souls and forecasts death, it's a pretty safe bet who that huntsman will be. Once again we find the Devil stepping into a tradition that had previously existed without him.

Death and the Maiden

In other accounts the hellhounds take second place, and the Devil is at the centre of the story. Between Okehampton and Tavistock lies a low bleak hill, once an open heath. Though a good road lay over it, people would cross Heathfield as fast as they could, and only in the hours of daylight, for queer stories were told about what could be seen there at night. A Tavistock woman had collected some provisions to be sold at Okehampton market and went to bed early, planning to rise first thing the next morning; in the excitement she got up shortly before midnight, and set out, with two stout panniers on either side of her horse, and a heavy cloak to keep out the winter chill. She was jogging along over the heath when she heard the distant cry of hounds and soon after saw a hare running pell-mell towards her. She waited for it to pass by, but the hare seemed suddenly to lose its fear; it leapt up onto a stone bank and began to twist and turn around. The old woman, who had not forgotten the poaching escapades of her young days, thought this was too good an opportunity to miss, so, deftly catching the animal behind its head, she popped it into one of her pannier baskets and banged down the wicker lid.

Meanwhile the hounds were calling, louder and more insistent, and looking across the waste she saw them getting close. These were no ordinary pack; the horns on their heads and the flames in their eyes told her that much, and besides, there was a burning smell when they whisked their phosphorescent tails. But some people have a way with dogs, and the old woman let them scurry and sniff about her without alarm. She was more concerned by the sight of the huntsman, who seemed dark even in that midnight darkness. The little light that shone from the red eyes of the hounds showed horns under his cap and a strange-shaped leg in the saddle. He pulled his horse up besides her, and asked 'Where is the hare?' His sulphurous breath frosted in the winter air, as the woman answered, with the fluency of the habitual liar, 'Ah, *that* hare. Her were running fast, weren't she? Happen her'd be halfway to Holyeat by now. Lydford, maybe.' And hearing this, the dark huntsman spurred on his horse and raced away into the dark.

Got out of that one well, thinks the woman, as she soothes her horse and rides him downhill, away from the haunted waste. But next thing she knows, the pannier basket at her back is creaking and rocking, and as she stops to tie it down, the lid pops open and out comes a beautiful lady all in white, who gets down off the pannier with that dignity which comes naturally to all ladies, even those who have recently been a hare. That was my fate, she says, because of certain things which – oh never mind what I did, but I was condemned to be chased night after night, and when I was caught: well, I won't tell you. Not pleasant. But it was also foretold that if ever once I got behind their tails, the torment should be at an end, and now through your kindness my hardships are over, and I cannot thank you enough. You will have cause to remember me, for from this day your hens shall all lay two eggs where before they laid one, and your cows give twice as much milk, and your husband contradict you half as often in anything you say. Goodbye![16]

So the tale was told by Mary Colling of Tavistock, one of many stories that she shared with her friend and employer Anna Bray. Unlike most English local legends, it is a one-off: nothing quite like it appears in the county collections of folk tales.[17] But six centuries earlier, and far away in the Rhineland, we find a story that is clearly a distant cousin of the one that Mary Colling knew.

A knight was riding homewards down a lonely road. It was well before dawn, but he could see his way clearly in the moonlight. Suddenly he heard the distant sound of a woman screaming. Appalled, he reined in his horse and soon saw her running pell-mell towards him, all in white. The woman snatched at his arm and begged for protection; the knight leapt down from the horse, pulled out his sword and swore that he would save her, come what may. And then he heard the echoes of a hunting horn, louder and fiercer than any he had ever known, and soon afterwards the baying of hounds. The woman trembled terribly and would have returned to her flight, but the knight would not abandon her. Because her hair was long and loose, he clutched a handful and twisted it round his left arm, with his sword at the ready in his right. But he was not prepared for what he saw next – the infernal huntsman. Shuddering, he stood his ground, but the sight was too much for the woman, who screamed and twisted, and finally in an agony of fear tore her hair out by the roots and fled once more. The huntsman instantly set off after her, and the hounds after him. Soon the knight saw them return. She was slung over the saddle of the dark rider, her bruised feet trailing on one side, her bleeding head on the other; so they rode away, getting smaller and smaller in the moonlight. The knight passed on, morning came, and he was at the door of his own hall. Servants came out to greet him and take his horse away, and he told them what he had seen, and showed them the handful of bloody hair. 'We do not know, we cannot say,' they muttered. 'We only know that last night, between moonrise and morn, the priest's woman died.' 'Take me where she is,' said the knight, and they took him to her, stretched out all in white, her hair long and loose around her; and it was the same as the hair in his hand, and there was a bare bloody patch on her crown.[18]

So we read in the compendium of miracles by the Cistercian chronicler Caesarius of Heisterbach. He was probably better as a monk than a storyteller: at all events he bungles the plot by introducing a second identification motif which I've left out – the beautiful shoes of which the woman had been so proud, which were buried with her at special request, and in which she after-wards runs in the moonlight. You don't need the hair *and* the shoes; I suspect that he had heard two separate versions, one for each, and absent-mindedly spliced them together. I'd also bet that, although this is very much a sermon-story with a traditional moral, it was first told by lay parishioners and not by monks. The clue lies in the revelation that the damned fugitive is the priest's mistress. It is hard, if you come from any religious tradition but the Catholic, to understand the visceral loathing felt by the village faithful for a woman who slept with a priest. It was not just that she was a partner in his sin: she was corrupting everything the priest did, polluting the celibate power that should protect the village against illness and darkness. In real life, she got some protection through her special status, but after death she was fair game for vindictive stories, just like a wicked steward or an unjust magistrate.

They take a kinder view in Anglican Tavistock; the lady in white gets away, and though she still confesses to some nameless past crime, at the end she seems something of a good fairy, or at least a beneficent witch, not a screaming ghost. But the frame of the two stories is identical: lonely road, traveller at night, figure running towards them, the hunt seen with the huntsman, and then the attempted rescue (successful or otherwise). To fill in the gaps, we can turn to Scotland, which has two similar stories in which the fugitive is a warlock or hag, running in terror to escape the black horseman, but seen at last as a limp body thrown across his saddle, just as in the thirteenth-century version.[19] The Scots take their Deil seriously, and do not provide happy endings for the damned.

But even when descent and variation can be traced from the medieval Rhineland to nineteenth-century Britain, the origin of these stories remains doubtful. As we saw earlier, hunting was not the usual way that medieval people imagined devils and their pursuit of souls. But from the thirteenth century stories abounded in the German-speaking world about a supernatural figure – otherworldly, not diabolical – who was a hunter, with wild maidens, forest fairies or elf-women as his quarry. He goes under different names in different stories – Fasolt, Orkîse or simply *der Wilder Jäger*, the wild huntsman.[20] Despite this variation, the tradition had consistent themes and survived into modern times, extending into Denmark and the Netherlands. Throughout this region, the same group of stories is told again and again about the hunter and his pursuit of the pitiful little moss-wives, who beg some midnight traveller to protect them but are taken in the end. It is easy to see how a Christian moralist could expand on this theme, especially if they thought that all fairy beings were really disguised devils anyway.

But was the *Wilde Jagd* ever known in England? The closest parallels come from the barren heights of Dartmoor. We have seen how the supernatural pack of hounds, elsewhere a purely auditory phenomenon and consisting only of yelping dogs, was provided in this region with a matching huntsman whose whip could be heard cracking loudly above the tumult. One story goes further, and describes his appearance.

> A person who was passing at night over the moors above Widecombe, heard them sweep through the valley below him with a great cry and shouting; and when he reached the highest point of the hill, he saw them pass by, with the Master behind – a dark gigantic figure, carrying a long hunting pole at his back, and with a horn slung round his neck. When they reached the ancient earthwork of Hembury Fort – which rises on a high wooded hill above the Dart – the Master blew a great blast upon his horn, and the whole company sank into the earth.[21]

Hunting poles were necessary equipment for the chase in this part of the world, used to vault over any stream too wide to be jumped; we have already seen one being carried by the Devil on Bodmin Moor. The supernatural takes its cue from local practice, so that the fiend or phantom runs after his hounds on foot, as human hunters must in this landscape of mire and clitter where it would be suicidal to ride to hounds. This is quite different from the German legends, in which the huntsman is always mounted and seen pounding overhead through the sky, not running behind his pack down some overgrown Devon lane. But there is one story that seems to link the two traditions.

A Share in the Game

A farmer had been out west of the moor, and was riding back through Two Bridges. He had done well in his buying and selling: most of the money was stashed away in his pocket, but enough had been left for drinks at the Saracen's Head, with a final chaser to protect him against the cold night air. Setting out at last, he was a little unsteady, but the horse was sober, and after all it was the horse that was doing the walking. They took the road as far as Postbridge and then struck out north over barren ground. Thick blankets of fog blew over the moor, parted every now and then by gusts of wind that let the moon shine uninterrupted over the bleak terrain. The path dipped to cross a little stream and then rose up the slope beyond, heading for a broken ring of old grey stones. The farmer had been half-asleep, just about balanced on his sturdy horse, when he was startled into wakefulness by the sound of a hunting horn. No huntsman should have been out in such a place, at such an hour. A moment later his suspicions were confirmed when the hounds of the moor swept past him, swift, undeviating, silent. And after them came their black master.

It was a sight that would have made a softer man, or a soberer one, fall from his horse in terror, but moorland farmers are a tough breed, and this one had been well warmed inside, so he just leaned back in the saddle and hailed his fellow traveller. 'Been hunting, have 'ee? Didst kill?' The huntsman turned to him, his face shadowed in the moonlight, and soft as the whispering wind said, 'Yes – take that!' Tossing a ragged game bag into the farmer's lap, the

Two Bridges, Dartmoor.

hunter turned and sped behind his pack into darkness and distance. Well, there's a turn-up for the books, thinks the farmer. Wonder what it is. Bigger than a hare, it is, smaller than a deer, and drat this fog, it's come down again and I can't see a thing in front of me.

Before long the horse plods downhill, from heather to furze, from furze to windswept trees, and at last to the farmer's own front door, where his household are waiting for his homecoming. 'Bring us a light,' he shouts, 'hold it high, 'cause I want you to look at something. Look at *this*,' he says, thrusting his hand into the tattered bag, and pulling out into the unpitying light – a baby. His own child, dead and cold.[22]

Such is the story as it was passed down by the great Devon folklorist Sabine Baring-Gould. Like the Tavistock story it is a one-off, never recorded again in this area, and with no parallels elsewhere in England. However, Baring-Gould was helpful enough to provide his sources. He was told the story by a lady from Dartmouth; she heard it from her father, George Bidder, who said he remembered hearing it in the 1810s, when he was a boy and used to hang around the forge at Moretonhampstead, listening to the blacksmith's tales. So we can take the tale back some two generations before it was written down, but it is not at all certain that the story we read on the page is what the blacksmith told young George. Bidder had left the village by the time he was a teenager, got himself an education and made a living first as an engineer and then as a parliamentary witness on railway companies before retiring to Devon.

So this is a third-hand story, and even its written versions are inconsistent: though one of them begins, as we have seen, with the farmer at Two Bridges, the other places the beginning of his journey at Widecombe, 7 miles to the east. But some confusion was natural when the second and third tellers of the tale were no longer living on the moor. Both they and the fourth link in the chain, Baring-Gould himself, came from the Victorian middle classes, and familiarity with literature would explain details such as the stone circle through which the black hounds run, a very Gothic touch.

If those grey Druid stones sound like a romantic embellishment, then so does the parting of the clouds to reveal the moon, famously brought into play in Bürger's *Lenore*. Might the story itself owe something to familiarity with books? The *Wilde Jagd* was a popular theme in German Romanticism, and here we often find the motif by which a bold or rash or drunken peasant shouts 'Hunter, what sport?' and in return is flung – something. Usually it turns out to be rotten meat, or the dismembered quarters of one of the little moss-wives. That still leaves out the plot development by which the quarry proves to be the rash man's own son. It is true that, according to an earlier tradition, the Wish Hounds were supposed to be hunting the souls of unbaptized children. But the structure of the story, with its father on a haunted midnight ride that will lead to a dreadful discovery, has more than a hint of German literature, especially Goethe's poem *Erlkönig*, written in 1782. Widely read as a poem, it was made famous when set to music by Schubert in 1815, with its simple and terrible ending: *das Kind war tot*, the child was dead.

It looks as if the original tale told by the blacksmith of Moretonhampstead, whatever it was, has been modified so much by literature that it now represents an outlier of German tradition in southwestern England. As for the other one-off story, about the old woman heading to market over Heathfield and her rescue of the lady in white, I am inclined to suspect an Irish origin, because it was originally a Catholic sermon story, and it seems much more likely that the tale would survive in a region which kept up the tradition of Catholic preaching than that it could go underground for four hundred years in Protestant England. Certainly there were stories very close to Caesarius' monitory tale of the priest's mistress being told in nineteenth-century Ireland.[23]

Not that this in any way discounts the stories as folklore; they have long since been accepted by Devon people and are part of what everyone knows about the dark hunter. It's simply that at Tavistock and Two Bridges we are able, for once, to trace the migration of local legends in detail. Tale-types do not spread by themselves, like stains on a carpet: they are picked up and deliberately imitated by people who heard them in one place and think they would fit another, with a little modification to make them more gruesome (the child is dead), or less (the lady is saved). At the centre of the region where a migratory legend is popular, motifs are swapped to and fro by storytellers who are all close to each other, and their mutual influences are impossible to pick out. But on the outskirts we get a glimpse of who was imitating whom.

When Wordsworth writes

For overhead are sweeping Gabriel's Hounds
Doomed with their impious Lord, the flying Hart,
To chase for ever, on aerial grounds!

he is versifying something he had been told by Mitchell, the nightwatchman at Coleorton near Loughborough.[24] But the sounds that the old man heard on his rounds have been fused with a theme from Bürger, the German poet who made supernatural huntsmen into the stuff of literature. These hounds were heard in Derbyshire as well, where we are told that Gabriel was a gentleman condemned to follow his hounds every night in the sky until Doomsday, as a punishment for having hunted on Sunday.[25] Again this explanation of Gabriel's Hounds does not come direct from the folk; it appears in a novel of rural life, with a footnote that explains the idiomatic phrase by reference to the German legend. It looks as if the name of the Gabriel ratchets is native English, but their identification as the pack of a wicked hunter doomed to chase in the sky forever is a literary import. Stories about this sinner belong to Germany and France, where he is known as the *chasseur maudit*, the Cursed Huntsman. It is true that Ilmington in Warwickshire was haunted by a squire who insisted on hunting on Sundays, despite all warnings, until one day the earth swallowed him up, hounds and all, but he appeared as an ordinary, ground-level ghost.[26] In Cleveland the apparition was of aerial hounds, but they were explained without any story of blasphemy, as the pack of a gentleman

> who was so inordinately fond of the pleasures of the chase, and so jealous about the hounds who had ministered to them, that, on his deathbed, he gave orders they should all be killed and buried with him, that no-one else should benefit by them as he himself would no longer be able.[27]

Poor dogs! Someone should have got in touch with the RSPCA, but as that didn't exist then, they did the next best thing and consigned the perpetrator to a miserable afterlife. You can see from the scattered and inconsistent nature of these reports that

England is at the further limits of *chasseur maudit* traditions, just as it lies outside the heartland of the *Wilde Jagd*. There may be good historical reasons for this. In a thickly populated country, there wasn't much left to hunt by the eighteenth and nineteenth centuries, apart from foxes. And the setting of a fox hunt – the gallop over fence and field, the flushing of old Charlie out of some isolated spinney and his eventual fate with half the county looking on – relied on particular social relationships between gentry, labourers and the tenant farmers who formed the middle rank between them: not just the visible ritual of pinks and hunt breakfasts, but the backstage arrangements by which the Master squared up with the men whose gates and hedges had been broken. In a feudal setting, where there is no third class to buffer the peasantry from their lords, they are much more likely to consign the proud trampler of their fields to Hell.

In at the Kill

Significantly, one of the few English stories to link hunting with the Devil refers to a time when deer were the usual quarry, as they were on the Continent. Lushill House lies between Swindon and the meadows of the upper Thames, a rich landscape which still provided shelter and grazing for deer in the seventeenth century. The house was owned by one of the Parker family, a passionate hunter who had hung its walls with antlers of the great stags he had taken over the years, but there was one stag which he could never take. However swift the dogs, however tireless the huntsmen, it always outran the pack. One day Squire Parker swore a terrible oath that he would chase that elusive stag and not rest until he had its antlers in his hands. The next day dawned fair, and the hunt set out full of confidence. All the day the dogs cried loud as they swept through the hills, tumbled down into the Thames water and raced out once more through thicket and scrub.

One by one the hunting party fell away, broken by the endless chase, until at last there were only two riding to hounds: Parker himself and a strange companion who had joined the hunt at daybreak and now continued tireless as when he began, his eyes bright with the light of a pursuer who sees the quarry fall at last. They ran, and the stag ran before them; in its windings and turnings it had come at last in the fading light to Lushill House. On the lawns of his own demesne, Parker leapt from his horse in a last convulsive bound and grasped its antlers. And then all at once there was no stag, no hunt and no strange horseman; only a sheet of lightning rippling through the sky and thunder echoing like a belly-laugh. The next day the terrified servants stepped out onto the lawn and there lay Squire Parker, a pair of old antlers in his hand.[28]

Pity Squire Parker – his original offence, Sunday hunting perhaps or some other disregard of religion, has dropped out of the story altogether, and nothing is left but that strange chase. The idea of the hunter becoming the hunted is a natural twist to the story. It is there in Bürger's poem, though Wordsworth may have rejected the theme as a little too lurid. Others were less scrupulous. In Cornwall, a little to the west of Saltash lies the village of St Germans, with its priory church looking over the silted waters of the Tiddy. Among the ornaments of the church is a fourteenth-century misericord, a tilted seat with carvings under the ledge. This one shows a hunter; he is on foot, with his quarry (a hare, or something like it) hanging from a stick over his shoulder. In front are six small dogs, perhaps greyhounds, and behind two larger ones, perhaps mastiffs. They all look much the same but the carver was not interested in recording medieval dog breeds; if we believe the story, he has left a moral memorial to future ages. For this is an image of Dando the hunter.

The church had wide lands in those days, and Dando hunted them through and through. He cared little for property and nothing for people, as long as he ran down whatever he was pursuing; fences were broken and corn trampled flat before it could come to harvest; if they were on the scent of hart or hind, the dogs would run through the little tended plots of the cottagers, with the horses galloping after them until all was pounded into mud. So Dando was not a popular man. Curses trailed him as he ran, curses that were deeper than they were loud, for the poor have learnt to keep their anger silent. Not that Dando cared. He was a man who knew how to enjoy life in his own way, and if years of good living had left him a bit heavy in the saddle, while the exertions of the hunt seemed to need more hard drinking each day, well, these were pleasures in their own kind. He did not like being thwarted, and had long since disregarded the restraint that would have kept him from his favourite pastime on the Sabbath.

So it happened that one Sunday he set out with his companions, all as reckless of the day as himself, and it was a good day in its own way, with parcel after parcel of game sent back to hang in the larder at St Germans. It was late when at last he drew to a halt, pulling up his horse on a little hill above the Lynher, and calling for a drink. There was none – well, none apart from water, which wasn't what he had in mind – and Dando's face turned dark as he shouted, 'Drink! Where in Hell can I get a drink?'

A smartly dressed hunter dismounted and strolled over. He wasn't one of the usual crew; the lord of another estate, Dando supposed, come to see the fun. Smiling, the stranger held up a gilded flask and said, 'I have brought that drink at your request and you will find it warms you. Will you take it, friend? Will you drink it to the dregs?' – all of which sounded vaguely challenging, and Dando was too proud to resist a challenge. So he seized the flask and drank it down. Queer liquor to be sure. He had thought he could take his drink, but all at once his head was swimming and everything seemed far away. He looked down and there was that cocky fellow again, pulling a hare out of his game bag. 'That's mine,' he slurred, his voice suddenly out of control. The stranger looked him coolly in the eye: 'You are in my place now, everything is mine.' Dando swung a punch at him, but there was no strength in the hand that held the reins and he toppled from the saddle. The stranger picked up his corpulent body, as lightly as hunter ever lifted a quail or partridge, put one foot in the stirrup and swung himself and his human burden into the saddle. The black horse snorted and was off, followed by Dando's barking dogs, and not even the sparks that flew from its hooves could deter the angry pack from following their old master. They rode until they came to the river, where the horse made one smooth leap, coming down midstream in a sheet of flame. For a moment the waters boiled convulsively, and then there was nothing to be seen, neither rider nor horse nor dogs nor Dando himself. But men say that on a Sunday by the banks of the Lynher, the sound of hounds in chase can still be heard, and the distant horn of their master.[29]

So they tell the tale, or so at any rate it is told by Robert Hunt, the chronicler of Cornish legends. If we had more than one source,

The Lynher, St Germans.

it would be easier to know what mattered most in the original versions – Dando's drunkenness and gluttony, or his contempt for the common people, or just his infringement of Sunday's sacred rest. Hunt makes much of Dando's vices as a priest, and has him domineering over layfolk and taking advantage of the confessional to absolve faults like his own, but I doubt whether these were in the tale before he got hold of it. True, it's based on a carving in a medieval priory church, but that may not have meant much to nineteenth-century villagers, whereas Hunt seldom resisted the temptation to have a dig at the old church. He even introduces degenerate Catholic clergymen into the story of Tregeagle, which is pushing things when you consider that the historical steward died in 1680. Medieval settings for local legends are often suspect, as we have seen, and so are unusual names. 'Dando' was borrowed from the story of the dandy dogs, which had been published ten years earlier.

Cross-fertilization between these legends in the nineteenth-century local collections has obscured most of their original distinctiveness. The failure of the folklorists, which they regarded as their greatest success, was to treat all the tales as aspects of one single overarching story. Whether writing about hounds heard barking overhead, or the Devil hunting a soul, or the ghost of a landowner riding to hounds after his death, or a spectral figure who is neither ghost nor Devil, they never fail to tell you that these are aspects of the Wild Hunt. Originally this simply translated the *Wilde Jagd* of Germany and adjoining territories, and that really is a coherent tradition. It rides at midwinter, is heard passing overhead, must not be looked at or obeyed, shuns holy things, chases supernatural figures and so on; the details repeat, one here, one there, until we feel that behind the multiplicity there is one consistent imagination. But Victorian folklorists, coming from countries where this tradition was unknown anyway, used it as a catch-all term for dozens of quite different supernatural traditions involving dogs, riders, sounds overhead or maybe just a phantom coach.

They thought they had seized the secret of these legends, that they had discovered a single pagan origin for them all. In times so ancient that they were beyond written history, there was supposed to have been a single Wild Huntsman – Odin or someone like that – who rode through the skies with his hounds and warriors in a hunt for souls. Gradually this stem tradition had branched out into hundreds of variants: phantom armies, demon huntsmen, Gabriel ratchets, ghosts of the chase. But the conclusions are wrong because the theory is false. Folklore is not a tree but a lattice; stories are continually crossing over and exchanging motifs with each other, developing new variants or dying out, acquiring fresh heroes and forgetting old ones. Stories that were once sacred mysteries have become children's entertainments, and stories told for a joke have been made into foundational myth. Four thousand years ago the latticework of folklore was as complex as it is today, and in four thousand years' time it will be equally complex and unimaginably different, with no master clue to explain how it got from here to there.

The Devil is eternal, but the people who tell stories about him are creatures of time. Like no other creature, we can play games of the imagination with the facts of this world and the next. We can turn gold into leaves and leaves into gold; we can build and unbuild the everlasting hills; we can work the miracles that will save despair. We can punish the wickedness of this world beyond the grave; we can let the cleverness of the simple defeat the anger of the proud; we can change anything in our imagination. We can even imagine being better people than we are now, and perhaps that will rescue us from our own demons in the end.

REFERENCES

1 His Work Undone: The Devil's Ambitious Projects Fail

1 John Cary, *Cary's New and Correct English Atlas* (London, 1787), *s.l.* Sussex.
2 Thomas Yeakell and William Gardner's map of 1778–83 shows the hill fort as Poor Man's Walls.
3 William Hamper, 'The Devil's Dyke: A Sussex Legend', *Gentleman's Magazine*, LXXX(1) (1810), pp. 513–14.
4 John Aubrey, *Monumenta Britannica*, ed. Rodney Legg and John Fowles (Milborne Port, 1980), vol. II, pp. 923–4, and *The Natural History and Antiquities of Surrey* (London, 1718–19), vol. IV, p. 187. The *Monumenta* was compiled between 1663 and 1693, *Surrey* between 1673 and 1692.
5 Snorri Sturluson, *The Prose Edda*, trans. Jean Young (Berkeley, CA, 1954), pp. 66–7.
6 Martin Puhvel, 'The Legend of the Church-Building Troll in Northern Europe', *Folklore*, LXXII/4 (1961), pp. 567–83.
7 *The Elder Edda*, trans. Paul Taylor and W. H. Auden (London, 1969), pp. 79–83.
8 *The Family Memoirs of the Reverend William Stukeley*, ed. William Lukis (Durham, 1882–5), vol. III, p. 75; Margaret Gelling, *The Place-Names of Berkshire* (Cambridge, 1973–6), vol. I, p. 4; Albert Hugh Smith, *The Place-Names of the West Riding of Yorkshire* (Cambridge, 1961–3), vol. III, p. 63; Charles Henry Hartshorne, *Salopia antiqua* (London, 1841), p. 136.
9 Commonplace book of Richard Shanne, *c.* 1611, in BL Additional MS 38599 f. 98v, quoted in Adam Fox, *Oral and Literate Culture in England, 1500–1700* (Oxford, 2000), pp. 235–6.
10 'Vulgi enim fabellas, qui has *"Cacodaemonum sagittas"* vocant, quibus antiquas urbes confixerunt, libens omitto', William Camden,

Britannia (London, 1590), p. 566. 'Daemonum sagittas', in the earlier edition of 1586, p. 406.

11 Aubrey Burl, 'The Devil's Arrows, Boroughbridge, North Yorkshire', *Yorkshire Archaeological Journal*, LXIII (1991), pp. 1–24, at pp. 12–13 proposes a late seventeenth-century date for the legend, but this is about a hundred years out.

12 Jabez Allies, *The Antiquities and Folk-Lore of Worcestershire* (London, 1856), p. 306; Benjamin Gibbons, *Notes and Suggestions for a History of Kidderminster* (Kidderminster, 1859), pp. 54–5. Allies has only one pair of shoes rather than a sack.

13 George Griffith, *Going to Markets and Grammar Schools* (London, 1870), vol. I, pp. 194–209.

14 Charlotte Burne, *Shropshire Folk-Lore: A Sheaf of Gleanings* (London, 1883), p. 4; other versions are to be found in Thomas Wright, 'On the Local Legends of Shropshire', *Collectanea Archaeologica*, I (1862), pp. 50–66, and Hiram Howell, *The Wrekin Legend and Other Poems* (Shrewsbury, 1894), pp. 20–31.

15 William Williams, *Observations of the Snowdon Mountains* (London, 1802), pp. 98–9.

16 Burne, *Shropshire Folk-Lore*, p. 4; Jacqueline Simpson, *The Folklore of the Welsh Border* (London, 1976), p. 15.

17 Ella Mary Leather, *The Folk-Lore of Herefordshire* (Hereford, 1912), pp. 1–2. Another version can be found further west, at Castell Gwynionydd in Cardiganshire: Chris Barber, *More Mysterious Wales* (Newton Abbot, 1986), p. 42.

18 Charles Gillman, 'Cam's Pike', *Notes and Queries*, 10th ser., 2 (1904), p. 110; Roy Palmer, *The Folklore of Gloucestershire* (Tiverton, 1994), p. 35.

19 John Powell, 'Folklore Notes from South-West Wilts', *Folk-Lore*, XII/1 (1901), pp. 71–83, at pp. 78–9; this version is in standard English, but the original dialect was later published by C. V. Goddard, 'Wiltshire Folklore Jottings', *Wiltshire Archaeological Magazine*, 50 (1942–4), p. 31.

20 'The Legend of Silbury Hill', *Belgravia Annual* (London, 1869), pp. 81–4.

21 Will Meade, *The Ballads of a Moonraker* (Devizes, 1935), pp. 49–51.

22 Robert Heanley, 'Silbury Hill', *Folk-Lore*, 24 (1913), p. 524. Another version is told of *Sidbury* Hill, but this just uses a similar name to justify repeating the story: Katy Jordan, *The Haunted Landscape: Folklore, Ghosts and Legends of Wiltshire* (Bradford-on-Avon, 2000), p. 40.

23 Leslie Grinsell, *Folklore of Prehistoric Sites in Britain* (Newton Abbot, 1976), p. 119.

24 Edmund Bogg, *A Thousand Miles of Wandering along the Roman Wall* (Leeds, 1898), pp. 229–30.

25 A poem by F. Whalley originally published in the *Lonsdale Magazine* of 1821 and reproduced in Jonathan Otley, *Concise Description of the English Lakes* (London, 1849), pp. 178–80.

26 John Hutton, *A Tour to the Caves, in the Environs of Ingleborough and Settle* (London, 1781), p. 9.

27 *Wensleydale Rambles* by J. Routh (1878), p. 4, quoted in Eliza Gutch, *County Folk-Lore II: Examples of Printed Folk-Lore Concerning the North Riding of Yorkshire, York and the Ainsty* (London, 1901), p. 19; Edmund Bogg, *From Edenvale to the Plains of York; or, A Thousand Miles in the Valleys of the Nidd and Yore* (Leeds, n.d. [1894]), pp. 193–4.

28 David Ogilvy, *A General Itinerary of England and Wales* (London, 1804), col. 245. It remained Kilgram Bridge on the Ordnance Survey (os) map.

29 Thomas Whellan, *History and Topography of the City of York and the North Riding of Yorkshire* (Beverley, 1857–9), vol. II, p. 453; *The Guardian*, 26 November 1997.

30 Bogg, *Edenvale to the Plains of York*, p. 274.

31 Quoted in Askew Roberts, *The Gossiping Guide to Wales* (London, 1879), p. 33. The earliest publication I can find, *Sporting Magazine*, 2nd ser., 8 (1821), p. 248, must already be at a remove from the original, as the names are mispelled.

32 Catherine Hutton, *Reminiscences of a Gentlewoman of the Last Century*, ed. Catherine Beale (Birmingham, 1891), pp. 48–9; Hywel Wyn Owen and Richard Morgan, *Dictionary of the Place-Names of Wales* (Llandysul, 2007), pp. 122–3.

33 Quoted in Christopher Hibbert, *The Grand Tour* (London, 1987), p. 100.

34 Roberts, *Gossiping Guide to Wales*, p. 33.

35 Christopher Woodward, *In Ruins* (London, 2002), p. 151.

36 Charles Tomkins, *A Tour to the Isle of Wight* (London, 1796), vol. II, p. 119.

37 1894 os at NZ 839 113.

38 1861 os at NZ 422 838 (the Bridge) and 423 389 (the Scar); 1897 os at NZ 436 396 (the Lapstone); William Brockie, *Legends and Superstitions of the County Durham* (Sunderland, 1886), p. 174.

39 Bedfordshire Archives 0/47.

40 1882 os at so 863 856.

41 1890 os at sz 016 877.

42 Ralph Whitlock, *Whitlock's Wessex* (Bradford-on-Avon, 1975), p. 35.

2 Down Tumbled the Stones: Landscapes Shaped by the Devil's Hand

1 The exhibition ran in 2018–19, and for the private view I'm grateful to the organizers of 'Living in a Magical World, Inner Lives: Emotions, Identity and the Supernatural, 1300–1900'.

2 George Lyman Kittredge, *Witchcraft in Old and New England* (Cambridge, MA, 1929), p. 209 (Dowsing), pp. 158, 211 (Wycherley).

3 Charles Beard, *The Romance of Treasure Trove* (London, 1933), p. 57.

4 *The Journeys of Celia Fiennes*, ed. Christopher Morris (London, 1949), p. 242.

5 *The Natural History and Antiquities of Surrey* (London, 1718–19), vol. III, p. 185; Eric Parker, *Highways and Byways in Surrey* (London, 1908), pp. 186–7.

6 *Historia Cantabrigiensis Academicae*, 47, in *The Works of John Caius*, ed. E. S. Roberts (Cambridge, 1912).

7 William Camden, *Britannia* (London, 1607), p. 360.

8 John Chambers, ed., *A General History of the County of Norfolk* (Norwich, 1829), vol. II, p. 704; 1884 os at TF 923 171; 1886 os at TG 347 252.

9 Leslie Grinsell, *The Ancient Burial-Mounds of England* (London, 1936), p. 43.

10 W. G. Clarke, *In Breckland Wilds* (London, 1925), p. 164.

11 Daniel Defoe, *A Tour thro' the Whole Island of Great Britain*, ed. G.D.H. Cole (London, 1927), vol. II, p. 592, from the 1724–6 version of this much-revised book.

12 Arthur Quiller-Couch, *The Mayor of Troy* (London, 1906), pp. 74–5.

13 Eleanor G. Hayden, *Travels round Our Village* (London, 1905), p. 12; John Edward Field, *The Myth of the Pent Cuckoo* (London, 1913), p. 84.

14 Margaret Eyre, 'Folklore Notes from St Briavel's', *Folk-Lore*, 13 (1902), pp. 170–77, at p. 171; Roy Palmer, *The Folklore of Gloucestershire* (Tiverton, 1994), p. 142.

15 Charlotte Burne, *Shropshire Folk-Lore: A Sheaf of Gleanings* (London, 1883), pp. 22–3.

16 Charles Warne, *Ancient Dorset* (Bournemouth, 1872), p. 6.

17 Alexandra Walsham, *The Reformation of the Landscape: Religion, Identity, and Memory in Early Modern Britain and Ireland* (Oxford, 2011), p. 364.

18 Thomas Newbigging, *History of the Forest of Rossendale* (Rawtenstall, 1893), pp. 271–2.

19 1854 os at SE 075 594 and Thomas Parkinson, *Yorkshire Legends and Traditions* (London, 1888), vol. I, p. 125; W. Self Weeks, 'Some Legendary Stories and Folk-Lore of the Clitheroe District', *Transactions of the Lancashire and Cheshire Antiquarian Society*, 34 (1916), pp. 77–110, at p. 86, for which see David Barrowclough and John Hallam, 'The Devil's Footprints and Other Folklore: Local Legend and Archaeological Evidence in Lancashire', *Folklore*, CXIX/1 (2008), pp. 93–102, at pp. 93–4.

20 *Memoirs of the First Forty-Five Years of the Life of James Lackington* (London, 1792), pp. 469–70; Arthur L. Humphreys, *Materials for the History of the Town of Wellington* (London, 1899), pp. 240–41.

21 William Bentinck Forfar, *Kynance Cove; or, The Cornish Smugglers* (London, 1865), pp. 97–8; *Black's Guide to the Duchy of Cornwall* (Edinburgh, 1871), p. 368.

22 Leslie Grinsell, *Folklore of Prehistoric Sites in Britain* (Newton Abbot, 1976), p. 175.

23 Hywel Wyn Owen and Ken Lloyd Gruffydd, *Place-Names of Flintshire* (Cardiff, 2017), pp. 45–6; 1898 os at SH 758 234.

24 'The Devil, too, in so far as he comes into Irish folklore, is a much less grotesque figure . . . He does not construct bridges . . . and few or none of the curious freaks of nature as seen in rocks, chasms and the like are attributed to him': Douglas Hyde, *Legends of Saints and Sinners* (London, 1915), pp. viii–ix.

25 John Aubrey, *Monumenta Britannica*, ed. Rodney Legg and John Fowles (Milborne Port, 1980), vol. I, p. 95.

26 *Stukeley's Stonehenge*, ed. Aubrey Burl and Neil Mortimer (London, 2005), p. 108.

27 Hunt's story was recorded by John Wood in 1747, and Caroline Lybbe Powys in 1776: see Leslie Grinsell, *The Legendary History and Folklore of Stonehenge* (Guernsey, 1973), pp. 14–15, and Christopher Chippindale, *Stonehenge Complete* (London, 1994), p. 40.

28 Travel notes of the 1590s in *An Itinerary Written by Fynes Moryson Gent* (London, 1617), vol. III, p. 142.

29 Francesca M. Wilson, *Strange Island: Britain through Foreign Eyes, 1395–1940* (London, 1955), p. 44. The original comedy is French, by Saint-Evremond.

30 'The Devil replaces giants in English folklore just as Arthur does in Welsh folklore': Richard Hayman, *Riddles in Stone: Myths, Archaeology and the Ancient Britons* (London, 1997), p. 32.

31 T. W. Webb, *Memorials of the Civil War as It Affected Herefordshire* (London, 1879), vol. II, pp. 333–4; John Duncumb et al., *Collections towards the History and Antiquities of the County of Hereford* (Hereford, 1804–1915), vol. II/I, p. 189 (this volume 1812).

32 Frank Latham, ed., *Delamere: The History of a Cheshire Parish* (Delamere, 1991), pp. 54–5.

33 Robert Hunt, *Popular Romances of the West of England* (London, 1865), vol. I, p. 202.

34 William Bottrell, *Traditions and Hearthside Stories of West Cornwall* (Penzance, 1879–80), vol. I, pp. 171–2.

35 Philip Ahier, *The Legends and Traditions of Huddersfield and Its District* (Huddersfield, 1940–45), vol. I, p. 15.

36 Hester Pinney, 'The Devil's Jumps', *Somerset and Dorset Notes and Queries*, 21 (1933–5), p. 68.

37 G. Rome Hall, 'On Ancient British Remains near Birtley and Barrasford, North Tyne', *Archaeologia Aeliana*, 2nd ser., 7 (1876), pp. 3–17, at pp. 10–11.

38 Kingsley Palmer, *The Folklore of Somerset* (London, 1976), p. 75; Ralph Whitlock, *The Folklore of Devon* (London, 1977), p. 17; Palmer, *Folklore of Gloucestershire*, p. 52.

39 Kai Roberts, *Folklore of Yorkshire* (Stroud, 2013), pp. 78–9.

40 Leslie Grinsell, 'Sussex Barrows', *Sussex Archaeological Collections*, 75 (1934), pp. 216–75, at p. 239.

41 Jacqueline Simpson, *The Folklore of Sussex* (London, 1973), p. 63.

42 S., 'Thursley Church', *Gentleman's Magazine*, 69 (1799), pp. 921–2.

43 Jennifer Westwood and Jacqueline Simpson, *The Lore of the Land: A Guide to England's Legends, from Spring-Heeled Jack to the Witches of Warboys* (London, 2005), p. 713.

44 H. Thornhill Timmons, *Nooks and Corners of Shropshire* (London, 1899), pp. 35–6.

45 Richard Barham (as 'Thomas Ingoldsby'), *The Ingoldsby Legends* (London, 1864), p. 96.

46 'The familiar Beelzebub of popular culture [is] an imbecile easily duped by humans. Such an approach did not preclude fear of the devil. It probably served rather to exorcize it': Robert Muchembled, *A History of the Devil from the Middle Ages to the Present*, trans. Jean Birrell (Cambridge, 2003), p. 191.

47 His immediate source was the story of the two Stephens in the *Dialogues* of Gregory the Great.

48 William Harrison Ainsworth, *Ovingdean Grange: A Legend of the South Downs* (London, 1860), pp. 186–98.

49 Doris Jones-Baker, *The Folklore of Hertfordshire* (London, 1977), p. 118; Jon Raven, *The Folklore of Staffordshire* (London, 1978), p. 21; Andrew Collins, *The Running Well Mystery* (privately printed, 1983), pp. 8–10; Enid Porter, *The Folklore of East Anglia* (London, 1974), pp. 134–6; James Bowker, *Goblin Tales of Lancashire* (London, n.d. [1878]), p. 221; John Harland and Thomas Wilkinson, *Lancashire Legends* (London, 1873), pp. 5–7.

3 Have at Thee! Churches Shifted, Targeted and Raided by the Devil

1 Percy Stone, *Legends and Lays of the Wight* (London, 1912), pp. 19–24, adapted with some assistance from Abraham Elder in *Bentley's Miscellany*, 4 (1839), pp. 255–62.

2 F. S., 'Churchdown', *Notes and Queries*, 1st ser., 12 (1855), pp. 341–2. The folk tale is ML 7060 in Reidar Thoralf Christiansen, *The Migratory Legends: A Proposed List of Types with a Systematic Catalogue of the Norwegian Variants* (Helsinki, 1958), pp. 201–9.

3 The church-moving version is from Anna Bray, *A Description of the Part of Devonshire Bordering on the Tamar and the Tavy* (London, 1836–8), vol. I, p. 252; the merchant's vow usually appears as an independent origin story but a version that combines the two can be found in Aileen Skinner, *Tales of the Tors* (London, 1939), pp. 28–31. I am grateful to Tim Sandals of Legendary Dartmoor for this reference.

4 J. P. Hervey, 'The Devil in Sussex', *Sussex County Magazine*, 17 (1943), p. 356.

5 Llewellynn Jewitt, 'The Devil and Church Building', *Notes and Queries*, 2nd ser., 4 (1857), p. 357.

6 A. Hadrian Allcroft, *The Circle and the Cross: A Study in Continuity* (London, 1927–30), vol. II, p. 329; A. Chambers, 'The Devil's Churchyard: An Iron Age enclosure at Checkendon, Oxon., 1979–81', *Oxoniensa*, 51 (1986), pp. 25–30.

7 J. B. Partridge, 'Cotswold Place-Lore and Customs: I', *Folk-Lore*, XXIII/4 (1912), pp. 332–42, at pp. 337–9.

8 John Thurman, 'On Ancient British Barrows, Especially Those of Wiltshire and the Adjoining Counties: 1: Long Barrows',

Archaeologia, XLII/1 (1869), pp. 161–244, at p. 243; *Transactions of the Bristol and Gloucestershire Archaeological Society*, 5 (1880–81), p. 19.

9 Mark Antony Lower, *A Compendious History of Sussex: Topographical, Archaeological and Anecdotal* (Lewes, 1870), vol. I, p. 196.

10 Robert Pitcairn, *Criminal Trials in Scotland* (Edinburgh, 1829–33), vol. 1/2, p. 240.

11 Ethel Rudkin, 'Lincolnshire Folklore: III', *Folk-Lore*, XLV/2 (1934), pp. 144–57, at pp. 146, 153–4.

12 Margaret Eyre, 'Folklore Notes from St Briavel's', *Folk-Lore*, 13 (1902), pp. 170–77, at p. 171; Arthur Clarke, *The Wye Valley and Royal Forest of Dean: Official Guide* (*c*. 1960).

13 Roy Palmer, *The Folklore of Gloucestershire* (Tiverton, 1994), p. 142.

14 *Gawain*, ll. 2185–8, in *Pearl, Cleanness, Patience: Sir Gawain and the Green Knight*, ed. A. C. Cawley and J. J. Anderson (London, 1962).

15 Thomas Crofton Croker, *Fairy Legends and Traditions of the South of Ireland* (London, 1825–8), vol. III, pp. viii–x.

16 W. Benham, 'The Winchester Hill, Hants', *Antiquary*, 19 (1889), p. 73; R. Pearse Chope, 'Thirty-Fourth Report on Devonshire Folklore', *Transactions of the Devonshire Association*, 66 (1934), pp. 73–91, at p. 76; Treadway Nash, *Collections for the History of Worcestershire* (London, 1781–99), vol. II appendix, p. 128.

17 Jeremy Harte, 'Churches Moved by Night', *At the Edge*, 2 (1996), pp. 1–7.

18 T. Rupert Jones, 'The Devil's Stone, at Staple Fitz-Paine', *Somerset and Dorset Notes and Queries*, 1 (1888–9), p. 153; A.C.G. Cameron, 'In Reference to the Sarsens or Greyweather-Sandstones at Staple Fitzpaine, near Taunton', *Proceedings of the Somerset Natural History and Archaeological Society*, 54 (1908), pp. 153–9; Kingsley Palmer, *Oral Folk-Tales of Wessex* (Newton Abbot, 1973), pp. 73, 105–6, 110–12.

19 'Every story in which the Devil or a giant tries to crush a church with a huge rock, or smother a town under a hill, could once have been . . . a proof that God providentially saves the community from attacks by evil beings': Jacqueline Simpson, 'God's Visible Judgements', *Landscape History*, VIII/1 (1986), pp. 53–8, at p. 56.

20 T. S. Turner, *History of Aldborough and Boroughbridge* (London, 1853), pp. 66–7; Thomas Parkinson, *Yorkshire Legends and Traditions* (London, 1888), vol. I, p. 118.

21 James Orchard Halliwell, *Popular Rhymes and Nursery Tales* (London, 1849), pp. 195–6.

22 C. H. Nutt, 'Popular Names of Tumuli', *Antiquary*, 6 (1882), p. 135.
and Leslie Grinsell, *Folklore of Prehistoric Sites in Britain* (Newton
Abbot, 1976), p. 138; Robert Plot, *The Natural History of Oxford-
Shire* (Oxford, 1677), p. 343; 'The Devil's Coytes', in John Aubrey,
Monumenta Britannica, ed. Rodney Legg and John Fowles
(Milborne Port, 1980), vol. II, p. 822; William Henry Greene, *Jack o'
Kent and the Devil: Stories of a Welsh Border Hero Told in Verse*, ed.
E. W. Greene (Chepstow, n.d. [1974]), pp. 14–15. For more stone-
throwing stories, see R. Bruce Boswell, 'Footprints of the Devil
in Our Own Country', *Pall Mall Magazine*, 5 (1895), pp. 555–64, at
pp. 561–3.

23 Oliver Padel, 'Cornwall and the Matter of Britain', in *Arthur in the
Celtic Languages: The Arthurian Legend in Celtic Literatures and
Traditions*, ed. Ceridwen Lloyd-Morgan and Eric Poppe (Cardiff,
2019), pp. 263–80, at p. 267.

24 Grinsell, *Folklore of Prehistoric Sites*, p. 168.

25 Tony Deane and Tony Shaw, *The Folklore of Cornwall* (London,
1975), p. 107.

26 William Henry Hudson, *A Shepherd's Life* (London, 1921),
pp. 254–5, except for the detail of the seven churches, which I
have introduced from the *Itinerarium Curiosum* as quoted by
Stuart Piggott in *William Stukeley: An Eighteenth-Century
Antiquary* (Oxford, 1950), p. 74.

27 John Camp, *In Praise of Bells* (London, 1988), p. 96.

28 Charles Harper, *The Ingoldsby Country* (London, 1906), pp. 233–4.

29 Neil Arnold, *Kent Urban Legends: The Phantom Hitch-Hiker and
Other Stories* (Stroud, 2013), pp. 76–7.

30 R. Bruce Boswell, 'Diabolical Folk-Lore in Divers Places',
Gentleman's Magazine, 281 (1896), pp. 472–85, at p. 479; Mary
Hopkirk, *Danbury: Historical Notes and Records of the Village of
Danbury in the County of Essex* (Chelmsford, 1945), pp. 33, 37, 72.

31 *Johannis de Trokelowe et Henrici de Blaneforde necnon Quorundam
Anonymorum Chronica*, ed. Henry Thomas Riley (London, 1866),
p. 340; Andrew Collins, *The Knights of Danbury* (privately printed,
1985), p. 17.

32 *Memorials of St Dunstan, Archbishop of Canterbury*, ed. William
Stubbs (London, 1874), p. 174.

33 Richard Barham (as 'Thomas Ingoldsby'), *The Ingoldsby Legends*
(London, 1864), p. 182 – the Lay of St Nicholas, admittedly, not
that of St Dunstan, but equally memorable.

34 Jacqueline Simpson, *The Folklore of Sussex* (London, 1973), pp. 63–4.

35 'It was you against the Devil: you alone': Jeffrey Burton Russell, *Mephistopheles: The Devil in the Modern World* (Ithaca, NY, 1986), pp. 31–2.

4 There Stood the Stranger: Rash Deals and Binding Promises with the Devil

1 Charlotte Burne, *Shropshire Folk-Lore: A Sheaf of Gleanings* (London, 1883), pp. 4–5; earlier found in Thomas Wright, 'On the Local Legends of Shropshire', *Collectanea Archaeologica*, 1 (1862), p. 54.

2 Leslie Grinsell, *Folklore of Prehistoric Sites in Britain* (Newton Abbot, 1976), p. 157.

3 Burne, *Shropshire Folk-Lore*, pp. 4–5.

4 Wright, 'Local Legends of Shropshire', p. 56.

5 Mary Webb, *The Golden Arrow* (London, 1916), p. 24.

6 Richard Ridge, *Shropshire Highland Folk Tales* (privately printed, 1937), pp. 13–17. The folk tale is ATU 815* in Hans-Jörg Uther, *The Types of International Folktales: A Classification and Bibliography Based on the System of Antti Aarne and Stith Thompson* (Helsinki, 2004), vol. 1, pp. 456–7.

7 Tom Wall, *The Singular Stiperstones: Landscape, Reminiscence, Literature and Wildlife* (privately printed, 2014), p. 101.

8 F. Grice, *Folk Tales of the North Country: Drawn from Northumberland and Durham* (London, 1944), pp. 143–7.

9 Margaret Eyre, 'Folklore of the Wyre Valley', *Folk-Lore*, 16 (1905), pp. 162–79, at p. 174.

10 C. W. Whistler, 'Local Traditions of the Quantocks', *Folk-Lore*, 19 (1908), pp. 31–51, at pp. 41–2.

11 John Lloyd Warden Page, *An Exploration of Exmoor and the Hill Country of West Somerset* (London, 1890), pp. 90–93.

12 James Obelkevich, *Religion and Rural Society: South Lindsey, 1825–1875* (Oxford, 1976), p. 276.

13 John Merrifield (as 'J. M.'), 'Devonshire Folk Lore', *Notes and Queries*, 1st ser., 3 (1851), p. 404.

14 Katharine Briggs, *A Dictionary of British Folk-Tales in the English Language* (London, 1970–71), B1, p. 153.

15 T. A. Davies, 'Folklore of Gwent: Monmouthshire Legends and Traditions', *Folk-Lore*, 48 (1937), pp. 41–59, at pp. 58–9.

16 'Satan . . . was well acquainted with the secrets of nature and might counterfeit an effect when he could not reproduce it directly':

Keith Thomas, *Religion and the Decline of Magic: Studies in Popular Beliefs in Sixteenth- and Seventeenth-Century England* (London, 1971), p. 304.

17 William Bottrell, *Traditions and Hearthside Stories of West Cornwall* (Penzance, 1879–80), vol. III, pp. 3–11.

18 Herbert Halpert, 'The Devil and the Fiddle', *Hoosier Folklore Bulletin*, 2 (1943), pp. 39–43.

19 R. Bruce Boswell, 'More Diabolical Folk-Lore Relating to Definite Localities', *Gentleman's Magazine*, 283 (1897), pp. 443–60, at pp. 449–50.

20 Robert Hunt, *Popular Romances of the West of England* (London, 1865), vol. I, pp. 241–5.

21 Anna Bray, *A Description of the Part of Devonshire Bordering on the Tamar and the Tavy* (London, 1836–8), vol. II, pp. 281–5.

22 Walter Joyce, *Moorside Tales and Talk* (London, 1935), p. 75, Molland; Alfred Williams, *Round about the Upper Thames* (London, 1922), p. 67, Watchfield; Burne, *Shropshire Folk-Lore*, p. 598, Munslow.

23 Roy Palmer, *The Folklore of the Black Country* (Woonton, Almeley, 2007), pp. 40–41.

24 S. J. Swainson, 'Langford Budville Revel (and Devil)', *Somerset and Dorset Notes and Queries*, 20 (1930–32), pp. 245–6.

25 A. R. Bickford, 'Boulder outside Shebbear Church', *Devon and Cornwall Notes and Queries*, 24 (1950/51), p. 17.

26 Jeremy Harte, 'The Devil's Stone at Shebbear', *FLS News*, 89 (2019), pp. 10–12.

27 Jessica Lofthouse, *North-Country Folklore* (London, 1976), p. 58.

28 James Henry Dixon (as 'T.Q.M.') in William Hone, *The Table Book* (London, 1827), pp. 258–61.

29 Thomas Sternberg, 'Popular Stories of the English Peasantry: V', *Notes and Queries*, 1st ser., 5 (1852), pp. 601–4.

30 Margaret Ann Courtney, 'Cornish Folk-Lore: I', *Folk-Lore Journal*, V/I (1887), pp. 14–61, at p. 27; *Dorset Year Book* (1932), p. 159.

31 Sidney Oldall Addy, *Household Tales with Other Traditional Remains Collected in the Counties of York, Lincoln, Derby and Nottingham* (London, 1895), pp. 23–4.

32 Sabine Baring-Gould, and John Fisher, *The Lives of the British Saints* (London, 1907–13), vol. II, pp. 157–61.

33 David Shankland, 'Integrating the Past: Folklore, Mounds and People at Çatalhöyük', in *Archaeology and Folklore*,

ed. Amy Gazin-Schwartz and Cornelius Holtorf (London, 1999),
pp. 139–57, at p. 151.

34 Willem de Blécourt, 'Sabbath Stories: Towards a New History
of Witches' Assemblies', in *The Oxford Handbook of Witchcraft
in Early Modern Europe and Colonial America*, ed. Brian Levack
(Oxford, 2013), pp. 84–100, at p. 95.

35 Willem de Blécourt, 'The Flying Charm – to Cologne in the
Wine Cellar: On the History of a Scholarly Legend', *Incantatio*,
8 (2019), pp. 9–28.

5 Off in a Sheet of Flame: Fighting the Devil and Escaping His Clutches

1 A fused retelling from L., 'Ancient Tradition at Tolleshunt-
Knights, Essex', *Sporting Magazine*, 42 (1813), pp. 21–4; Sidney
Hartland, 'Supernatural Change of Site', *Folk-Lore*, VIII (1897),
pp. 177–8; John Atkinson, 'Supernatural Change of Site', *Folk-Lore*,
VIII (1897), pp. 279–80; and Jessie K. Payne, *A Ghost Hunter's Guide
to Essex* (Romford, 1987), pp. 9–10. The lower legs of the effigy are
now missing, along with the dogs.

2 Alan Wykes, *Reading: A Biography* (London, 1970), p. 106.

3 Jessica Lofthouse, *North-Country Folklore* (London, 1976), p. 58.

4 Charlotte Burne, *Shropshire Folk-Lore: A Sheaf of Gleanings*
(London, 1883), pp. 154–5; cf. p. 644.

5 Ella Mary Leather, *The Folk-Lore of Herefordshire* (Hereford, 1912),
p. 107.

6 James John Hissey, *Over Fen and Wold* (London, 1898), p. 399.

7 Enid Porter, *Cambridgeshire Customs and Folklore* (London, 1969),
pp. 55–7; Ethel Rudkin, 'Lincolnshire Folklore: 1', *Folk-Lore*, XLIV/3
(1933), pp. 189–214, at pp. 198–200.

8 James Wentworth Day, *In Search of Ghosts* (London, 1969),
pp. 67–8.

9 G. W. Pattison, 'Adult Education and Folklore', *Folk-Lore*, LXIV/3
(1953), pp. 424–6, at p. 426. Maureen James has been researching
the history of these toadmen, and I owe much to her.

10 J. P. Hervey, 'St Leonards Forest and Its Legends', *Sussex County
Magazine*, 15 (1941), pp. 154–6.

11 James John Hissey, *On Southern English Roads* (London, 1896),
pp. 32–3.

12 Thomas Sternberg, *The Dialect and Folk-Lore of Northamptonshire*
(London, 1851), pp. 174–5.

13 L. F. Newman, 'Some Notes on the Folklore of Cambridgeshire and the Eastern Counties', *Folk-Lore*, LVI/3 (1945), pp. 287–93, at p. 288.

14 William E. A. Axon, *The Black Knight of Ashton* (Manchester, n.d. [1870]).

15 There is a copy in the Folger Shakespeare Library, https://luna.folger.edu.

16 James Wentworth Day, *Essex Ghosts* (Bourne End, 1973), pp. 2–6. Four years earlier (*In Search of Ghosts*, p. 149) Day had given the same story in quite different words; like all folklorists in the days before sound recording, he was retelling from notes, not transcribing an actual performance.

17 Thomas Quiller-Couch, 'The Longstone: A Cornish Legend', *Notes and Queries*, 6th ser., 7 (1883), pp. 323–4.

18 W. J. Watkins, 'A Cycle of Stories Current in Radnorshire', *Folk-Lore*, XLIII/4 (1932), pp. 424–7.

19 'Pearmain', 'Davies of Rivon', *Bye-Gones Relating to Wales and the Border Counties*, 9 (1888), pp. 105–6.

20 Mabel Peacock, *Tales and Rhymes in the Lindsey Folk-Speech* (Brigg, 1886), p. 67–71.

21 Sternberg, *Folk-Lore of Northamptonshire*, pp. 140–41.

22 Thomas Keightley, *The Fairy Mythology* (London, 1850), p. 113. He writes Lujhmân in error for the Lúghmân of his source, Charles Masson, *Narrative of Various Journeys in Balochistan, Afghanistan and the Panjab* (London, 1842), vol. III, pp. 297–8; in this version the locals have just taken up farming, and are outsmarted by the Shaitan, not vice versa.

23 Steve Roud, *The Penguin Guide to the Superstitions of Britain and Ireland* (London, 2003), p. 257; Sarah Bartels, '"A terrific ogre": The Role of the Devil in Victorian Popular Belief', *Folklore*, CXXVIII (2017), pp. 271–91, at p. 278.

24 'French peasants saw life as a contest between God, the sun, rain, earth, man, sheep, dog, vine, cabbage and carrot on the one side; and on the other, the Devil, moon, hail, sea, monkey, wolf, fox, brambles and thistles': G. R. Quaife, *Godly Zeal and Furious Rage: The Witch in Early Modern Europe* (London, 1987), p. 59.

25 Wrotham is named on a postcard of *c.* 1910; Dilwyn on the Tithe Apportionment of 1837, plot 301.

26 J. T. Llewellyn Prichard, *The Llandrindod Guide* (Llandrindod, 1826), p. 237.

27 Ethel Rudkin, 'Lincolnshire Folklore: IV', *Folk-Lore*, XLV (1934), pp. 249–67, at p. 250.

28 T. D. Davidson, 'The Untilled Field', *Agricultural History Review*, III (1955), pp. 20–25; Robert Smith, *The Road to Maggieknockater: Exploring Aberdeenshire and the North-East through Its Place Names* (Edinburgh, 2004), pp. 65–6.

29 Timothy Easton, 'Apotropaic Symbols and Other Measures for Protecting Buildings against Misfortune', in *Physical Evidence for Ritual Acts, Sorcery and Witchcraft in Christian Britain: A Feeling for Magic*, ed. Ronald Hutton (London, 2016), pp. 39–67, at p. 50.

30 H.E.H. Gillett, 'Some Saws and Proverbs of Norfolk', in *Bygone Norfolk*, ed. William Andrews (London, 1898), pp. 201–28, at pp. 227–8. As noted by Jennifer Westwood and Jacqueline Simpson, *The Lore of the Land: A Guide to England's Legends, from Spring-Heeled Jack to the Witches of Warboys* (London, 2005), p. 524, Gillett misunderstood some of what he was being told.

31 Westwood and Simpson, *Lore of the Land*, pp. 520–21.

6 Neither Inside nor Outside: Raising the Devil and Laying Him Afterwards

1 Michael Aislabie Denham, *The Denham Tracts*, ed. James Hardy (London, 1892), vol. II, pp. 117–18.

2 Edmund Sandford, *A Cursory Relation of All the Antiquities and Familyes in Cumberland*, ed. Richard Ferguson (Kendal, 1890), p. 31.

3 *Denham Tracts*, vol. II, p. 116.

4 George Stovin, 'Lindholme, a Reputed Hermit's Cell', *Gentleman's Magazine*, 17 (1747), p. 23.

5 William Stonehouse, *The History and Topography of the Isle of Axholme* (London, 1839), pp. 393–4.

6 Ella Mary Leather, *The Folk-Lore of Herefordshire* (Hereford, 1912), pp. 163–4; cf. Beatrix Wherry, 'Wizardry on the Welsh Border', *Folk-Lore*, XV/1 (1904), pp. 75–86, at p. 85; T. A. Davies, 'Folklore of Gwent: Monmouthshire Legends and Traditions', *Folk-Lore*, XLVIII/1 (1937), p. 42.

7 'John ap John', 'Dafydd of Rivon', *Bye-gones Relating to Wales and the Border Counties*, 2nd ser., 1 (1889–90), pp. 349–50; also in Leather, *Folklore of Herefordshire*, p. 165, and William Henry Greene, *Jack o' Kent and the Devil: Stories of a Welsh Border Hero Told in Verse*, ed. E. W. Greene (Chepstow, n.d. [1974]), collected from the original poems published in the *Chepstow Weekly Advertiser* at various dates before the author's death in 1893.

8 Greene, *Jack o' Kent*.

9 Vince Russett, 'Sir John Hauteville: A Wessex Giant', *Picwinnard*, 10 (1979), pp. 20–23.

10 Richard King, 'Local Rhymes and Proverbs of Devonshire', *Notes and Queries*, 1st ser., 2 (1850), pp. 511–12; most recently in John Hayward, *Dartmoor 365* (Lytchett Matravers, 1991), p. 117.

11 Leslie Grinsell, *Folklore of Prehistoric Sites in Britain* (Newton Abbot, 1976), pp. 98, 99, 103, 112–13 (Battlegore, Compton Bishop, Porlock, Mottistone).

12 John Billingsley, *Folk Tales from Calderdale: Place Legends and Lore from the Calder Valley* (Hebden Bridge, 2007), pp. 39–43.

13 Greene, *Jack o' Kent*; Leather, *Herefordshire*, p. 166; Davies, 'Folklore of Gwent', p. 43.

14 W. J. Watkins, 'A Cycle of Stories Current in Radnorshire', *Folk-Lore*, XLIII/4 (1932), pp. 424–7; Ida Gandy, *An Idler on the Shropshire Borders* (Shrewsbury, 1970), pp. 79–80.

15 Watkins, 'Stories Current in Radnorshire', p. 427.

16 Davies, 'Folklore of Gwent', p. 43; Wherry, 'Wizardry on the Welsh Border', p. 86; also Leather, *Herefordshire*, p. 163.

17 Charles Keyser, 'Notes on the Churches of Frilsham, Yattendon, Ashampstead, Hampstead Norris and Aldworth: IV', *Berkshire, Buckinghamshire and Oxfordshire Journal*, XXI (1915), pp. 97–108, at p. 107.

18 William Henderson, *Notes on the Folklore of the Northern Counties of England and the Borders* (London, 1866), pp. 343–4. This story was omitted from the later 1879 edition.

19 Theo Brown, *The Fate of the Dead: A Study in Folk Eschatology in the West Country after the Reformation* (Cambridge, 1979), pp. 52–3.

20 Margaret Ann Courtney, 'Cornish Folk-Lore: I', *Folk-Lore Journal*, V/1 (1887), pp. 14–61, at p. 23.

21 John Harland and Thomas Wilkinson, *Lancashire Folk-Lore* (London, 1867), p. 83.

22 Charlotte Burne, 'Reminiscences of Lancashire and Cheshire when George IV Was King', *Folk-Lore*, XX/2 (1909), pp. 203–7, at p. 205.

23 John Harland and Thomas Wilkinson, *Lancashire Legends* (London, 1873), pp. 241–3, based on an earlier versified version; cf. James Bowker, *Goblin Tales of Lancashire* (London, n.d. [1878]), pp. 120–28, 257.

24 W. Self Weeks, 'Some Legendary Stories and Folk-Lore of the Clitheroe District', *Transactions of the Lancashire and Cheshire Antiquarian Society*, 34 (1916), pp. 82–4.

25 Jessica Lofthouse, *North-Country Folklore* (London, 1976), pp. 55–6.

26 Brown, *Fate of the Dead*, pp. 25–6, 42–4.

27 Peter Landreth as 'The Chronicler', *Legends of Lancashire* (London, 1841), pp. 91–154; the story survives only in this verbose period piece, so I have parted with my usual respect for the text and tried to reconstruct something closer to the original tale. The main changes were to reduce Landreth's inflated cast of characters and to supply a motive for the action taking place within 24 hours.

7 Woman's Wit Is Better than Man's: Maidens and Mothers Beat the Devil

1 John Aubrey, *Monumenta Britannica*, ed. Rodney Legg and John Fowles (Milborne Port, 1980), vol. III, p. 360.

2 Matthew Alexander, *More Surrey Tales* (Newbury, 1986), pp. 29–30.

3 Henry Richards Luard, ed., *Annales Monastici* (London, 1864–9), vol. II, pp. 284–5; Owen Manning and William Bray, *The History and Antiquities of the County of Surrey* (London, 1804–14), vol. III, p. 140. The modern form of the name has been influenced by the proverbial 'Ludlam's dog'.

4 John Walker Ord, *The History and Antiquities of Cleveland* (London, 1846), pp. 429–30.

5 Henry Burstow, *Reminiscences of Horsham*, ed. J. Poole (Horsham, 2016), pp. 78–81.

6 Alfred Williams, *Folk-Songs of the Upper Thames* (London, 1923), p. 211. The ballad is number 278 in Francis James Child, *The English and Scottish Popular Ballads* (Boston, MA, 1882–98). It is 160 in the Roud Folk-Song Index, https://catalogue.efdss.org.

7 'The Devill and the Scold', in *The Roxburghe Ballads*, ed. William Chappell and Joseph Ebsworth (London, 1869–99), vol. II, pp. 367–71.

8 Chappell and Ebsworth, *Roxburghe Ballads*, vol. II, pp. 335–6.

9 Bodleian, Harding B 11(878). The ballad is Roud v4803.

10 Jesse Salisbury, *A Glossary of Words Used in South-East Worcestershire* (London, 1894–6), pp. 73–5.

11 *The Wonder; or, The Devil Outwitted* (Dublin, 1736); this is based on '*La chose impossible*' from *Nouveaux contes de Monsieur de la Fontaine* (Amsterdam, 1676).

12 Bodleian, Harding B 4(58) and Douce Ballads 2 f. 175v. The ballad is Roud v643; oral versions are discussed by Ian Spring, 'The Devil and the Feathery Wife', *Folklore*, XCIX/2 (1988), pp. 139–45. The folk tale is ATU 1091 in Hans-Jörg Uther, *The Types of International*

Folktales: A Classification and Bibliography Based on the System of Antti Aarne and Stith Thompson (Helsinki, 2004), vol. II, pp. 34–5.

13 Bodleian, Douce Prints s 9 (p74) and Douce Ballads 3 (37A). The ballad is Roud v4809. The folk tale is ATU 1133 in Uther, *Types of Folktales*, vol. II, pp. 43–4.

14 'The Plymouth Tragedy', Bodleian, Harding B 2(58). The ballad is Roud 622.

15 William Bottrell, *Traditions and Hearthside Stories of West Cornwall* (Penzance, 1879–80), vol. III, pp. 12–20.

16 P.F.S. Amery et al., 'Fifteenth Report of the Committee on Devonshire Folk-Lore', *Transactions of the Devonshire Association*, 30 (1898), pp. 90–96, at pp. 93–4.

17 Katharine Briggs, *A Dictionary of British Folk-Tales in the English Language* (London, 1970–71), B1, p. 45.

18 Williams, *Folk-Songs of the Upper Thames*, p. 37. The ballad is number 1 in Child, *English and Scottish Popular Ballads* (1882–98).

19 The ballad is number 243 in Child, *English and Scottish Popular Ballads*, where the Devil versions are listed as 243D to G. The transmission history is discussed in John Burrison, '"James Harris" in Britain since Child', *Journal of American Folklore*, LXXX/317 (1967), pp. 271–84. I have combined different versions to produce a single narrative; the hills of Heaven appear in Scottish texts, but the dramatic ending comes from a Bert Lloyd performance apparently based on the song as sung by Marina Russell of Upwey.

8 Amid the Shrieking of the Storm: The Devil Appears to Carry off Sinners

1 Anna Bray, *A Description of the Part of Devonshire Bordering on the Tamar and the Tavy* (London, 1836–8), vol. I, pp. 310–14; Samuel Rowe, *A Perambulation of the Antient and Royal Forest of Dartmoor* (Plymouth, 1848), pp. 134–5; Ruth St Leger-Gordon, *The Witchcraft and Folklore of Dartmoor* (London, 1965), pp. 117–18.

2 *The Harleian Miscellany* (London, 1809), vol. I, pp. 220–28.

3 W. A. Leighton, 'Early Chronicles of Shrewsbury, 1372–1603', *Transactions of the Shropshire Antiquarian and Natural History Society*, 3 (1880), pp. 239–352, at p. 255.

4 *Report on the Manuscripts of the Marquess of Downshire 4: Papers of William Trumbull the Elder* (Historical MSS Commission 75, 1940), p. 19.

5 Katharine Briggs, *Pale Hecate's Team* (London, 1962), p. 161.

6 John Powell, 'Folklore Notes from South-West Wilts', *Folk-Lore*, XII/1 (1901), p. 74; Theo Brown, *The Fate of the Dead: A Study in Folk Eschatology in the West Country after the Reformation* (Cambridge, 1979), p. 62.

7 Tattersall Wilkinson and J. F. Tattersall, *Memories of Hurstwood, Burnley, Lancashire: With Tales and Traditions of the Neighbourhood* (Burnley, 1889), pp. 50–51.

8 'The fiend's power was ... limited by the belief that he could harm only those who led outwardly wicked lives': Darren Oldridge, *The Devil in Tudor and Stuart England* (Stroud, 2010), pp. 85–6.

9 Frederick Hancock, *The Parish of Selworthy in the County of Somerset: Some Notes on Its History* (Taunton, 1897), p. 234.

10 George Roberts, *The History of Lyme-Regis, Dorset* (Sherborne, 1823), p. 103; Francis Bickley, *Where Dorset Meets Devon* (London, 1911), p. 31.

11 John Ashton, *Chap-Books of the Eighteenth Century* (London, 1882), pp. 33, 56, 66, 443; Michael Goss, '"Strange and wonderful news ...": Broadsides, Tabloids, Folklore and Fortean Phenomena', *Fortean Studies*, 1 (1994), pp. 182–97, at pp. 194–5.

12 David Stevens, 'Stanton Drew and Its Tradition', *Notes and Queries*, 1st ser., 4 (1851), pp. 3–4; this summarizes a verse telling, *The Petrified Wedding*, published locally in about 1850.

13 Leslie Grinsell, *The Folklore of Stanton Drew* (Guernsey, 1973), pp. 5–10.

14 Sam Menefee, 'The "Merry Maidens" and the "Noce de Pierre"', *Folklore*, LXXXV/1 (1974), pp. 23–42.

15 Percy Manning, 'Stray Notes on Oxfordshire Folklore', *Folk-Lore*, XIII/3 (1902), pp. 288–95, at p. 294.

16 Kingsley Palmer, *Oral Folk-Tales of Wessex* (Newton Abbot, 1973), p. 112.

17 Ralph Whitlock, *The Folklore of Wiltshire* (London, 1976), p. 159.

18 J. B. Partridge, 'Cotswold Place-Lore and Customs: I', *Folk-Lore*, XXIII/4 (1912), pp. 332–42, at p. 339.

19 Steve Roud, *The Penguin Guide to the Superstitions of Britain and Ireland* (London, 2003), p. 344.

20 Thomas Geering, *Our Parish: A Medley* (Lewes, 1884), pp. 145–8.

21 Francis Young, *Peterborough Folklore* (Norwich, 2017), p. 127.

22 Iona Opie and Moira Tatem, *A Dictionary of Superstitions* (Oxford, 1989), p. 29.

23 Charlotte Latham, 'Some West Sussex Superstitions Lingering in 1868', *Folk-Lore Record*, 1 (1878), pp. 1–67, at p. 14.

24 Roy Vickery, *A Dictionary of Plant Lore* (Oxford, 1995), pp. 45–6; Roud, *Superstitions*, p. 39; Donald Watts, *Elsevier's Dictionary of Plant Lore* (Cambridge MA, 2007), pp. 35–6.

25 Angelina Parker, 'Oxfordshire Village Folklore: II', *Folk-Lore*, XXXIV/4 (1923), pp. 322–33, at p. 328. The badger story was already current in the Middle Ages: Arturo Graf, *The Story of the Devil*, trans. Edward Noble Stone (London, 1931), p. 104.

26 Terence Whitaker, *Lancashire's Ghosts and Legends* (London, 1980), p. 112.

27 Powell, 'Folklore from South-West Wilts', p. 74.

28 Dorset County Museum: MS annotations by C. V. Goddard to Worthington's *Chideock*, made 1890–96.

29 Marianne Dacombe, *Dorset Up Along and Down Along* (Dorchester, 1935), p. 112. As she tells it, it is the Devil who drops the card and shows his hoof, but I've assimilated this to the standard version.

30 Martin Puhvel, 'The Legend of the Devil-Haunted Card Players in Northern Europe', *Folklore*, LXXVI/1 (1965), pp. 33–8. The folk tale is ML 3015 in Reidar Thoralf Christiansen, *The Migratory Legends: A Proposed List of Types with a Systematic Catalogue of the Norwegian Variants* (Helsinki, 1958), pp. 24–8.

31 H. J. Rose, 'The Devil at a Card-Party', *Folk-Lore*, XXXVII/4 (1926), p. 395; J.R.W. Coxhead, *The Devil in Devon* (Bracknell, 1967), pp. 12–13; Aubrey Parke, 'The Folklore of Sixpenny Handley, Dorset', *Folk-Lore*, LXXIV/3 (1942–3), pp. 481–7, at p. 486.

32 Kai Roberts, *Folklore of Yorkshire* (Stroud, 2013), p. 77; Craig Weatherhill and Paul Devereux, *Myths and Legends of Cornwall* (Wilmslow, 1994), p. 103.

33 'One recognised the Devil by outward signs': P. G. Maxwell-Stuart, *Satan: A Biography* (Stroud, 2008), p. 133.

34 C.J.R., 'Halter-Devil Chapel, Derbyshire', *Notes and Queries*, 4th ser., 4 (1869), p. 8.

9 To Chase Forever: The Devil Is a Huntsman, and Souls Are His Prey

1 The Roche episode of the Tregeagle cycle appears in William Bottrell, *Traditions and Hearthside Stories of West Cornwall* (Penzance, 1879–80), vol. III, p. 15; Robert Hunt, *Popular Romances of the West of England* (London, 1865), vol. I, pp. 138–9; Margaret Ann Courtney, 'Cornish Folk-Lore: II', *Folk-Lore Journal*, V/2 (1887), pp. 85–112, at p. 101.

2 Bottrell, *Traditions and Hearthside Stories of West Cornwall*, vol. III,
   p. 14. Other versions (Bottrell, vol. II, p. 225, Hunt, *Popular
   Romances*, vol. I, p. 145) place the incident with the child later in
   the cycle.

3 Bottrell, *Traditions of West Cornwall*, vol. II, pp. 225–6.

4 Hunt, *Popular Romances*, vol. I, pp. 133–42; Jennifer Westwood and
   Jacqueline Simpson, *The Lore of the Land: A Guide to England's
   Legends, from Spring-Heeled Jack to the Witches of Warboys* (London,
   2005), p. 117.

5 'Avon Lea', 'Hampshire Folk-Lore', *Notes and Queries*, 1st ser.,
   12 (1855), p. 100; Thomas William Shore, *A History of Hampshire,
   Including the Isle of Wight* (London, 1892), p. 172; David Horovitz,
   The Place-Names of Staffordshire (privately printed, 2005), p. 229;
   Jill Lucas, *Spinning Jenny and Devil's Darning Needle* (privately
   printed, 2002).

6 Thomas Quiller-Couch, 'The Folk-Lore of a Cornish Village: II',
   Notes and Queries, 1st ser., 11 (1855), pp. 457–9.

7 John Rhys, *Celtic Folklore, Welsh and Manx* (Oxford, 1901), vol. I,
   pp. 215–16.

8 Gerald of Wales, *The Journey through Wales/ The Description
   of Wales*, trans. Lewis Thorpe (London, 1978), pp. 116–17.

9 London, British Library, Yates Thomson MS 13, ff. 146v to 148.

10 *Inferno* Canto 13, ll. 112–31.

11 *The Anglo-Saxon Chronicle*, ed. and trans. Dorothy Whitelock
   (London, 1961), p. 194.

12 Elias Owen, *Welsh Folk-Lore: A Collection of the Folk-Tales and
   Legends of North Wales* (Oswestry, 1896), pp. 125–7.

13 Joseph Wright, *The English Dialect Dictionary* (London, 1898)
   s.vv. Gabriel Hound, Gabriel Ratchet.

14 Theo Brown, *The Fate of the Dead: A Study in Folk Eschatology
   in the West Country after the Reformation* (Cambridge, 1979), p. 37.

15 John Merrifield (as 'J. M.'), 'Devonshire Folk Lore', *Notes and
   Queries*, 1st ser., 3 (1851), p. 404.

16 Anna Bray, *A Description of the Part of Devonshire Bordering
   on the Tamar and the Tavy* (London, 1836–8), vol. II, pp. 279–81.

17 Two parallel stories from Gloucestershire and Somerset are
   simply literary retellings from Bray's book: Katharine Briggs,
   The Folklore of the Cotswolds (London, 1974), p. 140, and
   Katharine Briggs, *A Dictionary of British Folk-Tales in the
   English Language* (London, 1970–71), B1, p. 103, from the
   notorious Ruth Tongue.

18 Caesarius of Heisterbach, *The Dialogue on Miracles*, trans. Henry
    von Essen Scott and C. C. Swinton Bland (New York, 1929),
    vol. II, pp. 306–7.

19 Hugh Miller, *Scenes and Legends of the North of Scotland*
    (Edinburgh, 1835), pp. 415–17; Henry Brereton, *Gordonstoun:
    Ancient Estate and Modern School* (Edinburgh, 1968), pp. 73–4.

20 Claude Lecouteux, *Phantom Armies of the Night: The Wild Hunt
    and the Ghostly Processions of the Undead*, trans. Jon E. Graham
    (Rochester, VT, 2011), pp. 65–70.

21 Richard King, 'The Wish or Wisked Hounds of Dartmoor',
    The Athenaeum (1847), pp. 334–5.

22 Sabine Baring-Gould, *A Book of the West* (London, 1899–1902),
    vol. I, pp. 183–4; *A Book of Folk-Lore* (London, 1913), p. 74.

23 Douglas Hyde, *Legends of Saints and Sinners* (London, 1915),
    pp. 187–9.

24 *The Cornell Wordsworth: Poems, in Two Volumes, and Other Poems,
    1800–1807*, ed. Jared Curtis (Ithaca, NY, 1983), p. 245, with notes
    at p. 422.

25 Frances Verney, *Stone Edge* (London, 1868), p. 207.

26 J. Harvey Bloom, *Folk Lore, Old Customs and Superstitions
    in Shakespeare Land* (London, n.d. [1929]), p. 106.

27 John Atkinson, *A Glossary of the Cleveland Dialect* (London, 1868),
    p. 203.

28 Alfred Williams, *Round about the Upper Thames* (London, 1922),
    p. 205.

29 Robert Hunt, *Popular Romances of the West of England* (London,
    1865), vol. I, pp. 247–51.

BIBLIOGRAPHY

Addy, Sidney Oldall, *Household Tales with Other Traditional Remains Collected in the Counties of York, Lincoln, Derby and Nottingham* (London, 1895)

Ahier, Philip, *The Legends and Traditions of Huddersfield and Its District* (Huddersfield, 1940–45)

Ainsworth, William Harrison, *Ovingdean Grange: A Legend of the South Downs* (London, 1860)

Alexander, Matthew, *More Surrey Tales* (Newbury, 1986)

Allcroft, A. Hadrian, *The Circle and the Cross: A Study in Continuity* (London, 1927–30)

Allies, Jabez, *The Antiquities and Folk-Lore of Worcestershire* (London, 1856)

Amery, P.F.S., et al., 'Fifteenth Report of the Committee on Devonshire Folk-Lore', *Transactions of the Devonshire Association*, 30 (1898), pp. 90–96

The Anglo-Saxon Chronicle, ed. and trans. Dorothy Whitelock (London, 1961)

Arnold, Neil, *Kent Urban Legends: The Phantom Hitch-Hiker and Other Stories* (Stroud, 2013)

Ashton, John, *Chap-Books of the Eighteenth Century* (London, 1882)

Atkinson, John, *A Glossary of the Cleveland Dialect* (London, 1868)

——, 'Supernatural Change of Site', *Folk-Lore*, VIII (1897), pp. 279–80

Aubrey, John, *Monumenta Britannica*, ed. Rodney Legg and John Fowles (Milborne Port, 1980)

——, *The Natural History and Antiquities of Surrey* (London, 1718–19)

'Avon Lea', 'Hampshire Folk-Lore', *Notes and Queries*, 1st ser., 12 (1855), p. 100

Axon, William E. A., *The Black Knight of Ashton* (Manchester, n.d. [1870])

Barber, Chris, *More Mysterious Wales* (Newton Abbot, 1986)

Barham, Richard (as 'Thomas Ingoldsby'), *The Ingoldsby Legends* (London, 1864)

Baring-Gould, Sabine, *A Book of the West* (London, 1899–1902)

—, *A Book of Folk-Lore* (London, 1913)

—, and John Fisher, *The Lives of the British Saints* (London, 1907–13)

Barrowclough, David, and John Hallam, 'The Devil's Footprints and Other Folklore: Local Legend and Archaeological Evidence in Lancashire', *Folklore*, cxix/1 (2008), pp. 93–102

Bartels, Sarah, '"A terrific ogre": The Role of the Devil in Victorian Popular Belief', *Folklore*, cxxviii (2017), pp. 271–91

Beard, Charles, *The Romance of Treasure Trove* (London, 1933)

Benham, W., 'The Winchester Hill, Hants', *Antiquary*, 19 (1889), p. 73

Bickford, A. R., 'Boulder outside Shebbear Church', *Devon and Cornwall Notes and Queries*, 24 (1950/51), p. 17

Bickley, Francis, *Where Dorset Meets Devon* (London, 1911)

Billingsley, John, *Folk Tales from Calderdale: Place Legends and Lore from the Calder Valley* (Hebden Bridge, 2007)

Black's Guide to the Duchy of Cornwall (Edinburgh, 1871)

Bloom, J. Harvey, *Folk Lore, Old Customs and Superstitions in Shakespeare Land* (London, n.d. [1929])

Bogg, Edmund, *From Edenvale to the Plains of York; or, A Thousand Miles in the Valleys of the Nidd and Yore* (Leeds, n.d. [1894])

—, *A Thousand Miles of Wandering along the Roman Wall* (Leeds, 1898)

Boswell, R. Bruce, 'Footprints of the Devil in Our Own Country', *Pall Mall Magazine*, 5 (1895), pp. 555–64

—, 'Diabolical Folk-Lore in Divers Places', *Gentleman's Magazine*, 281 (1896), pp. 472–85

—, 'More Diabolical Folk-Lore Relating to Definite Localities', *Gentleman's Magazine*, 283 (1897), pp. 443–60

Bottrell, William, *Traditions and Hearthside Stories of West Cornwall* (Penzance, 1879–80)

Bowker, James, *Goblin Tales of Lancashire* (London, n.d. [1878])

Bray, Anna, *A Description of the Part of Devonshire Bordering on the Tamar and the Tavy* (London, 1836–8)

Brereton, Henry, *Gordonstoun: Ancient Estate and Modern School* (Edinburgh, 1968)

Briggs, Katharine, *Pale Hecate's Team* (London, 1962)

—, *A Dictionary of British Folk-Tales in the English Language* (London, 1970–71)

—, *The Folklore of the Cotswolds* (London, 1974)

Brockie, William, *Legends and Superstitions of the County Durham* (Sunderland, 1886)

Brown, Theo, *The Fate of the Dead: A Study in Folk Eschatology in the West Country after the Reformation* (Cambridge, 1979)

Burl, Aubrey, 'The Devil's Arrows, Boroughbridge, North Yorkshire', *Yorkshire Archaeological Journal*, LXIII (1991), pp. 1–24

Burne, Charlotte, *Shropshire Folk-Lore: A Sheaf of Gleanings* (London, 1883)

——, 'Reminiscences of Lancashire and Cheshire when George IV Was King', *Folk-Lore*, XX/2 (1909), pp. 203–7

Burrison, John, '"James Harris" in Britain since Child', *Journal of American Folklore*, LXXX/317 (1967), pp. 271–84

Burstow, Henry, *Reminiscences of Horsham*, ed. J. Poole (Horsham, 2016)

C.J.R., 'Halter-Devil Chapel, Derbyshire', *Notes and Queries*, 4th ser., 4 (1869), p. 8

Caesarius of Heisterbach, *The Dialogue on Miracles*, trans. Henry von Essen Scott and C. C. Swinton Bland (New York, 1929)

Caius, John, *The Works of John Caius*, ed. E. S. Roberts (Cambridge, 1912)

Camden, William, *Britannia* (London, 1586)

——, *Britannia* (London, 1590)

——, *Britannia* (London, 1607)

Cameron, A.C.G., 'In Reference to the Sarsens or Greyweather-Sandstones at Staple Fitzpaine, Near Taunton', *Proceedings of the Somerset Natural History and Archaeological Society*, 54 (1908), pp. 153–9

Camp, John, *In Praise of Bells* (London, 1988)

Cary, John, *Cary's New and Correct English Atlas* (London, 1787)

Chambers, A., 'The Devil's Churchyard: An Iron Age Enclosure at Checkendon, Oxon., 1979–81', *Oxoniensia*, 51 (1986), pp. 25–30

Chambers, John, ed., *A General History of the County of Norfolk* (Norwich, 1829)

Chappell, William, and Joseph Ebsworth, eds, *The Roxburghe Ballads* (London, 1869–99)

Child, Francis James, *The English and Scottish Popular Ballads* (Boston, MA, 1882–98)

Chippindale, Christopher, *Stonehenge Complete* (London, 1994)

Christiansen, Reidar Thoralf, *The Migratory Legends: A Proposed List of Types with a Systematic Catalogue of the Norwegian Variants* (Helsinki, 1958)

Clarke, W. G., *In Breckland Wilds* (London, 1925)

Collins, Andrew, *The Running Well Mystery* (privately printed, 1983)

——, *The Knights of Danbury* (privately printed, 1985)

Courtney, Margaret Ann, 'Cornish Folk-Lore: I', *Folk-Lore Journal*, v/1 (1887), pp. 14–61

——, 'Cornish Folk-Lore: II', *Folk-Lore Journal*, v (1887), pp. 85–112

Coxhead, J.R.W., *The Devil in Devon* (Bracknell, 1967)

Croker, Thomas Crofton, *Fairy Legends and Traditions of the South of Ireland* (London, 1825–8)

Dacombe, Marianne, *Dorset Up Along and Down Along* (Dorchester, 1935)

Davidson, T. D., 'The Untilled Field', *Agricultural History Review*, III (1955), pp. 20–25

Davies, T. A., 'Folklore of Gwent: Monmouthshire Legends and Traditions', *Folk-Lore*, XLVIII/1 (1937), pp. 41–59

Day, James Wentworth, *In Search of Ghosts* (London, 1969)

——, *Essex Ghosts* (Bourne End, 1973)

Deane, Tony, and Tony Shaw, *The Folklore of Cornwall* (London, 1975)

De Blécourt, Willem, 'Sabbath Stories: Towards a New History of Witches' Assemblies', in *The Oxford Handbook of Witchcraft in Early Modern Europe and Colonial America*, ed. Brian Levack (Oxford, 2013), pp. 84–100

——, 'The Flying Charm – to Cologne in the Wine Cellar: On the History of a Scholarly Legend', *Incantatio*, VIII (2019), pp. 9–28

Defoe, Daniel, *A Tour thro' the Whole Island of Great Britain*, ed. G.D.H. Cole (London, 1927)

Denham, Michael Aislabie, *The Denham Tracts*, ed. James Hardy (London, 1892)

Duncumb, John, et al., *Collections towards the History and Antiquities of the County of Hereford* (Hereford, 1804–1915)

Easton, Timothy, 'Apotropaic Symbols and Other Measures for Protecting Buildings against Misfortune', in *Physical Evidence for Ritual Acts, Sorcery and Witchcraft in Christian Britain: A Feeling for Magic*, ed. Ronald Hutton (London, 2016), pp. 39–67

The Elder Edda, trans. Paul Taylor and W. H. Auden (London, 1969)

Eyre, Margaret, 'Folklore Notes from St Briavel's', *Folk-Lore*, XIII/2 (1902), pp. 170–77

——, 'Folklore of the Wyre Valley', *Folk-Lore*, XVI/2 (1905), pp. 162–79

F. S., 'Churchdown', *Notes and Queries*, 1st ser., 12 (1855), pp. 341–2

Field, John Edward, *The Myth of the Pent Cuckoo* (London, 1913)

Fiennes, Celia, *The Journeys of Celia Fiennes*, ed. Christopher Morris (London, 1949)

Forfar, William Bentinck, *Kynance Cove; or, the Cornish Smugglers*
(London, 1865)

Fox, Adam, *Oral and Literate Culture in England, 1500–1700*
(Oxford, 2000)

Gandy, Ida, *An Idler on the Shropshire Borders* (Shrewsbury, 1970)

Geering, Thomas, *Our Parish: A Medley* (Lewes, 1884)

Gelling, Margaret, *The Place-Names of Berkshire* (Cambridge, 1973–6)

Gerald of Wales, *The Journey through Wales/The Description of Wales*,
trans. Lewis Thorpe (London, 1978)

Gibbons, Benjamin, *Notes and Suggestions for a History of Kidderminster*
(Kidderminster, 1859)

Gillett, H.E.H., 'Some Saws and Proverbs of Norfolk', in *Bygone
Norfolk*, ed. William Andrews (London, 1898), pp. 201–28

Gillman, Charles, 'Cam's Pike', *Notes and Queries*, 10th ser., 2 (1904),
p. 110

Goddard, C.V., 'Wiltshire Folklore Jottings', *Wiltshire Archaeological
Magazine*, 50 (1942–4), p. 31

Goss, Michael, '"Strange and wonderful news . . .": Broadsides, Tabloids,
Folklore and Fortean Phenomena', *Fortean Studies*, 1 (1994), pp. 182–97

Graf, Arturo, *The Story of the Devil*, trans. Edward Noble Stone
(London, 1931)

Greene, William Henry, *Jack o' Kent and the Devil: Stories of a Welsh
Border Hero Told in Verse*, ed. E. W. Greene (Chepstow, n.d. [1974])

Grice, F., *Folk Tales of the North Country: Drawn from Northumberland
and Durham* (London, 1944)

Griffith, George, *Going to Markets and Grammar Schools* (London, 1870)

Grinsell, Leslie, 'Sussex Barrows', *Sussex Archaeological Collections*,
75 (1934), pp. 216–75

——, *The Ancient Burial-Mounds of England* (London, 1936)

——, *The Folklore of Stanton Drew* (Guernsey, 1973)

——, *The Legendary History and Folklore of Stonehenge* (Guernsey, 1973)

——, *Folklore of Prehistoric Sites in Britain* (Newton Abbot, 1976)

Gutch, Eliza, *County Folk-Lore II: Examples of Printed Folk-Lore
Concerning the North Riding of Yorkshire, York and the Ainsty*
(London, 1901)

Hall, G. Rome, 'On Ancient British Remains near Birtley and Barrasford,
North Tyne', *Archaeologia Aeliana*, 2nd ser., 7 (1876), pp. 3–17

Halliwell, James Orchard, *Popular Rhymes and Nursery Tales* (London,
1849)

Halpert, Herbert, 'The Devil and the Fiddle', *Hoosier Folklore Bulletin*,
2 (1943), pp. 39–43

Hamper, William, 'The Devil's Dyke: A Sussex Legend', *Gentleman's Magazine*, 80(1) (1810), pp. 513–14

Hancock, Frederick, *The Parish of Selworthy in the County of Somerset: Some Notes on Its History* (Taunton, 1897)

Harland, John, and Thomas Wilkinson, *Lancashire Folk-Lore* (London, 1867)

—, and —, *Lancashire Legends* (London, 1873)

Harley, Edward, *The Harleian Miscellany* (London, 1809)

Harper, Charles, *The Ingoldsby Country* (London, 1906)

Harte, Jeremy, 'Churches Moved by Night', *At the Edge*, 2 (1996), pp. 1–7

—, 'The Devil's Stone at Shebbear', *FLS News*, 89 (2019), pp. 10–12

Hartland, Sidney, 'Supernatural Change of Site', *Folk-Lore*, VIII (1897), pp. 177–8

Hartshorne, Charles Henry, *Salopia antiqua* (London, 1841)

Hayden, Eleanor G., *Travels round Our Village* (London, 1905)

Hayman, Richard, *Riddles in Stone: Myths, Archaeology and the Ancient Britons* (London, 1997)

Hayward, John, *Dartmoor 365* (Lytchett Matravers, 1991)

Heanley, Robert, 'Silbury Hill', *Folk-Lore*, XXIV/4 (1913), p. 524

Henderson, William, *Notes on the Folklore of the Northern Counties of England and the Borders* (London, 1866)

Hervey, J. P., 'St Leonards Forest and Its Legends', *Sussex County Magazine*, 15 (1941), pp. 154–6

—, 'The Devil in Sussex', *Sussex County Magazine*, 17 (1943), p. 356

Hibbert, Christopher, *The Grand Tour* (London, 1987)

Hinds, A. B., ed., *Report on the Manuscripts of the Marquess of Downshire 4: Papers of William Trumbull the Elder* (Historical MSS Commission 75, 1940)

Hissey, James John, *On Southern English Roads* (London, 1896)

—, *Over Fen and Wold* (London, 1898)

Hone, William, *The Table Book* (London, 1827)

Hopkirk, Mary, *Danbury: Historical Notes and Records of the Village of Danbury in the County of Essex* (Chelmsford, 1945)

Horovitz, David, *The Place-Names of Staffordshire* (privately printed, 2005)

Howell, Hiram, *The Wrekin Legend and Other Poems* (Shrewsbury, 1894)

Hudson, William Henry, *A Shepherd's Life* (London, 1921)

Humphreys, Arthur L., *Materials for the History of the Town of Wellington* (London, 1899)

Hunt, Robert, *Popular Romances of the West of England* (London, 1865)

Hutton, Catherine, *Reminiscences of a Gentlewoman of the Last Century*, ed. Catherine Beale (Birmingham, 1891)

Hutton, John, *A Tour to the Caves, in the Environs of Ingleborough and Settle* (London, 1781)

Hyde, Douglas, *Legends of Saints and Sinners* (London, 1915)

Jewitt, Llewellynn, 'The Devil and Church Building', *Notes and Queries*, 2nd ser., 4 (1857), p. 357

'John ap John', 'Dafydd of Rivon', *Bye-Gones Relating to Wales and the Border Counties*, 2nd ser., 1 (1889–90), pp. 349–50

Jones, T. Rupert, 'The Devil's Stone, at Staple Fitz-Paine', *Somerset and Dorset Notes and Queries*, 1 (1888–9), p. 153

Jones-Baker, Doris, *The Folklore of Hertfordshire* (London, 1977)

Jordan, Katy, *The Haunted Landscape: Folklore, Ghosts and Legends of Wiltshire* (Bradford-on-Avon, 2000)

Joyce, Walter, *Moorside Tales and Talk* (London, 1935)

Keightley, Thomas, *The Fairy Mythology* (London, 1850)

Keyser, Charles, 'Notes on the Churches of Frilsham, Yattendon, Ashampstead, Hampstead Norris and Aldworth: IV', *Berkshire, Buckinghamshire and Oxfordshire Journal*, XXI (1915), pp. 97–108

King, Richard, 'The Wish or Wisked Hounds of Dartmoor', *The Athenaeum* (1847), pp. 334–5

—, 'Local Rhymes and Proverbs of Devonshire', *Notes and Queries*, 1st ser. 2 (1850), pp. 511–12

Kittredge, George Lyman, *Witchcraft in Old and New England* (Cambridge, MA, 1929)

L., 'Ancient Tradition at Tolleshunt-Knights, Essex', *Sporting Magazine*, 42 (1813) pp. 21–4

La Fontaine, Jean, *Nouveaux contes de Monsieur de la Fontaine* (Amsterdam, 1676)

Lackington, James, *Memoirs of the First Forty-Five Years of the Life of James Lackington* (London, 1792)

Landreth, Peter, as 'The Chronicler', *Legends of Lancashire* (London, 1841)

Latham, Charlotte, 'Some West Sussex Superstitions Lingering in 1868', *Folk-Lore Record*, 1 (1878), pp. 1–67

Latham, Frank, ed., *Delamere: The History of a Cheshire Parish* (Delamere, 1991)

Leather, Ella Mary, *The Folk-Lore of Herefordshire* (Hereford, 1912)

Lecouteux, Claude, *Phantom Armies of the Night: The Wild Hunt and the Ghostly Processions of the Undead*, trans. Jon E. Graham (Rochester, VT, 2011)

Leighton, W. A., 'Early Chronicles of Shrewsbury, 1372–1603',
   *Transactions of the Shropshire Antiquarian and Natural History
   Society*, 3 (1880), pp. 239–352
Lofthouse, Jessica, *North-Country Folklore* (London, 1976)
Lower, Mark Antony, *A Compendious History of Sussex: Topographical,
   Archaeological and Anecdotal* (Lewes, 1870)
Luard, Henry Richards, ed., *Annales Monastici* (London, 1864–9)
Lucas, Jill, *Spinning Jenny and Devil's Darning Needle* (privately
   printed, 2002)
Manning, Owen, and William Bray, *The History and Antiquities
   of the County of Surrey* (London, 1804–14)
Manning, Percy, 'Stray Notes on Oxfordshire Folklore', *Folk-Lore*,
   XIII/3 (1902), pp. 288–95
Masson, Charles, *Narrative of Various Journeys in Balochistan,
   Afghanistan and the Panjab* (London, 1842)
Maxwell-Stuart, P. G., *Satan: A Biography* (Stroud, 2008)
Meade, Will, *The Ballads of a Moonraker* (Devizes, 1935)
Menefee, Sam, 'The "Merry Maidens" and the "Noce de Pierre"',
   Folklore, LXXXV/1 (1974), pp. 23–42
Merrifield, John (as 'J.M.'), 'Devonshire Folk Lore', *Notes and Queries*,
   1st ser., 3 (1851), p. 404
Miller, Hugh, *Scenes and Legends of the North of Scotland*
   (Edinburgh, 1835)
Moryson, Fynes, *An Itinerary Written by Fynes Moryson Gent*
   (London, 1617)
Muchembled, Robert, *A History of the Devil from the Middle Ages
   to the Present*, trans. Jean Birrell (Cambridge, 2003)
Nash, Treadway, *Collections for the History of Worcestershire*
   (London, 1781–99)
Newbigging, Thomas, *History of the Forest of Rossendale*
   (Rawtenstall, 1893)
Newman, L. F., 'Some Notes on the Folklore of Cambridgeshire and
   the Eastern Counties', *Folk-Lore*, LVI/3 (1945), pp. 287–93
Nutt, C. H., 'Popular Names of Tumuli', *Antiquary*, 6 (1882), p. 135
Obelkevich, James, *Religion and Rural Society: South Lindsey, 1825–1875*
   (Oxford, 1976)
Ogilvy, David, *A General Itinerary of England and Wales* (London, 1804)
Oldridge, Darren, *The Devil in Tudor and Stuart England* (Stroud, 2010)
Opie, Iona, and Moira Tatem, *A Dictionary of Superstitions*
   (Oxford, 1989)
Ord, John Walker, *The History and Antiquities of Cleveland* (London, 1846)

Otley, Jonathan, *Concise Description of the English Lakes* (London, 1849)

Owen, Elias, *Welsh Folk-Lore: A Collection of the Folk-Tales and Legends of North Wales* (Oswestry, 1896)

Owen, Hywel Wyn, and Ken Lloyd Gruffydd, *Place-Names of Flintshire* (Cardiff, 2017)

——, and Richard Morgan, *Dictionary of the Place-Names of Wales* (Llandysul, 2007)

Padel, Oliver, 'Cornwall and the Matter of Britain', in *Arthur in the Celtic Languages: The Arthurian Legend in Celtic Literatures and Traditions*, ed. Ceridwen Lloyd-Morgan and Eric Poppe (Cardiff, 2019), pp. 263–80

Page, John Lloyd Warden, *An Exploration of Exmoor and the Hill Country of West Somerset* (London, 1890)

Palmer, Kingsley, *Oral Folk-Tales of Wessex* (Newton Abbot, 1973)

——, *The Folklore of Somerset* (London, 1976)

Palmer, Roy, *The Folklore of Gloucestershire* (Tiverton, 1994)

——, *The Folklore of the Black Country* (Woonton, Almeley, 2007)

Parke, Aubrey, 'The Folklore of Sixpenny Handley, Dorset', *Folk-Lore*, LXXIV/3 (1942–3), pp. 481–7

Parker, Angelina, 'Oxfordshire Village Folklore: II', *Folk-Lore*, XXXIV/4 (1923), pp. 322–3

Parker, Eric, *Highways and Byways in Surrey* (London, 1908)

Parkinson, Thomas, *Yorkshire Legends and Traditions* (London, 1888)

Partridge, J. B., 'Cotswold Place-Lore and Customs: I', *Folk-Lore*, XXIII/4 (1912), pp. 332–42

Pattison, G. W., 'Adult Education and Folklore', *Folklore*, LXIV/3 (1953), pp. 424–6

Payne, Jessie K., *A Ghost Hunter's Guide to Essex* (Romford, 1987)

Peacock, Mabel, *Tales and Rhymes in the Lindsey Folk-Speech* (Brigg, 1886)

Pearl, Cleanness, Patience, Sir Gawain and the Green Knight, ed. A. C. Cawley and J. J. Anderson (London, 1962)

'Pearmain', 'Davies of Rivon', *Bye-Gones Relating to Wales and the Border Counties*, 9 (1888), pp. 105–6

Pearse Chope, R., 'Thirty-Fourth Report on Devonshire Folklore', *Transactions of the Devonshire Association*, 66 (1934), pp. 73–91

Piggott, Stuart, *William Stukeley: An Eighteenth-Century Antiquary* (Oxford, 1950)

Pinney, Hester, 'The Devil's Jumps', *Somerset and Dorset Notes and Queries*, 21 (1933–5), p. 68

Pitcairn, Robert, *Criminal Trials in Scotland* (Edinburgh, 1829–33)

Plot, Robert, *The Natural History of Oxford-Shire* (Oxford, 1677)

Porter, Enid, *Cambridgeshire Customs and Folklore* (London, 1969)
—, *The Folklore of East Anglia* (London, 1974)
Powell, John, 'Folklore Notes from South-West Wilts', *Folk-Lore*,
    XII/1 (1901), pp. 71–83
Prichard, J. T. Llewellyn, *The Llandrindod Guide* (Llandrindod, 1826)
Puhvel, Martin, 'The Legend of the Church-Building Troll in
    Northern Europe', *Folklore*, LXXII/4 (1961), pp. 567–83
—, 'The Legend of the Devil-Haunted Card Players in Northern
    Europe', *Folklore*, LXXVI/1 (1965), pp. 33–8
Quaife, G. R., *Godly Zeal and Furious Rage: The Witch in Early Modern
    Europe* (London, 1987)
Quiller-Couch, Arthur, *The Mayor of Troy* (London, 1906)
Quiller-Couch, Thomas, 'The Folk-Lore of a Cornish Village: II',
    Notes and Queries, 1st ser., II (1855), pp. 457–9
—, Thomas, 'The Longstone: A Cornish Legend', *Notes and Queries*,
    6th ser., 7 (1883), pp. 323–4
Raven, Jon, *The Folklore of Staffordshire* (London, 1978)
Rhys, John, *Celtic Folklore, Welsh and Manx* (Oxford, 1901)
Ridge, Richard, *Shropshire Highland Folk Tales* (privately printed, 1937)
Riley, Henry Thomas, ed., *Johannis de Trokelowe et Henrici de Blaneforde
    necnon Quorundam Anonymorum Chronica* (London, 1866)
Roberts, Askew, *The Gossiping Guide to Wales* (London, 1879)
Roberts, George, *The History of Lyme-Regis, Dorset* (Sherborne, 1823)
Roberts, Kai, *Folklore of Yorkshire* (Stroud, 2013)
Rose, H. J., 'The Devil at a Card-Party', *Folk-Lore*, XXXVII/4 (1926),
    p. 395
Roud, Steve, *The Penguin Guide to the Superstitions of Britain and
    Ireland* (London, 2003)
Rowe, Samuel, *A Perambulation of the Antient and Royal Forest
    of Dartmoor* (Plymouth, 1848)
Rudkin, Ethel, 'Lincolnshire Folklore: I', *Folk-Lore*, XLIV/3 (1933),
    pp. 189–214
—, 'Lincolnshire Folklore: III', *Folk-Lore*, XLV/2 (1934), pp. 144–57
—, 'Lincolnshire Folklore: IV', *Folk-Lore*, XLV/3 (1934), pp. 249–67
Russell, Jeffrey Burton, *Mephistopheles: The Devil in the Modern World*
    (Ithaca, NY, 1986)
Russett, Vince, 'Sir John Hauteville: A Wessex Giant', *Picwinnard*,
    10 (1979), pp. 20–23
S., 'Thursley Church', *Gentleman's Magazine*, 69 (1799), pp. 921–2
Salisbury, Jesse, *A Glossary of Words Used in South-East Worcestershire*
    (London, 1894–6)

Sandford, Edmund, *A Cursory Relation of All the Antiquities and Familyes in Cumberland*, ed. Richard Ferguson (Kendal, 1890)

Shankland, David, 'Integrating the Past: Folklore, Mounds and People at Çatalhöyük', in *Archaeology and Folklore*, ed. Amy Gazin-Schwartz and Cornelius Holtorf (London, 1999), pp. 139–57

Shore, Thomas William, *A History of Hampshire, Including the Isle of Wight* (London, 1892)

Simpson, Jacqueline, *The Folklore of Sussex* (London, 1973)

——, *The Folklore of the Welsh Border* (London, 1976)

——, 'God's Visible Judgements', *Landscape History*, VIII/1 (1986), pp. 53–8

Skinner, Aileen, *Tales of the Tors* (London, 1939)

Smith, Albert Hugh, *The Place-Names of the West Riding of Yorkshire* (Cambridge, 1961–3)

Smith, Robert, *The Road to Maggieknockater: Exploring Aberdeenshire and the North-East through Its Place Names* (Edinburgh, 2004)

Spring, Ian, 'The Devil and the Feathery Wife', *Folklore*, XCIX/2 (1988), pp. 139–45

St Leger-Gordon, Ruth, *The Witchcraft and Folklore of Dartmoor* (London, 1965)

Sternberg, Thomas, *The Dialect and Folk-Lore of Northamptonshire* (London, 1851)

——, 'Popular Stories of the English Peasantry: v', *Notes and Queries*, 1st ser., 5 (1852), pp. 601–4

Stevens, David, 'Stanton Drew and Its Tradition', *Notes and Queries*, 1st ser., 4 (1851), pp. 3–4

Stone, Percy, *Legends and Lays of the Wight* (London, 1912)

Stonehouse, William, *The History and Topography of the Isle of Axholme* (London, 1839)

Stovin, George, 'Lindholme, A Reputed Hermit's Cell', *Gentleman's Magazine*, 17 (1747), p. 23

Stubbs, William, ed., *Memorials of St Dunstan, Archbishop of Canterbury* (London, 1874)

Stukeley, William, *The Family Memoirs of the Reverend William Stukeley*, ed. William Lukis (Durham, 1882–5)

——, *Stukeley's Stonehenge*, ed. Aubrey Burl and Neil Mortimer (London, 2005)

Sturluson, Snorri, *The Prose Edda*, trans. Jean Young (Berkeley, CA, 1954)

Swainson, S. J., 'Langford Budville Revel (and Devil)', *Somerset and Dorset Notes and Queries*, 20 (1930–32), pp. 245–6

Thomas, Keith, *Religion and the Decline of Magic: Studies in Popular Beliefs in Sixteenth- and Seventeenth-Century England* (London, 1971)

Thurman, John, 'On Ancient British Barrows, Especially Those of Wiltshire and the Adjoining Counties: 1 Long Barrows', *Archaeologia*, XLII/1 (1869), pp. 161–244

Timmons, H. Thornhill, *Nooks and Corners of Shropshire* (London, 1899)

Tomkins, Charles, *A Tour to the Isle of Wight* (London, 1796)

Turner, T. S., *History of Aldborough and Boroughbridge* (London, 1853)

Uther, Hans-Jörg, *The Types of International Folktales: A Classification and Bibliography Based on the System of Antti Aarne and Stith Thompson* (Helsinki, 2004)

Verney, Frances, *Stone Edge* (London, 1868)

Vickery, Roy, *A Dictionary of Plant Lore* (Oxford, 1995)

Wall, Tom, *The Singular Stiperstones: Landscape, Reminiscence, Literature and Wildlife* (privately printed, 2014)

Walsham, Alexandra, *The Reformation of the Landscape: Religion, Identity, and Memory in Early Modern Britain and Ireland* (Oxford, 2011)

Warne, Charles, *Ancient Dorset* (Bournemouth, 1872)

Watkins, W. J., 'A Cycle of Stories Current in Radnorshire', *Folk-Lore*, XLIII/4 (1932), pp. 424–7

Watts, Donald, *Elsevier's Dictionary of Plant Lore* (Cambridge, MA, 2007)

Weatherhill, Craig, and Paul Devereux, *Myths and Legends of Cornwall* (Wilmslow, 1994)

Webb, Mary, *The Golden Arrow* (London, 1916)

Webb, T. W., *Memorials of the Civil War as It Affected Herefordshire* (London, 1879)

Weeks, W. Self, 'Some Legendary Stories and Folk-Lore of the Clitheroe District', *Transactions of the Lancashire and Cheshire Antiquarian Society*, 34 (1916), pp. 77–110

Westwood, Jennifer, and Jacqueline Simpson, *The Lore of the Land: A Guide to England's Legends, from Spring-Heeled Jack to the Witches of Warboys* (London, 2005)

Whellan, Thomas, *History and Topography of the City of York and the North Riding of Yorkshire* (Beverley, 1857–9)

Wherry, Beatrix, 'Wizardry on the Welsh Border', *Folk-Lore*, XV/1 (1904), pp. 75–86

Whistler, C. W., 'Local Traditions of the Quantocks', *Folk-Lore*, XIX/1 (1908), pp. 31–51

Whitaker, Terence, *Lancashire's Ghosts and Legends* (London, 1980)

Whitlock, Ralph, *Whitlock's Wessex* (Bradford-on-Avon, 1975)

——, *The Folklore of Wiltshire* (London, 1976)

——, *The Folklore of Devon* (London, 1977)

Wilkinson, Tattersall, and J. F. Tattersall, *Memories of Hurstwood, Burnley, Lancashire: With Tales and Traditions of the Neighbourhood* (Burnley, 1889)

Williams, Alfred, *Round about the Upper Thames* (London, 1922)

——, *Folk-Songs of the Upper Thames* (London, 1923)

Williams, William, *Observations of the Snowdon Mountains* (London, 1802)

Wilson, Francesca M., *Strange Island: Britain through Foreign Eyes, 1395–1940* (London, 1955)

Woodward, Christopher, *In Ruins* (London, 2002)

Wordsworth, William, *The Cornell Wordsworth: Poems, in Two Volumes, and Other Poems, 1800–1807*, ed. Jared Curtis (Ithaca, NY, 1983)

Wright, Joseph, *The English Dialect Dictionary* (London, 1898)

Wright, Thomas, 'On the Local Legends of Shropshire', *Collectanea Archaeologica*, 1 (1862), pp. 50–66

Wykes, Alan, *Reading: A Biography* (London, 1970)

Young, Francis, *Peterborough Folklore* (Norwich, 2017)

PHOTO ACKNOWLEDGEMENTS

All photos are from the author's postcard collection.

INDEX

Page numbers in *italics* refer to illustrations